AF572168

8 —

THE COMPLETE BOOK OF

Vegetables

THE COMPLETE BOOK OF Vegetables

An illustrated guide to over 400 species and varieties of vegetables from all over the world

Tjerk Buishand · Harm P. Houwing · Kees Jansen

GALLERY BOOKS
An Imprint of W. H. Smith Publishers Inc.
112 Madison Avenue
New York City 10016

Adapted from the Dutch by Multimedia Publications (UK) Ltd

Translation: AGET Language Services, London
Design: Ron Putto, Matthew Ward
Production: Zivia Desai

First published in the Netherlands by Uitgeverij Het Spectrum BV, Parkvoorn 4, 3454 JR De Meern

First published in the United States of America 1986 by Gallery Books, an imprint of WH Smith Publishers Inc, 112 Madison Avenue, New York, NY 10016

Typeset by Keene Graphics Ltd, London, UK
Printed in Italy by Sagdos
ISBN 0 8317 9111 X

Contents

Introduction

What is a vegetable?

It is surprisingly hard to give a neat, precise definition of such an ordinary, everyday word. What, for instance, is the difference between fruit and vegetables? The distinction is not at all clear, particularly when we look at the 'fruit vegetables', the edible seed bodies of some plants. The fruits of such close relations as the melon and cucumber provide a good example of this confusion. They are both members of the *Cucurbitaceae* family, but we consider the melon to be a fruit and the cucumber to be a vegetable, and there is no obvious reason for this distinction.

Another possible criterion, the visible presence of the green pigment, chlorophyll, is not decisive either. There are vegetables where the chlorophyll is obscured by the presence of other pigments, such as the red of anthocyanin, or where the colouring has been removed by human intervention, as in the artificially blanched types of vegetables like white asparagus, seakale and witloof chicory. We also describe as vegetables some parts of plants that have very little chlorophyll or none at all, like the tubers and roots of potatoes, parsnips and carrots. What should one think of a 'vegetable' like the banana flower, the reproductive organ of the banana plant?

The term 'vegetable', in fact, stands for a large and varied number of plants and parts of plants that have in common their suitability for human consumption, and their significant contribution to our diet of vitamins and minerals, of starch and vegetable protein.

The vegetables of the Pharaohs

The cultivation of vegetables certainly goes back a long way, although not right back to the dawn of humanity. Our earliest ancestors were wandering hunters and gatherers who collected the vegetable part of their diet in a haphazard way wherever the plants happened to be growing. As far as we know, they began to cultivate plants only when they became farmers instead of hunters, abandoning their nomadic life for a settled existence.

We do not know the exact moment of this change-over, partly because this social revolution did not happen everywhere simultaneously. In the Near East large agricultural civilizations flourished for centuries while in the northern latitudes small groups continued to live by hunting and fishing.

Early signs of vegetable cultivation are to be found in Egypt. Tomb paintings tell us that peas, black radishes, onions and a kind of lettuce were all grown some 5,000 years ago along the banks of the Nile. Even older are the traces of beans and peppers that have been found in Mexican excavations. These show that pulse and fruit vegetables were commonly grown in the great Indian civilizations of the New World. In China and India too, farmers grew onions, black radishes and several kinds of cabbage thousands of years ago. No one knows if vegetables were grown at all in Europe at that time, although it is now one of the world's most important vegetable-producing areas. There are signs that there was some cultivation of plants discovered by food-gathering ancestors, though this was probably just on temporary little fields.

Only when the first outward-looking civilizations

Left: *the male flower of the banana plant shows how hard it is to define a 'vegetable'*
Below: *vegetables have been grown on the fertile banks of the Nile since earliest times*

arose in Europe — Greek and Roman — did the cultivation of vegetables begin to acquire some significance. At that time vegetables from other parts came to Europe via the early trade routes. A good example is the primitive cucumber, arriving in southern Europe from India and China around 150 BC. The first truly world-wide exchange of vegetables came in the period of the great voyages of discovery. Then, species like the potato and the tomato were brought from the New World to Europe as curiosities.

No vegetables for those who want to stay healthy

Vegetable cultivation did not become established immediately as a result of such discoveries. The history of European eating habits shows that until the nineteenth century vegetables, particularly leaf vegetables, were far from popular and only rarely cultivated. In the Middle Ages vegetables, and also fruit to some extent, were even regarded with disfavour. 'He who wishes to remain healthy will generally not eat very much fruit or vegetables', states a fourteenth-century text. Fruit had a specially bad name: until the seventeenth century doctors were convinced that fruit not only caused intestinal diseases but was also a major cause of plague. During a plague epidemic in 1655, the sale of plums, black cherries and cucumbers was forbidden.

Vegetable-eating was not really significant until the nineteenth century, and so growing vegetables was not an important activity. The few vegetables that were eaten in great quantities were dried beans and peas, onions, garlic, turnips, carrots, parsnips and some kinds of cabbage. There was little demand for leaf vegetables: it was not until the eighteenth century that the first lettuces appeared on the menu. Apart from meat and fish, the European population fed itself on bread and cheese and stews and soups, using the vegetable species just mentioned, plus grains, buckwheat and groats. Scurvy was a common disease for centuries, not only at sea but also ashore. It was particularly bad in northern Europe, where the lack of sunshine and fresh fruit led to a shortage of vitamin C, the cause of scurvy. Vegetables gained a place on southern European tables far earlier than they did in northern parts.

Scurvy ceased to be a widespread health problem only after the potato began to appear as part of the daily diet. Even in the eighteenth century it was not really popular, particularly among the better-off members of the community. Around 1750 a Dutch Burgermeister's wife berated her kitchen maid for bringing potatoes to the table without permission. Potatoes were for animals, said madam.

An 18th century Dutch vegetable grower sells his produce from his rowing-boat. He is holding carrots and strings of onions, and there are cabbages in the boat

Mendel, first of the improvers

It was not until about 1900 that vegetables began to be really appreciated. In a nineteenth-century German book on plant life, the author describes various European vegetable species, including many that are now forgotten or treated as exotic, like hop shoots. The few drawings of vegetables in his book are surprisingly primitive and clumsy, and this is true of almost all pictures of vegetables done before 1900.

This is not really unexpected. Most were seed-bearing plants and in those days their propagation was left entirely to nature. There was therefore no standardization, and during the process of natural selection changes occurred over and over again. You could not say 'as like as two peas', even though the plants they grew on belonged to the same species.

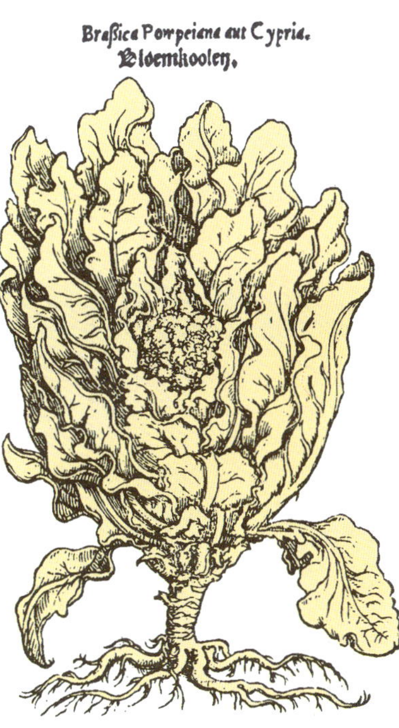

Left: *this drawing of a cauliflower plant from the* Herb Book *of Rembertus Dodonaeus (1554) shows how much vegetables have changed since Mendel's work on plant genetics*

Harvesting was an uncertain business, too. Disease, plague, storm, drought, and other factors beyond human control, decided whether there was to be plenty or not. These were all reasons for vegetables not being a permanent part of the daily diet. The consumer had to choose from whatever came to market, and in the winter months there was very little choice, and often very little of anything. The Augustinian monk Gregor Mendel (1822-1884), the founder of modern genetics, is really responsible for the dramatic changes that revolutionized food production. In the 1860s he carried out innumerable experiments in plant crossing in the garden of his monastery at Brunn (now Brno in Czechoslovakia). In doing so he discovered that the descendants of crosses inherited characteristics from the parent plants according to fixed rules. Some inherited the characteristics of one parent plant, while others inherited a combination of both. Mendel's discovery did not fit in with contemporary botanical views and his publications remained unnoticed and ignored. Only in 1900 were Mendel's laws rediscovered, and from then on the way was open for humans to intervene in the process of selection. People could now improve existing varieties of vegetables or develop new varieties as they wished. The improvement and expansion of the range has become more and more significant. The objectives are obvious. The improvers try to achieve greater uniformity, better resistance to disease, increased yield per plant. They also try to lengthen the period of cultivation, so that the plant can be grown all the year round (if possible), and they select out any characteristics likely to make it less attractive to the consumer.

Winter lettuce and water bubble

There are far too many success stories of vegetable improvement to mention here, so one really remarkable example will have to do — the cabbage lettuce. Under natural conditions this plant (itself a product of improvement) forms a proper head only when the weather is warm enough, and when the days are long. In northern Europe this means only during the summer time. Cultivation under glass, where the temperature can be raised artificially, still did not produce properly formed heads in autumn and winter because the light was not good enough. For years greenhouse lettuce was just a loose collection of leaves — you could not really call it a head. By endless crosses the improvers succeeded in developing a number of cabbage lettuce varieties that needed less daylight, and so could be grown under glass nearly all the year round.

The improvement of vegetables has been carried out to suit the best interests of the grower rather than the consumer. The consumer has certainly benefited from some improvements: many vegetables look more attractive, and prices have been kept low as a result of higher production. Even so, improvement is a mixed blessing, as the taste and quality of many vegetables have suffered as a result. The round tomato is one example, cultivated under glass and known in the trade contemptuously as water bubble — not much flesh and hardly any delicious tomato smell. Another example is the modern bean. Here the improvers have selected out the troublesome strings that used to make preparation so time-consuming, but the new varieties do not have nearly as much flavour as the old varieties with strings.

In many cases the loss of flavour is also caused by forced growth. This reduces the dry substance content of a plant, and it is this dry substance that contains the flavour, plus the vitamins and minerals.

The rich assortment of vegetables today is not just a result of improvement or of the rapid increase of cultivation under glass. Many popular vegetable types have spread to new areas, where the climate and soil suit them. All kinds of 'European' vegetables are now grown for export in African countries. These countries are not

Top: *the development of new varieties means that good quality cabbage lettuces can be grown in the greenhouse outside the normal season*
Bottom: *the market is usually the first place to sell exotic vegetables*

yet major exporters, but already they are able to supply us with fresh produce at times of the year when our own growers cannot.

The arrival of vegetables from far away

There have also been an increasing number of exotic vegetables available in European and North American shops since the early 1960s. Tourists have been travelling more widely and visiting new countries more often, and, after some hesitation, have learned to appreciate new flavours. As a result, there is a rising demand for vegetables such as paprikas, aubergines, artichokes and marmande tomatoes accelerated by immigrants creating a demand for the vegetables they are more used to. This was obviously a commercial attraction, and horticulturalists in the market-gardening countries, particularly Belgium and the Netherlands, began intensive experiments, trying to grow these new vegetables themselves. At first they grew them under glass, but at the same time they began to work towards improvements in appearance, uniformity and yield. Their extensive knowledge and expertise have led to success in many cases. Recently there has been some development of vegetables from even further away. Large groups of Asians and Africans arrived in Europe in the wake of de-colonization in the 1950s and 60s and the accompanying periods of unrest. New and totally unfamiliar vegetables began to appear in the shops. To begin with, they were imported from the country of origin and were sold only in shops specializing in tropical products. Demand increased, culinary trend-setters began to discover these new species, and so vegetable growers became interested too. Now history is repeating itself: scientific plant improvers have turned their attention to developing tropical vegetables such as pak-choi and the asparagus pea into varieties that can be grown in Europe.

In the market-gardening countries, this development is accompanied by another — technological progress. A spectacular example is the revolution in growing Witloof chicory. Until recently it was a winter vegetable, harvested between September and May, but now, with the new system of heating the plant roots, it is possible to harvest a superb witloof chicory crop in the summer too. The plants are grown in dark climate-controlled cells, heated in winter and cooled in summer. The roots are piled four to six deep in flat boxes, and water flows through, sometimes enriched with a plant food solution. Three or four weeks after the chicory roots have set, the heads can be harvested.

Methods like these are forerunners of what can only be described as a vegetable factory, an ingeniously structured, computer-controlled complex, where even the soil is replaced by another material, a so-called substrate. Here temperature, light, air, humidity, fertilization and disease can be completely controlled, so that even the yield can be calculated in advance. The new science of bio-technology is yet another factor in all this progress. Scientists can now manipulate the genetic material of a plant and so make more far-reaching changes than anything possible from the use of Mendel's laws. As an example of these new possibilities, a leading bio-technician stated boldly in 1985, 'If the consumer wanted to have a square tomato, we could supply it within a year.'

We cannot possibly foresee where these new developments will lead, but the rich assortment of vegetables in Europe, America and other wealthy parts of the world will increase with every year that passes.

Will this open the door to an unknown paradise? It will probably be a matter of taste.

Witloof chicory is forced in dark climate-controlled cells, and so can be bought all the year round

The cultivation of tomato plants on a substrate — a special material now used instead of earth. Vegetable growing is getting more and more like factory production

The main vegetable types

The expression vegetable now includes a far wider variety than the greens or pot-herbs used by our ancestors. The consumer used to say greens, meaning just those plants where only the leaf was eaten, like cabbages.

We now differentiate between a number of vegetable types. It is impossible to make a completely hard and fast classification, as some species may belong to several different types. The summary we provide here does at least give some picture of the wide variation in the present supply of vegetables.

Leaf vegetables are plants where mainly the leaf is eaten: lettuce, endive, spinach, sugar loaf and red-leaved chicory. They contain many vitamins and minerals, and are eaten both cooked and raw in countries with a temperate climate. In southern Europe there is a marked preference for leaf vegetables with a more bitter taste, like red-leaved chicory or radicchio.

Sprouting vegetables are the young shoots of various rapidly-germinating seed plants, especially from the *Papilionaceae* and *Cruciferae* families. Bean sprouts and alfalfa are popular examples. Sprouting vegetables are an important source of vitamins, especially in the winter, and are also rich in proteins and minerals. They can be grown on a small scale at home in a warm room, and only take a few days.

Aromatic vegetables contain volatile oils with a distinctive taste and smell. They are therefore often included among the kitchen spices: the borderline between vegetables and spices is often blurred with species such as chervil, parsley, dill, horse radish and aromatic vegetables from the tropics such as ginger.

Stem vegetables could really be put with the leaf vegetables. The plants in this group have fleshy leaf stems, like rhubarb, seakale, cardoon, or have above-ground tubers of the thickened leaf stem, like Florence fennel, or tubers of the thickened stalk, like kohlrabi. Bamboo and hop shoots can also be regarded as vegetables. A striking feature of this group is the adaptation of some species to cultivation in the dark. Using this method a white or light-coloured plant is produced. This blanching is used for asparagus, seakale, cardoon, celery and rhubarb.

Cabbage plants contain many minerals (including iron) and vitamins (mainly vitamin C). Recent tests have shown that they also have cancer-inhibiting properties. In countries with a temperate climate growers concentrate on species of cabbage with a long growing time, such as white, red and savoy cabbage, Brussels sprouts, kale and cauliflower. Where it is warmer, people tend to cultivate rapidly-growing cabbage species such as pak-choi, Chinese cabbage, radish, black radish and white garden turnip.

Onion species could be included among the aromatic vegetables because they contain volatile oils, or they could be included among the root and tuber plants. This is particularly true of the bulb-forming onion species, more widely grown than the non-bulb-forming leeks and Welsh onions. The bulb-forming species are sub-divided into white, yellow and red varieties. The sharp taste is caused by small quantities of disulphide. From time immemorial many onion species have been credited with medicinal properties.

Tuber and root plants are generally regarded as one group, but there is a clear difference. The tuber plants form, as well as roots, underground stems *(stolona)* that thicken at the top to form a tuber. Well-known examples are the potato (mainly in temperate countries) and the yam (a tropical plant). Other true tuber plants are the Jerusalem artichoke and the Japanese artichoke.

In the root plants the tap root is thickened and so, in some cases, is a part of the stem as well. This thickening may take the form of a tuber, as with kohlrabi, celeriac, garden turnip, radish, sweet potato, taro and cassava. With other plants there is no tuber, but the root itself is obviously thickened, as with scorzonera, carrot, parsnip, black radish and burdock.

Fruit vegetables are types of vegetables where the part that is eaten is mainly the fruit. The borderline between fruit and vegetables cannot always be clearly drawn. Fruit vegetables can be sub-divided into three important groups, the pulses (rich in nutrients, especially protein), the *Cucurbitaceae* (often with little flavour and few calories), and the fleshy, berry fruits of the *Solonaceae* or nightshade family, (including the tomato, paprika and aubergine). Sugar maize, okra and roselle can also be grouped with the fruit vegetables. A characteristic of fruit vegetables is their need for warmth: except for the pea and the broad bean, these plants need a high temperature for germination and growth. They are sensitive to frost and low temperatures, so should never be kept in the refrigerator.

Vegetables from all corners of the earth

After the cereal plants, vegetables are the most important source of food for the present world population. This book covers the wide assortment of vegetables now available in the Western world. The Food and Agriculture Organisation of the United Nations (FAO) publishes a *Production Year Book*, containing a wealth of production statistics for the interested reader. The list below, of the top twenty vegetable plants, was compiled from the 1984 edition. The figures can only be approximate, as they are generally based on commercial cultivation. In many countries amateur gardeners make a significant contribution, in some cases as much as 40 per cent of the country's annual yield. Some plants and their tonnages need a few words of explanation:

— the cabbage species include the red, white and savoy cabbages, Brussels sprouts, curly kale and Chinese cabbage. Cauliflower and broccoli belong in a separate category.
— plants like tomatoes, cucumbers and gherkins are grown almost exclusively in greenhouses in temperate regions.
— weights for green peas and beans include the pods. This category does not include the slicing and snap beans, as they do not make a major contribution to world food production.

The five leading vegetables of each continent

The map below shows world vegetable production, generally by continent. The Soviet Union has been treated as a single unit as it covers a large part of both Europe and Asia.

One disadvantage of this brief comparison is that small and medium-sized countries do not get a mention, even if they have a very high annual yield, but even so some striking facts emerge:

— the potato is by far the most important vegetable in the world. Europe, with Poland as its main producer, is responsible for at least one third of the world's production. Large quantities are also harvested in the Soviet Union and Asia. The African harvest is comparatively small — perhaps a programme of increased potato production could help with the food supply problems there.
— the cassava is easily the most important vegetable in Africa and South America, but the annual harvest in Thailand deserves a mention.
— the annual yield of sweet potatoes comes almost entirely from Asia, and 90 per cent of that harvest is Chinese. The sweet potato is eaten mainly in China, but also appears on the menu in Africa, especially in Rwanda.
— the tomato is also a very important food plant in all continents. The tomato and the potato, both members of the nightshade family, together feed a vast number of people around the world.

The top twenty vegetable plants worldwide

(all figures are 1000 metric tons)

Potatoes	312,209	Cucumbers/ Gherkins	11,758
Cassava	129,020	Dried peas	10,627
Sweet potatoes	117,337	Peppers	7,849
Soya beans	89,893	Taro	5,763
Tomatoes	58,592	Pumpkins/Gourds	5,631
Cabbage species	38,182	Aubergines	5,126
Yams	25,492	Cauliflowers	5,002
Onions	23,109	Fresh peas	4,603
Dried beans	15,469	Fresh beans	2,879
Carrots	12,126	Garlic	2,845

By major areas: the first figure is for total production in the area, the second for the area's major producer.

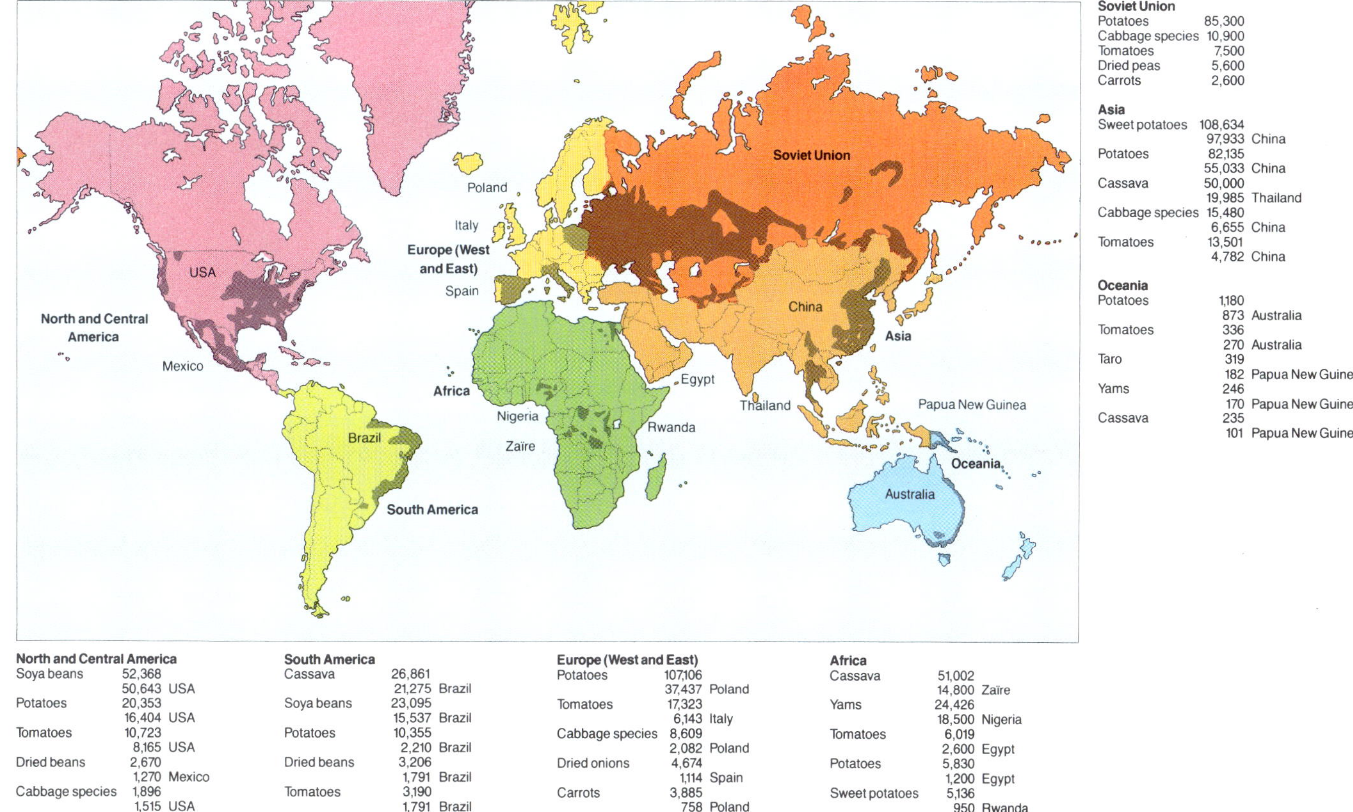

Aizoaceae

The ice plants or *Aizoaceae* generally have thick fleshy leaves and used to be regarded as members of the purslane family. Nowadays, however, botanists classify the 2,000 or so varieties as a separate family. Most *Aizoaceae* grow in South Africa, but there are some to be found in Australia and South America. The name is derived from the Greek *aizoon,* meaning eternal life, because many ice plant species are able to survive in extreme conditions, in torrid deserts and in barren steppes with very poor soil.

As far as we know, only two genera in the ice plant family contain vegetable species: *Mesembryanthemum* and *Tetragonia.*

The genus *Mesembryanthemum* is best known for ornamental plants: the fig marigold *(M. blandum),* a house plant with oblong matchstick-shaped green leaves and lilac flowers and the ice plant *(M. criniflorum)* often used in the garden as an edging plant where it blooms exuberantly and colourfully in a sunny position. The flowers of the garden ice plant are the main feature, while the leaves are far less conspicuous.

The one *Mesembryanthemum* species eaten as a vegetable, the edible plant *M. crystallinum* is quite different. The few white flowers are small and inconspicuous, while the leaves are strongly developed. This ice plant grows wild from the coasts of South Africa up to the Mediterranean and has also settled elsewhere. In some desert regions of Africa it is used to hold the sand in place. In a warm dry environment evaporation deposits salt crystals on the stems and leaves, and this gives the leaves a rather salty taste. With cultivated ice plants in northern regions, this taste is present only in plants grown under glass.

Of the 50 or so *Tetragonia* species only the New Zealand spinach *(T. tetragonioides)* is cultivated and eaten as a vegetable. It grows wild in Japan, Australia and New Zealand. It was from New Zealand that Sir Joseph Banks, who sailed with Captain Cook on his first voyage of discovery, took seed back to Britain. From Britain the plant gradually spread over western Europe. New Zealand spinach is an annual plant, flourishing on moist ground in a warm environment. It grows slowly and harvesting the leaves and the tops is very labour-intensive, so it is not widely grown, though cultivation has increased in the last few years.

Ice plant
(Mesembryanthemum crystallinum)
Annual low-growing herbaceous plant with green stems and thick, fleshy, juicy leaves. Flavour similar to spinach, but with a piquant, rather acid aftertaste.
ORIGIN: South-west Africa, Cape Province.
PRODUCTION: Mediterranean area, Portugal, France, Canary Isles, USA (California), Australia.
SEASON: When cultivated in northern regions in open ground, July to October. Cultivation under glass can extend the season.
USE: Cook like spinach or blend into soups. Can also be eaten raw.
STORAGE: As the young leaf contains a great deal of water, it soon becomes limp and cannot be stored for long.
NUTRITIONAL VALUE: 19 kcal, 3 g carbohydrate, 2 g protein, 0.3 g fat, 58 mg calcium, 2.6 g iron, 0.3 mg vitamin A, 30 mg vitamin C per 100 g serving.

New Zealand spinach
(Tetragonia tetragonioides)
Annual leafy plant with horizontally-spreading, many-branched stems. Only the fleshy, ribbed, triangular, dark-green leaves can be eaten.
ORIGIN: Australia, New Zealand, Polynesia, Japan.
PRODUCTION: All European countries with temperate climate, but not widely grown: much more important in the subtropics.
SEASON: Throughout the year from imports and cultivation under glass. Open ground cultivation in northern regions July to October.
USE: Wash stem tops and leaves thoroughly and boil for a short time. Can be used in all spinach recipes.
STORAGE: Very limited, like ordinary spinach.
NUTRITIONAL VALUE: Similar to ice plant.

△Ice plant, 9¼ in (235 mm) high ▽ New Zealand spinach, 5½ in (140 mm) across

Alliaceae
Onions

Onions *(Alliums)* used to be classed as members of the lily family *(Liliaceae)*, but nowadays botanists are undecided. One opinion is that they are a subdivision of the narcissus family *(Amaryllidaceae)*, but here we treat them as a separate family *(Alliceae)*.

There are about 500 varieties of onion. Some grow wild like the crow garlic *(Allium vineale)*, while others are popular vegetables — onions, spring onions (scallions in the US), leeks and garlic. Chives and chibol (Chinese chives) are popular as herbs. Shallots and silverskin onions are also cultivated, and other less well-known varieties — tree (Egyptian) onions *(A. cepa var. viviparum)*, pearl onions *(A. ampeloprasum var. holmense)*, and rakkyo *(A. chinense)*, much liked in Japan.

Crow garlic can be recognized as an Allium by the small underground 'onions' from which its stems sprout

Onions, leeks and garlic have a long history as food plants. The Chinese were growing them by 3,000 BC. Onions and garlic were certainly eaten by the pyramid-builders of Ancient Egypt. The Egyptians ate leeks, too, and the Greeks and Romans made them into soup. The Roman Empire spread onions, leeks and garlic throughout western Europe, and much later Columbus took onions to America.

Onions have also been known for their medicinal properties. They have been used to lower blood sugar, to stimulate the heart, to eliminate fat, to stimulate the production of bile and urine as well as to combat colds and viral infections. In the Middle Ages garlic was used to treat leprosy, and in the trenches of World War I sphagnum moss impregnated with garlic juice was used to treat infected wounds.

Leeks and garlic as we know them now are cultivars, not found in the wild. Botanists believe that leeks originate from *Allium ampeloprasum*, known in Germany as 'summer garlic'. The pearl onion is a narrow-leaved sterile variety of the leek, but does not develop a stem like a leek or a single large bulb like an onion. Instead it forms a cluster of small white bulbs. The silverskin onion is beginning to replace it as a cultivated species.

Very little is known of the shallot's history. It may have originated in the old Palestinian city of Ascalon, been brought to Europe by returning Crusaders and later taken to America.

The origins of the spring onion or scallion are also obscure, although the giant chive is probably its distant ancestor. The Japanese have developed varieties that have hollow green leaves like onions, but instead of forming bulbs they have broad stems like leeks. Another new variety, the Japanese winter onion, has been created by crossing different varieties and is now being exported.

Chives have been cultivated for centuries and have changed very little over the years. They probably spread through the northern hemisphere from a north Russian origin. Chibol (Chinese chives) are native to central and eastern Asia and are a popular crop in Japan, China, India, Nepal, Thailand and the Philippines, where both the leaves and the heads are used in cooking.

△ Shallot 'Ouddorp brown', $2\frac{1}{4}$ in (55 mm) long ▽ Shallot 'Dutch yellow', $3\frac{1}{8}$ in (80 mm) long

△ Shallot 'Santé', 3 in (75 mm) long

Varieties

Dutch yellow Large straw-coloured shallots with strong shoots. Bulbs keep well.

Ouddorp brown Small firm bulb with brown skin and transparent fleshy layers.

Santé A new variety with reddish-brown skin. Its strong leaf-growth, slow development and late ripening may cause problems in drying off and therefore reduce storage life.

Shallot
(Allium ascalonicum)
Oval or elongated bulb, formed by several clusters of bulblets on a common base, the whole surrounded by a dry brownish skin. Bulb size depends on variety. Colour ranges from yellow to reddish-brown. Flavour less pronounced than that of the onion.
ORIGIN: Probably Israel (Ascalon).
PRODUCTION: Various European countries, USA, Canada.
SEASON: All the year round. Green varieties sold in summer in bunches, dry bulbs sold in September to June.
USE: Fresh shallots for flavouring. The bulbs are eaten raw, boiled, baked or fried after removing the dry skin layers.
STORAGE: Dry bulbs, if stored carefully, will keep for about six months at freezing point. Fresh shallots with green stems will keep for about a week at 32 to 34°F (0 to 1°C).
NUTRITIONAL VALUE: 48 kcal, 11 g carbohydrate, 1.5 g protein, 0.3 g fat, 30 mg calcium, 0.5 mg iron, 10 mg vitamin C, per 100 g serving.

Seed onion and onion set

(Allium cepa)

The onion bulb consists of a number of fleshy layers covered with a few dry skins. The outermost layers may contain pigments that produce red, purple, yellow or variegated tints. These pigments are absent in white onions. The onion contains a great deal of sugar and a characteristic volatile oil that produces the typical onion taste. Depending on the composition of this oil, varieties are sweet, semi-sharp or sharp in taste.

ORIGIN: Probably central Asia, Pakistan and north-west India. The wild forms in these countries have much in common with present-day cultivated types.

PRODUCTION: Italy, Netherlands, France, Spain, Egypt, Israel, Poland, New Zealand, USA.

SEASON: Throughout the year.

USE: Usually only the dry bulb, peeled and eaten raw, baked or boiled as a vegetable or in soup.

STORAGE: Green onion sets will keep for two to three weeks at freezing point. Seed onions (depending on variety) five to seven months at 35 to 41°F (2 to 5°C) and can also be stored for up to ten months at 29 to 30°F (−2 to −1°C) when they must be thawed slowly before use.

NUTRITIONAL VALUE: 47 kcal, 10 g carbohydrate, 1 g protein, 0.3 g fat, 30 mg calcium, 0.5 mg iron, 0.125 mg vitamin B6, 10 mg vitamin C per 100 g serving.

INDUSTRIAL PROCESSING: Deep freezing, drying, making into powder. See also silverskin onion.

△ Left: onion 'Noordhollandse bloedrode', 3¼ in (83 mm) across △ Right: onion, 'Exhibition', 6¼ in (158 mm) across

△ Onion, 'Stuttgarter riesen', 3⅞ in (99 mm) across

△ Onion, 'Albion', 3 in (76 mm) across ▽ Onion, 'Brunswijker', 3 in (76 mm) across

Varieties

The difference between seed onions and onion sets is simply the difference in season and in firmness. Onion sets can be harvested earlier (July to August) than onions (September to October) and are somewhat softer because of their more rapid growth. Onion sets come only in yellow and red varieties, but the seed onion may also be white. White onions (chiefly originating in southern Europe) are the sweetest, red varieties are sharp, and the yellow are somewhere in between.

Yellow varieties

Buffalo early ripening, bulbous light yellow Japanese winter onion. Suitable for growing so-called spring onions (scallions). See spring onion.

Exhibition (Ailsa Craig type) This tall, round to pear-shaped yellow onion can reach a weight of 2 lb (1 kg). Flesh rather soft in texture and mild in flavour.

Hybrid varieties Various varieties such as Dino, Hyduro, Hyton. Similar to the better selections of the Rijnsburger (see below). Cultivated as seed onions.

Rijnsburger Bulbous onion that keeps well. To cultivate sets of this variety the plant material must be kept warm.

Senshyu yellow Mid-early spherical yellow Japanese winter onion. Sown in August and harvested early the following summer.

Sturon Spherical yellow onion developed from the Stuttgarter riesen (see below). Chiefly used for growing onion sets.

Stuttgarter riesen Dark yellow flat onion with firm skin. Used for pickling and for growing onion sets. The plant material of this variety can be stored cold.

Zittauer Old variety of flattish round yellow onion with good keeping qualities but not prolific. For cultivating onion sets the plant material must be kept in a warm place.

Red varieties

Brunswijker Dark blood-red flattish round onion that keeps well. When boiled the attractive tint changes to pink or greyish white. For cultivating onion sets the plant material must be prepared.

Noordhollandse bloedrode Flat to spherical purplish onion that also keeps well. The newer selections include the spherical Zur-Robal and the flattish round dark red, late Noro.

Renared Spherical light red Japanese winter onion with a firm leaf and a very mild flavour for a red onion. Also used for early cultivation of spring onions (see spring onion).

White varieties

Albion New white hybrid with high content of dry substance. Keeps well compared with other white onions.

White sweet Spanish Old variety of white onion, also well-known as Utah jumbo. Bulb quite moist when cooked.

△ Silverskin onion 'Barletta', max. ¾ in (20 mm) across

Silverskin onion
(Allium cepa)
Small white onions, obtained by sowing particular onion varieties thickly and deep in the soil, as the small onions turn green if they are not formed below ground. Fresh silverskin onions are seldom available, as they nearly all go for processing.

ORIGIN: As seed onions and onion sets.

PRODUCTION: Europe, USA.

SEASON: Mid-June to mid-August.

USE: In pickles and relishes.

STORAGE: Only a few days when fresh. Processed products keep for a long time.

NUTRITIONAL VALUE: Fresh, as seed onions and onion sets. In jars, 31 kcal, 7 g carbohydrate, 0.5 g protein, 0.1 g fat, 25 mg calcium, 0.6 mg iron, 3 mg vitamin C per 100 g serving.

INDUSTRIAL PROCESSING: Fermenting in brine, preserving in salt, deep-freezing. The larger onions — those over ⅞ inch (23 mm) across — are used for preserves. The taste is more sweet than sour: tartrazine or lactoflavine are added to give the yellow colouring.

Varieties

Pompei or **Allervroegste wonder** Very early small flattish round white onions with short fine leaf and thin neck.

Barletta or **St Jansui** Mid-early with sturdy leaf and thicker neck than the Pompei. Onions round to rather oblong.

△ Silverskin onion as spring onion, 13¾ in (350 mm) long including leaves

Spring onion or **scallion**
(Allium cepa)
Spring onions are onion sets of seed onions harvested when they are young and green. They are sold in bunches. Both spherical and non-spherical varieties are used for growing them. Some varieties, like Stuttgarter riesen and Sturon, produce spring onions when harvested early. Others, like some of the Japanese winter onions (Buffalo, Renared), are grown in pots during the spring. A non-spherical variety used for growing spring onions is White Lisbon, with rather heavy stiff leaves and a thick neck.
ORIGIN: As seed onions and onion sets.
PRODUCTION: As seed onions and onion sets.
SEASON: Cultivated under glass April to May, in open ground June to July.
USE: Chopped in salads or in soups.
STORAGE: One to two weeks at 35 to 41°F (2 to 5°C). Two to three weeks at freezing point.
NUTRITIONAL VALUE: For dry onions as seed onions and onion sets. For green onions, 36 kcal, 8.2 g carbohydrate, 1.5 g protein, 0.2 g fat, 51 mg calcium, 1 g iron, 2 mg vitamin A, 23 mg vitamin C per 100 g serving.

Welsh onion or **bunching onion**
(Allium fistulosum)
White, tightly-closed shaft (like a leek) and tubular hollow leaf (like an onion). Length of shaft depends on variety and method of cultivation. The original type splits easily and forms a flower stem quite early in the year. The more recent Japanese cultivars are almost entirely free from these faults.
ORIGIN: Probably northern China.
PRODUCTION: East Asia (Japan, Korea, Taiwan) and (to a limited extent) Europe.
SEASON: Throughout the year.
USE: When harvested young, shredded raw as salad onions. Later, cooked like leeks. Especially good for onion soup.
STORAGE: Two weeks at 35 to 41°F (2 to 5°C), three to four weeks at 30°F (−1°C).
NUTRITIONAL VALUE: 34 kcal, 6.5 g carbohydrate, 1.9 g protein, 0.4 g fat, 18 mg calcium, 27 mg vitamin C per 100 g serving.

Varieties

Ishikura Rapid-growing with long shaft and greyish-green leaves.

Kaigaro Firm dark green plant with long white shaft and no bulb.

Kincho Firm, dark green. Base of plant keeps particularly well.

Tsukuba Firm leaf and long shaft.

△ Welsh onion 'Kaigaro' 15⅜ in (390 mm) long

△ Leek 'Bulgarian giant' (young plant), $21\frac{1}{4}$ in (540 mm) long

△ Leek 'Swiss giant' (fully-grown), $20\frac{7}{8}$ in (530 mm) long

Leek
(Allium porrum)
Herbaceous plant with distinctive smell. Base of stem and leaf sheath form a white to greenish-white shaft. The leaf is long, flat and quite broad. Colour varies from light grey-green to dark bluish-green depending on variety.
ORIGIN: Probably eastern Mediterranean area. No known true wild leek. Ancestor probably *A. ampeloprasum*.
PRODUCTION: France, Belgium, Netherlands, Turkey, Egypt, Spain.
SEASON: Throughout year, peaking in October.
USE: Mostly the white shaft, but sometimes 4 to 6 inches (10 to 15 cm) of the green leaf is eaten as well. Cook as a vegetable or use in soups and savoury flans.
STORAGE: Young leeks a few weeks at 36 to 41°F (2 to 5°C). Autumn leeks up to four weeks at 32 to 34°F (0 to 1°C). Longer storage (four to eight weeks) at 30°F (−1°C).
NUTRITIONAL VALUE: 31 kcal, 5g carbohydrate, 2 g protein, 0.3 g fat, 60 mg calcium, 1 mg iron, 0.6 mg vitamin A, 25 mg vitamin C per 100 g serving.
INDUSTRIAL PROCESSING: Deep-freezing, drying, canning or bottling.

Varieties

Depending on shaft length, leaf colour, speed of growth and winter hardiness, varieties are subdivided into summer, autumn and winter leeks. Early varieties generally have a long shaft, light greyish-green leaves and a soft or loose structure. They usually cook rapidly. Late varieties have a rather short, thick shaft, dark greyish-green or bluish-green leaves and good winter hardiness. Varieties are classified here in season order.

Bulgarian giant Early variety with very long greenish-white shaft and light-coloured leaves.

Swiss giant Shaft shorter and whiter than Bulgarian giant. Leaves green to light green. Suitable for summer and early autumn cultivation.

Autumn giant Selections include Otima, Batom, Snowstar and Goliath. Some suitable for summer and early autumn cultivation, others for early and late autumn cultivation. All have thick shafts and broad, quite thick, greyish-green leaves.

Winter giant Quite broad greyish-green leaves and long, thick, rather lumpy shaft. Most winter giants are winter hardy.

Blue-green winter Winter hardy with dark greyish-green long narrow leaves. Shaft rather thick with more of a bulb than the autumn varieties.

△ Leek (winter type), $18\frac{1}{8}$ in (460 mm) long

△ Garlic (dry), white and purple type, 2⅜ in (60 mm) across ▽ Garlic (fresh), with part of stem, 7 in (180 mm) long

Garlic

(Allium sativum)

White or purplish, rather flat, angular dry bulbs with cloves. There are many varieties, but it is difficult to tell them apart.

ORIGIN: South-west and central Asia.

PRODUCTION: Regions with dry sunny climate: southern Europe (Spain, Italy, France, Greece), some eastern European countries (including Hungary), Argentina and Mexico.

SEASON: Dried bulbs throughout the year. Green plants March to August.

USE: Blend into many dishes (mainly from southern European, Asian and South American cuisines) either shredded or pressed.

STORAGE: Dried bulbs for several weeks. Fresh for about two weeks if kept in the salad compartment of the refrigerator.

NUTRITIONAL VALUE: 139 kcal, 29 g carbohydrate, 6.2 g protein, 0.2 g fat, 30 mg calcium, 1.3 mg iron, 10 mg vitamin C per 100 g serving.

INDUSTRIAL PROCESSING: Drying and making into powder.

△ Chives, 9¼ in (250 mm) long

Chives

(Allium schoenoprasum)
Fine tubular leaf, sold in bunches or in pots. Many different hybrid varieties, hard to tell apart.
ORIGIN: Probably northern Russia.
PRODUCTION: All areas with a temperate climate in Europe, Asia and South America.
SEASON: Throughout the year.
USE: As seasoning in soups, sauces, salads and other dishes.
STORAGE: Best used at once (unless supplied in pots).
NUTRITIONAL VALUE: 45 kcal, 8.4 g carbohydrate, 3.6 g protein, 0.7 g fat, 167 mg calcium, 13 mg iron, 0.3 mg vitamin A, 47 mg vitamin C per 100 g serving.
INDUSTRIAL PROCESSING: Some deep-freezing. Also used in canned soups.

Chinese chives

(Allium tuberosum)
Long narrow flat leaves with a slight taste of garlic. The white flowers are also edible (harvested in the bud) forming open umbrellas on bare stems.
PRODUCTION: Japan, Philippines, Thailand, northern India, USA (California).
SEASON: Throughout year.
USE: Leaves as seasoning in various dishes, mainly Indian and Chinese. The flower buds may be fried.
STORAGE: Use immediately.
NUTRITIONAL VALUE: Probably the same as ordinary chives.

△ Chinese chives (leaf and flower), 20⅛ in (510 mm) long

Amaranthaceae

The amaranth family *(Amaranthaceae)* came originally from the tropical regions of America, Africa and Asia, but has now spread over a large part of the world. Some varieties were deliberately spread because they were valuable as vegetables or decorative plants. Others travelled unnoticed in ships' cargoes, and seem to have adapted easily to other climates. Two amaranth varieties that now happily grow wild in northern regions are the white amaranth *(A. alba)* and *Amaranthus lividus*, cultivated in the sixteenth and seventeenth centuries around the Mediterranean as a vegetable, but after 1700 used only for pig food.

Several amaranth species are still grown as ornamental plants, but are no longer as popular as they were in the last century, for instance the purple loosestrife *(A. caudatus)* a sturdy plant with a red leaf, and the tricolor amaranth *(A. tricolor)*. The purple loosestrife comes originally from South America, where it is still cultivated as a food plant (in Peru, Bolivia, north-east Argentina, Suriname). It is also grown in Asia (China, India, Nepal, Afghanistan). The original form of the tricolor amaranth comes from tropical Asia and is known there as a leaf vegetable under the name *bajem*. This name may be connected with the *bhaji* a small-leaved wild amaranth *(A. spinosus)* eaten in Suriname.

The only amaranth variety on the market (in shops specializing in tropical products) is *A. dubius*, sometimes called Suriname amaranth or Chinese spinach. Among all amaranth varieties the leaf is eaten, prepared like spinach, even among the varieties grown as ornamental plants. The seed of some tropical varieties is also an important foodstuff, as the protein content is higher than that of grain.

Suriname amaranth or **Chinese spinach** *(Amaranthus dubius)* Rapid-growing annual producing plentiful large dark green soft leaves on juicy stems. Sometimes green and reddish plants are cultivated together. The plant itself may grow to a height of over 3 feet (1 metre). It has a fresh flavour.
ORIGIN: Probably Caribbean.
PRODUCTION: Tropical and subtropical regions of South America. In northern latitudes can be grown only under glass.
SEASON: Throughout the year.
USE: Wash the leaf and cook like spinach.
STORAGE: Very limited.
NUTRITIONAL VALUE: 43 kcal, 5.2 g protein, 340 mg calcium, 4.1 mg iron, 7.7 mg vitamin A, 120 mg vitamin C per 100 g serving.

Varieties

In countries where the amaranth is widely eaten as a vegetable, people distinguish between several different varieties. In the south of the United States the **Tampala** variety is grown, with narrow, oblong, dull green leaves. It is also grown in western Europe, but on a limited scale. **Bajem**, a variety cultivated in western Europe under glass, has light green, broad, rather lumpy leaves.

△ Suriname amaranth, 10½ in (265 mm) long

Araceae

Most members of the arum family *(Araceae)* are perennial plants. They grow mainly where there is plenty of water. Below ground they usually form tubers from a thick root stock and above ground large long-stemmed leaves. The small flowers are normally clustered closely together on a thick axis or spike surrounded by a half-open bractlet shaped like a skull.

Most of the 1,500 varieties originate in the tropics or subtropics, but some are indigenous to temperate regions. In Britain there are three interesting members of this family. The poisonous bog arum *(Calla palustris)*, formerly used as an emetic and as an antidote to snakebite; lords-and-ladies or cuckoo pint *(Arum maculatum)*, also poisonous, although the roots can be eaten after cooking; and the sweet flag or sweet sedge *(Acorus calamus)*. This was brought from Turkey to western Europe in the sixteenth century by an Austrian diplomat. It has an aromatic rootstock with curative properties. Marinaded in brandy it is a well-tried remedy for stomach disorders, effective even if the root has not been dug up in total silence on midsummer night between eleven and twelve o'clock, as early herbalists recommended!

Several well-known house plants belong to the *Araceae* family: the popular white arum *(Zantedeschia aethiopica)*, the monstera or Swiss cheese plant *(Philodendron pertussum)*, the dieffenbachia *(Dieffenbachia picta)* and the flamingo plant *(Anthurium scherzerianum)*.

Two members of the *Araceae* family are of great significance in Third World countries as a food crop and are cultivated in almost all tropical regions. These are the cultivars of the taro (originally from Asia) and the tannia. The tannia probably comes from the West Indies, where Christopher Columbus found it to be a staple food. Both the bulbs and the leaves of these two plants are eaten. Taro and tannia are regularly on sale in shops specializing in tropical products. Tannia is also grown in the greenhouse in northern regions, but the yield is relatively small.

The so-called elephant yam is seldom on the market, although eaten widely in Java. Another member of the *Araceae* family with an edible root is *Alocasia macrorrhiza*, a staple food in eastern Indonesia and New Guinea, but not yet exported.

Elephant yam
(Amorphophallus campanulatus)
Perennial with thick rough leaf stalk up to 5 feet (1.5 metres) long and spherical tubers compressed together with a diameter of 8 to 12 inches (20 to 30 cm) and a weight of up to 55 lb (25 kg).
ORIGIN: Asia.
PRODUCTION: Indonesia.
SEASON: From May (harvesting takes place after the south-west monsoon).
USE: Wash the tubers, cut into slices and boil or bake.
STORAGE: Three to four days in a cool dry place (not in the refrigerator).

△ Taro. The large one is $5\frac{1}{2}$ in (138 mm) from Thailand, the small one *(eddo)* is from China. Description on page 26

△ Tannia, 19¾ in (500 mm) long

Taro
(Colocasia esculenta)
Dirty-brown root stocks sold in bunches of five or six, mostly with a long piece of stem. The young green leaf is sometimes on sale too.
ORIGIN: South-east Asia, India.
PRODUCTION: Virtually all tropical lowlands.
SEASON: Large tubers (mainly from Thailand) throughout the year. Small round Chinese tubers *(Eddo)* mainly in summer.
USE: Peel, slice, wash in salt water, steam and eat. Try it with grated coconut and brown sugar.
STORAGE: Three to four months in cool dry place (not in the refrigerator).
NUTRITIONAL VALUE: 61 kcal, 4.1 g protein, 160 mg calcium, 1 mg iron, 5.5 mg vitamin A, 65 mg vitamin C per 100 g serving.

Tannia
(Xanthosoma sagittifolium)
Perennial plant — both green leaves and thick root stock are eaten. Tubers similar to those of taro.
ORIGIN: West Indies.
PRODUCTION: All tropical lowlands. In northern regions under glass in summer.
SEASON: Throughout year.
USE: Cook like other green vegetables. Mild flavour.
STORAGE: Leaves can be kept for a few days in the refrigerator.
NUTRITIONAL VALUE: 16 kcal, 2 g carbohydrate, 2 g protein, 180 mg calcium, 1.9 mg iron, 27 mg vitamin C per 100 g serving.

Basellaceae

The small family of *Basellaceae* numbers not more than twenty species, indigenous to Asia or tropical America. They are all winding, herbaceous climbing plants, often with large fleshy leaves.

Three genera from this family each provide one edible type. In South and Central America, people eat the leaves and tubers of *Anreda cordifolia* (syn. *Boussinqoultia cordifolia*), a plant known as Madeira vine and Mognonette vine, found also in southern Europe. *Ullucus tuberosus* from the South American Andes provides edible tubers rich in starch. Neither of these two vegetables is sold in western Europe, although *Ullucus* could be cultivated there under glass.

On sale sometimes are the large glossy leaves of the genus *Basella,* originally from south-east Asia, but now grown in Africa and tropical America. In northern regions these plants can be cultivated under glass. There are three species: *B. alba* with oval dark green leaves, *B. cordifolia* with heart-shaped dark green leaves, and *B. rubra* with oval to round red leaves. When cooked they are a soft and rather slimy vegetable.

Basella or **Ceylon spinach** (*Basella* sp.)
Large, glossy, rather fleshy leaves, dark green or red, depending on species, heart-shaped, round, or oval.
ORIGIN: South-east Asia.
PRODUCTION: Tropical regions of America, Africa and south-east Asia.
SEASON: Limited exports. In northern regions grown under glass in summer and autumn.
USE: Wash leaves and prepare like spinach or purslane. As it is rather slimy this vegetable becomes revolting if overcooked.
STORAGE: Very limited. Leaves easily become too warm and rot.
NUTRITIONAL VALUE: 19 kcal, 4.1 g carbohydrate, 1.6 g protein, 105 mg calcium, 1.6 mg iron, 3.5 mg vitamin A, 85 mg vitamin C per 100 g serving.
INDUSTRIAL PROCESSING: None. The coloured juice of the false fruit is used in dried form for colouring cakes.

△ *Basella alba*, 6¼ in (160 mm) long

Boraginaceae

The 2,000 or so species of the *Boraginaceae* family are indigenous to the non-tropical regions of the northern hemisphere. The stems and leaves of some species are covered with rough hairs, while others have leaves covered with soft hairs or completely smooth leaves. The family characteristic is the attractive flowers that are always arranged in two adjacent rows, pointing alternately right and left. Insects are attracted to these flowers by the rich nectar, so *Boraginaceae* are valued by beekeepers.

Many *Boraginaceae* have also made a name for themselves as medicinal plants. Plants used in medicines include *officinalis* in their Latin name, but this reputation is not always justified. The comfrey *(Symphytum officinalis)*, for example, certainly does contain substances in its leaves and root stock that seem to be effective against chronic infections and muscular pain, but it was once claimed that the plant also mended broken bones. Believers in 'signature lore' claimed to be able to read the curative powers of a plant from its external characteristics. The comfrey probably owes its reputation to the fact that the leaf stalk joins the stem with a kind of leg, and that was considered sure proof that it could heal broken legs. Similarly the lungwort *(Pulmonaria officinalis)* was used to treat complaints of the lung, because its leaves carry a whitish pattern of spots looking rather like human lungs.

The only vegetable plant in the family, borage *(Borago officinalis)*, also has curative powers. The sixteenth century Flemish botanist Rembert Dodoens (Dodonaeus) reported in his *Herb Book* that 'the flowers of this plant, steeped in wine, make people happy and joyful and that all sadness, depression and melancholy disappear. He was right about borage in that the plant contains substances that calm the nerves, stimulate the metabolism, and regulate sweating. It also has a diuretic effect and the juice can be used to help slow-healing wounds as well as rashes. In the pharmaceutical industry there is a demand for substances derived from borage seeds.

Borage is used mainly as a herb, though it can also be eaten as a vegetable, both the leaves and the pretty, light blue flowers (fresh or preserved), being much liked as an edible garnish. It is an annual, although often regarded as a perennial because the ripe seed falls to the ground and germinates easily the following year.

Borage

Borage
(Borago officinalis)
Sturdy annual herbaceous plant with rough hairy leaves and light blue flowers. Young leaves usually on sale, fresh cucumber-like taste.
ORIGIN: Mediterranean area.
PRODUCTION: Throughout Europe.
SEASON: May to October, sometimes earlier or later if grown under glass.
USE: Eat the leaf raw in salads or (finely chopped) on bread. May be cooked with other leaf vegetables such as spinach beet or cabbage. Use flowers as edible garnish. An aromatic tea can be brewed from the fresh or dried flowers.
STORAGE: A few days in thc salad compartment of the refrigerator.
NUTRITIONAL VALUE: Limited. Borage contains a salty, sticky juice, resinous substances, and a small quantity of volatile oil.

Chenopodiaceae

The goosefoot family *(Chenopodiaceae)* gets its name from the genus *Chenopodium*, a group that grows in all temperate and warm regions. Many species of this genus have leaves shaped rather like a goose's foot if you use a little imagination.

The family is interesting for several reasons. It is economically significant because it contains a number of vegetable plants, such as spinach, garden beet and chard. Many wild goosefoot species are edible and probably played a part in the diet of our ancestors, as primitive vegetables. In the eighteenth century the present-day sugar beet was developed from the older beetroot. Sugar beet has now overtaken sugar cane as the world's main sugar source. The family also contains a number of species that flourish closer to the sea than most other plants. These salt-loving plants include the glasswort and the annual seablite *(Suaeda maritima)*. The sea salt, so deadly to other plants, is necessary for their survival. In earlier times they were often burned to make a detergent from the alkaline ash.

Primitive vegetables of the goosefoot family are mostly to be found in the genus *Chenopodium* itself, growing throughout the world. There are several species that used to be widely grown as vegetables (and still are here and there), like the white goosefoot *(Chenopodium album)*, with a leaf eaten like spinach and seeds eaten like groats, the Good King Henry *(Ch. bonus-henricus)*, to be found near villages and other places where people used to live, and the red strawberry spinach *(Ch. foliosum)* from the mountainous regions of Spain and Portugal.

American wormseed oil was made from *Ch. anthelminticum* (growing in Central America and the south-eastern United States). No other remedy has ever been found to be so effective for roundworm and amoebic dysentery. The only disadvantage was the number of patients who died or were left as permanent invalids after too large a dose. In spite of its undoubted curative powers it is now used only by witch doctors and quacks. A similar species is *Ch. ambrosioides* from Suriname, where it is called 'worm mint'. The juice of the leaves and seeds, mixed with molasses, is also used for worming, but we have no information about any harmful side-effects.

The orache genus *(Atriplex)* occupies a place half-way between primitive and modern vegetables. The most important species is the orache *(A. hortenis)*, a predecessor of spinach. Probably developed from the wild shiny orache *(A. nitens)*, this plant was enjoyed by the Greeks and Romans.

The history of the beet also goes back a long way. There is a small number of wild species from the *Beta* genus in southern Europe, on the Cape Verde Islands and in west and central Asia. The ancestor of our modern beet varieties probably developed from crosses of these species.

There are various types of beet, and the oldest is most likely the Swiss chard *(B. vulgaris var. flavescens)*, with its thick, fleshy, edible leaf stems. According to some historians this plant grew in the palace gardens of King Merodach-Baladan II, who ruled over Babylonia about 700 BC. It is now cultivated mainly in central and southern Europe and at present the white-ribbed varieties are the most popular. The red-ribbed are also very old — they were described in 1554 by the botanist Dodonaeus from Mechelen. Chards are known botanically under the name *B. vulgaris var. vulgaris* and the young leaves are usually cooked like spinach.

Beets with fleshy roots are classified as *B. vulgaris var. conditiva*. The best-known is the red beetroot, that probably developed around 1500 along the coasts of the Mediterranean and then gradually penetrated further north. Dodonaeus reported the plant in the sixteenth century, and other writers of the period mention a 'Roman beet,' a 'foreign genus with a short, thick root, similar to kohlrabi, with an attractive red colour inside'.

In France, at the beginning of the seventeenth century, people realized that the juice of red beets contained sugar similar in taste to cane sugar. Half a century later the quality of beet sugar equalled that of cane sugar, and in 1802 a Swiss opened the world's first sugar beet factory in Silesia, but the cane sugar manufacturers made sure that the enterprise came to nothing. The Swiss innovator went bankrupt and died a beggar. It is really due to Napoleon that beet sugar is now the world's main sugar supplier. When there were problems with France's cane sugar imports the Emperor took up the Swiss idea, and French growers managed to increase the yield of their sugar beet. One of the most important vegetable plants in the goosefoot family now is spinach. The cultivated plant probably developed from the wild form *Spinacia tetrande*, still found in the Caucasus, Iran and Afghanistan. It is generally believed that this plant travelled westwards around 650 AD and arrived in Europe in the twelfth century.

The leaf of modern spinach varieties varies from triangular or arrow-shaped to oblong or oval, and there are smooth-leaved and curly-leaved varieties as well. In the United States the curly leaves are preferred, while Europeans grow the smooth-leaved varieties. The so-called New Zealand spinach is not a true spinach, but belongs to the iceplant family (see page 12).

Orache or **mountain spinach** *(Atriplex hortensis)*
A rapid-growing, annual leaf vegetable with yellow, green, red or multi-coloured leaves, covered with a powdery substance on the underside. Young leaf is cut off at ground level, older leaf is plucked.
ORIGIN: South-eastern Europe, Caucasus, central Asia.
PRODUCTION: Central and southern Europe.
SEASON: May to October. Earlier and later under glass.
USE: Thoroughly wash leaf to remove powder. Use raw in salads, boil like spinach or add to vegetable soup.
STORAGE: A few days at 36 to 41°F (2 to 5°C).
NUTRITIONAL VALUE: 20 kcal, 2 g carbohydrate, 2 g protein, 0.3 g fat, 70 mg calcium, 4 mg iron, 3 mg vitamin A, 30 mg vitamin C per 100 g serving.

△ Left: Gele melde, leaf 3⅞ in (98 mm) long △ Right: Groene melde, 5⅝ in (142 mm) long ▽ Rode melde, 13⅜ in (340 mm) long

Varieties

Gele melde Most often on sale, with large yellowish-green leaves. Runs to seed rapidly in summer, but leaves can still be eaten.

Groene melde Green to dark green, arrow-shaped leaves.

Rode melde Red-leaved with slower growth than the yellow or green varieties.

Bonte melde Seldom on sale, easily recognized by its multi-coloured leaves.

Garden beet or **table beet** *(Beta vulgaris, var. conditiva)* A biennial plant that forms an edible tuber in the first year. The tuber is formed by the thickening of the lower part of the stem and the upper part of the root. There are flat, round, long and intermediate beetroots. The most important type is the round, red beet, but there are also varieties with white, yellow or reddish-white ringed flesh. The red colouring consists mainly of betanine.
ORIGIN: Mediterranean.
PRODUCTION: Mainly countries with a temperate climate, such as West Germany, the Netherlands, Poland, Scandinavia and northern parts of the USA.
SEASON: Throughout the year. May to July young beets in bunches with leaves, July to May fully-grown beets without leaves.
USE: On sale both raw and cooked. Raw beets should be boiled; ready-cooked beets can be sliced and used in salads or pickles.
STORAGE: Cooked beetroots a few days at 32 to 34°F (0 to 1°C). Raw beets for two weeks at the same temperature. Raw beets without leaves will keep for a few months at 38 to 41°F (3 to 5°C).
NUTRITIONAL VALUE: 37 kcal, 7 g carbohydrate, 2 g protein, 0.2 g fat, 400 mg potassium, 100 mg sodium, 40 mg phosphorus, 30 mg calcium, 1 mg iron, 5 mg vitamin C per 100 g serving.
INDUSTRIAL PROCESSING: Pickling, small beets whole, large ones sliced. Beetroot juice.

△ Garden beet 'Egyptische platronde', 4¼ in (110 mm) across

Varieties

Egyptische platronde An early variety, good for producing beets in bunches. The flattish-round tuber is purplish-red, often with obvious white rings. The faster the plants have grown, the lighter the colour.

Gladoro An early variety with little leaf and a fairly round tuber. Red fleshed, also used for early cultivation of beets in bunches.

Detroit or **Kogel** A principal variety (with many selections) with a round to conical tuber and attractive red flesh. Sown later than the two already mentioned. Beets come on to the market in autumn or are stored for sale later. Some selections are more resistant to developing shoots, are sown earlier, and are on sale in the summer.

△ Garden beet 'Formanova', $5\frac{1}{2}$ in (140 mm) long

Formanova An intermediate variety with a reasonably good red colour. On the market quite late, as it is liable to form shoots and so is not suitable for early cultivation. Much used for even slicing, especially in Scandinavia.

Lange donkerrode An old variety and a slow grower. This long, heavy beet has a smooth skin and attractive dark red flesh. Mainly intended for storage and sale in the winter. The professionals have abandoned it in favour of round varieties.

Crapaudine A long red beetroot with a rough, bark-like skin. By autumn the red colour has improved, earlier it is not so good.

Burpee's golden A rather early, round beet with smooth orange skin and bright yellow flesh, turning whitish when over ripe. Mainly grown by amateur gardeners.

Albine veredura Quite a late, round beet, with dark leaves and a thick tail, developed especially for use in fish salads. The flesh is white, so it does not colour the fish red.

Chioggia A sweet, round beet with smooth, light red skin and flesh composed of alternate white and pinkish rings. Used extensively in Italy as an early bunch beetroot.

△ Garden beet 'Burpee's golden', $3\frac{3}{4}$ in (95mm) across ▽ Garden beet 'Chioggia', 3 in (75 mm) across

△ Swiss chard 'Gele witribbige', 20½ in (520 mm) long

Swiss chard or **seakale beet** *(Beta vulgaris, var. flavescens)* Biennial with large leaves that may be red or light to dark green. The thick, wide, ribbed leaf stems are eaten.
ORIGIN: Mediterranean.
PRODUCTION: Central and southern Europe.
SEASON: June to October.
USE: Remove the soft tissue from the inside of the leaf, cut the leaf stems into pieces and boil or stew.
STORAGE: Bare leaf stems a few weeks at 32 to 34°F (0 to 1°C) and in high humidity. If kept too dry the leaves become fibrous and tough.
NUTRITIONAL VALUE: 28 kcal, 3 g carbohydrate, 3 g protein, 0.4 g fat, 87 mg calcium, 4 mg iron, 2 mg vitamin A, 35 mg vitamin C per 100 g serving.

Varieties

Lucullus Quite a robust variety with thick, fleshy, yellowish-green leaf stems and yellowish-green curly leaves. The ribs are not very fibrous, and the young leaves can be eaten too.

Gele witribbige A robust variety with broad, fleshy, white leaf stems and yellowish-green, smooth leaves. The ribs become fibrous more quickly than Lucullus.

Donkergroene gekrulde witribbige A variety with broad, fleshy, white leaf stems and dark green curly leaves. Ribs rapidly become fibrous.

Donkergroene gladde witribbige A decorative variety with broad, white leaf stems and tiny, dark green, smooth leaves. Ribs soon become fibrous.

Rhubarb chard A very decorative red-leaved variety with thick, fleshy, red leaf stems, very tasty, looking rather like rhubarb.

△ Swiss chard 'Donkergroene gekrulde witribigge', $20\frac{1}{8}$ in (510 mm) long

△ Swiss chard 'Donkergroene gladde witribigge', $19\frac{5}{8}$ in (499 mm) long

△ Swiss chard 'Rhubarb chard', $19\frac{1}{4}$ in (490 mm) long

Spinach beet
(Beta vulgaris, var. vulgaris v/h cicla)
Green or red leaf vegetable. The young leaf is cut off just above ground level, and the cut stem produces new shoots so that after two or three weeks the leaf can be harvested again.
ORIGIN: Mediterranean; Asia Minor.
PRODUCTION: Mostly grown by amateur gardeners.
SEASON: Seldom on market.
USE: Lightly boil young leaves and eat like spinach.
STORAGE: Very limited, as the young leaf rapidly becomes limp.
NUTRITIONAL VALUE: 28 kcal, 2 g carbohydrate, 3 g protein, 0.4 g fat, 87 mg calcium, 4 mg iron, 2 mg vitamin A, 35 mg vitamin C per 100 g serving.

Varieties

Gewone groene An old variety with smooth, green leaves and thin, green leaf stems. Only suitable for cultivating young leaves. Leaf production high.

Lucullus Yellowish-green curly leaves and stiff leaf stems. Eating quality better than gewone groene, but fewer leaves produced.

Rhubarb chard A red spinach beet, later than the other two varieties, with a lower yield and less prolific growth, but very good quality for eating.

△ Spinach beet 'Gewone groene', $9\frac{3}{4}$ in (250 mm) long

Glasswort
(Salicornia europaea)
Annual plants with no leaves, but branching, fleshy, green or reddish stems. Only suitable for eating when young. Plants on the market after July should only be used as a decoration on fish dishes.
ORIGIN: North Sea coasts of north-west Europe.
PRODUCTION: North-west Europe.
SEASON: April to July.
USE: Boiled, especially good with fish.
STORAGE: Two to three weeks in the refrigerator.
INDUSTRIAL PROCESSING: Bottling.

△ Glasswort, about $4\frac{3}{4}$ in (110 mm) long

Spinach
(Spinacia oleracea)
A rapid-growing, annual, herbaceous plant, with green leaves eaten when young. The 'seed' is made up of loose fruit parts that come out of the ground with the germinating plants, or come from pollen grains of the male plants.
ORIGIN: Caucasus, Iran, Afghanistan.
PRODUCTION: Europe, North America, western Asia.
SEASON: Throughout the year.
USE: Wash thoroughly and eat raw or boiled. Do not keep any left-overs of cooked spinach, as the nitrate in the leaf can be converted into poisonous nitrite.
STORAGE: Very limited. Leaf soon becomes limp. Will keep for four to eight days at 32 to 34°F (0 to 1°C).
NUTRITIONAL VALUE: 20 kcal, 2 g protein, 0.4 g fat, 2 g carbohydrate, 150 mg calcium, 2.8 mg iron, 3.1 mg vitamin A, 11 mg vitamin C per 100 g serving.
INDUSTRIAL PROCESSING: Deep-freezing (whole leaves, chopped or puréed), canned or bottled (puréed), preserved baby foods.

△ Spinach 'Winterreuzen', 5¾ in (144 mm) long including stem ▽ Spinach 'Resistoflay', 5¼ in (135 mm) long including stem

Varieties

Early varieties
Prickly-seeded, rapid -growing varieties are often used for early sowing in open ground. Later in the spring round-seeded varieties follow, resistant to downy mildew.

Breedblad scherpzaad A fairly broad, smooth, bright green leaf with a moderately pointed top.

Resistoflay A round-seeded variety for early spring and autumn cultivation, with a stiff, darkish green leaf. Resistant to some forms of downy mildew.

Wolter A rapid-growing, round-seeded hybrid for early spring and late autumn cultivation. Oval-round, mid-green leaf with a long stem. Resistant to downy mildew.

Summer varieties
In summer, spinach plants quickly run to seed, so slower-growing varieties are sown.

Mazurka A round-seeded hybrid with firm, darkish green leaves, fairly resistant to downy mildew.

Bloomsdale An old, round-seeded variety from America with dark green, very lumpy leaves. The plants are robust and resistant to mosaic disease, but are sensitive to downy mildew.

Winter varieties
These are sown at the end of August or the beginning of September and harvested in spring, so they need to be winter hardy.

Winterreuzen An old round-seeded variety of French origin, with an upright, arrow-shaped leaf and long leaf stems. Susceptible to false mildew.

Compositae

The family of the *Compositae* is one of the largest in the plant kingdom. It includes more than 1,000 genera and some 2,000 species. A characteristic of these plants is their inflorescence. Each 'flower' is made up of a large number of small, tubular and ribbon-like flowerettes. A frequent characteristic is also the garland of sepals that, on ripening, unfolds from the seeds like a fluffy parachute. This enables the seeds to travel great distances, carried by the wind. Another feature of the *Compositae* is that they produce a whitish milky juice with a bitter taste.

Well-known and typical *Compositae* are the marguerite, dandelion, sunflower and chrysanthemum. Many species are thought to have curative powers and in some cases they have, for instance camomile and milfoil. In the case of coltsfoot, 'colt' may be a corruption of 'cough', as it is indeed used to soothe coughs.

For such a large plant family, there are relatively few species eaten as vegetables and developed by nurserymen into cultivars. One of the most important types of vegetable economically is the lettuce. This genus includes several types grown on a large scale. No true wild form of our cultivated lettuce is known, but probably all cultivars derive in one way or another from the so-called wild lettuce *(Lactuca serriola)*, found in various parts of western Europe, western Asia, and north Africa.

Lettuce has been cultivated for many centuries. Our earliest information dates from around 550 BC when the plant was eaten in Egypt and at the Persian court as a cooked vegetable. The plants depicted in murals were probably primitive cos lettuce types. Shredding lettuce and other non-cabbage types have existed for nearly two thousand years. We find the first mention of cabbage lettuce in 1540, but the crisphead or iceberg lettuce is much younger, dating only from the nineteenth century.

We can distinguish the following varieties of lettuce:

Stem lettuce This form was developed in China, between 600 and 900 AD. They selected for plants with relatively small leaves and a long fleshy stem with an edible pith. In Asia these stems are cut off at ground level and sold in bunches with the leaves removed. In 1938 an American firm of seedsmen obtained some seed from Tibet, and in 1941 brought the results on to the market as a new vegetable called celtuce (a combination of celery and lettuce). Since this lettuce has in fact nothing to do with celery, we are calling it stem lettuce.

Cabbage lettuce This is by far the most important variety of lettuce. All cabbage or butterhead varieties and all crisphead varieties belong to this group. Cabbage lettuce and butterhead lettuce both have thin soft leaves that rapidly lose their crispness once picked. The colour of the leaf varies from yellowish-green to dark green. Sometimes anthocyanin is present and may colour the leaf red, especially during drought and at low temperatures. For a long time anthocyanin was regarded as undesirable, but now some people like it. Crisphead or iceberg lettuce is a type of cabbage lettuce with a thick crispy leaf that remains firm for a long time after harvesting. Crisphead lettuce was introduced into the United States in 1894 under the name iceberg. Improvement in the 1930s led to the development of the more hardy type familiar to us today, that can withstand long-distance transport.

The sea aster is a 'wild' vegetable from the coasts of the North Sea. Some market gardeners are now trying to grow it commercially

Loose-leaf lettuce The terms loose-leaf lettuce, curly lettuce, oakleaf lettuce, shredding lettuce and misticanza refer to various non-heading types of lettuce with frizzy or sharply-indented leaves. The species containing anthocyanin (with red leaves) seems to be becoming more popular. Shredding lettuce and misticanza are picked and sold as young leaves.

Cos lettuce or **Romaine lettuce** Probably the oldest form of lettuce as a cultivated plant. The heads are oblong and closed at the top. Growers used to bind the heads with raffia to produce a good yellow colouring. The leaf of this lettuce is rather stringy and not particularly suitable for eating raw, so it is often stewed.

Cichorium is another *Compositae* genus supplying vegetables. One of the best-known cultivars in this genus is the endive, probably developed from the wild form *C. pumilum* from the Mediterranean area. The Greeks and Romans knew the endive as a leaf vegetable and the sixteenth-century botanist Dodonaeus mentions a domesticated endive: a plant with large, long, broad, whitish-green, soft leaves. We now recognize three distinct varieties: curled endive *(var. crispum)*, slicing endive *(var. endivia)*, and whole-leaf or broad-leaf endive *(var. latifolium)*. In southern Europe curled endive is widely grown, but the whole-leaf type is cultivated further

The dandelion is related to the lettuce and the scorzonera and can be eaten as a vegetable

north. Slicing endive is grown for the processing industry, but not widely.

Wild chicory *(C. intybus),* with its large light blue flowers, grows on grass verges and along river banks throughout Europe, north Africa and western Asia. This is the origin of the chicory root *(C. intybus var. sativum),* grown to mix with coffee, and several other varieties, greenleaf chicory, sugar loaf, red-leaved chicory or radicchio, and witloof chicory. The Egyptians, the Greeks and the Romans all used chicory leaves as a vegetable. Dodonaeus, in the sixteenth century, describes both a domesticated chicory and a wild chicory with red leaf ribs. The cultivation of witloof is more recent, dating from the nineteenth century. It was discovered around 1850 that white (blanched) plants could be grown in a dark cellar. Because the centre of witloof culture is in Belgium, the vegetable is also known as Brussels chicory.

The *Compositae* family also includes thistles. Two of these are eaten: the artichoke, 'queen of vegetables', and the less well-known cardoon. Both species originate in the Mediterranean area, and are grown there still. As there is no wild form of the artichoke known, we assume it has been developed from the cardoon. We enjoy the fleshy flower buds of the artichoke, and the young leaf stems of the cardoon before it has produced any shoots.

Another vegetable from the *Compositae* family is the scorzonera, with its long, black, fleshy, edible roots. The plant probably derives its name from *escorzonera,* the Spanish for poisonous snake. The cylindrical black roots were used in earlier times as a cure for snakebite, but this probably has more to do with their appearance than their efficacy. Black (true) scorzonera is sometimes incorrectly called oatroot, which should strictly be reserved for the roots of the salsify *(Tragopogon porrifolius)* that are fleshy and edible with a light-coloured skin. They are also known as white scorzonera, and their woolly-haired roots are even more difficult to clean than the true scorzonera's. The salsify grows wild in southern Europe and is seldom cultivated. The edible branched white roots of *Scolymus hispanicus,* the Spanish oyster plant, a biennial from southern Europe, are similar to 'white scorzonera'.

Four other *Compositae* are known as vegetables, but have no great economic significance. The sea aster is a salt-loving species from the North Sea coast of Europe and the salt steppes of central and eastern Europe, north Africa and central Asia. The leaf is mainly gathered on mud flats in the Netherlands, but attempts have been made to improve the plant and to cultivate it in brackish types of soil.

Also in the process of improvement is the burdock, a plant from Europe and Asia that has also made its home in North America. It owes its name to its burrs, the hairy fruit that cling to clothes and fur. Varieties have been produced in Japan with thick straight black roots, rather like scorzonera. In Japan, Taiwan and California cultivation of the edible burdock is quite significant. The garland chrysanthemum is edible and valued as a vegetable in southern China, Japan, Taiwan and California, and now people are trying to grow this species in the Mediterranean area as well.

The leaves of the dandelion are also eaten. If the root balls (without leaves) are stored in a dark place they develop whitish-yellow leaflets known as mole salad. In earlier times people used to search the meadows in spring for the naturally blanched leaves of the wild dandelion. Tests are being carried out in Finland to extract the bitter substance from the dandelion, which could be used as a cheaper alternative to quinine in the production of tonic water (quinine water).

Finally, there is the Jerusalem artichoke, discovered in 1605 in the New World and brought to Europe two years later, when this heliotropic plant was given its name, a corruption of *girasol,* turning to the sun. It was grown in the Netherlands in the seventeenth century and then exported to Britain. The cultivation of these edible tubers is increasing, as nowadays they are processed to give alcohol fructose.

The various types of vegetable from the *Compositae* family are described on the following pages in alphabetical order of their Latin names.

△ Burdock, 15¾ in (400 mm) long ▽ Sea aster, 4¼ in (110 mm) long

Burdock
(Arctium lappa)
These strong plants have bare stems and large, fairly rough leaves. They form long, straight, fleshy, edible roots, rather like scorzonera.
ORIGIN: Europe and Asia.
PRODUCTION: Mainly Japan, also Taiwan and USA (California).
SEASON: September to December.
USE: Wash, peel and boil the roots. You can use the scorzonera recipe.
STORAGE: Roots that are not too old can be kept for a few weeks at 32 to 34°F (0 to 1°C) and in high humidity. Old roots soon become spongy and woody.

Varieties

Nakanomiya early An early variety. In Japan the roots grow to 30 inches (75 cm), but in northern regions only to a maximum of 16 inches (40 cm).

Watanabe early A rapid-growing variety with the same root length as above.

Takinogawa long A somewhat later variety with longer roots — in Japan 35 to 39 inches (90 to 100 cm).

Sea aster
(Aster tripolium)
Oblong fleshy leaves arranged in rosettes, about 4¾ inches (12 cm) long. They are gathered at an early stage for eating. In summer the leaves of the flowering plants are tough and tasteless.
ORIGIN: Europe and Asia.
PRODUCTION: Most are gathered locally in the wild, particularly in the Netherlands. A few specialized nurseries are beginning to cultivate this species and are trying to produce uniform and productive cultivars.
SEASON: April to June. May be extended in future.
USE: Wash young leaves and cook like a leaf vegetable. Often served with oysters or mussels.
STORAGE: After harvesting will keep for a few weeks at 32 to 34°F (0 to 1°C) in high humidity.

Garland chrysanthemum
(Chrysanthemum coronarium)
Rapid-growing, annual herbaceous plant, about 40 inches (1 metre) tall. If regularly pruned the plant keeps on forming new young edible shoots.
ORIGIN: Southern China. Probably also southern Portugal and Mediterranean countries.
PRODUCTION: Mainly southern China and Taiwan. Also Japan and USA (California).
SEASON: From May to October. Earlier and later when grown under glass in northern regions.
USE: Cook leaves of young plants as a vegetable or use in soups. Later the flowers are edible as well.
STORAGE: A few days at 34°F (1°C) and in high humidity.
NUTRITIONAL VALUE: 74 mg calcium, 4.2 g iron, 45 mg vitamin C, 3 mg vitamin A, 0.15 mg vitamin B1, 0.3 mg vitamin B2 per 100 g serving.

△ Garland chrysanthemum, $7\frac{1}{2}$ in (190 mm) long ▽ Endive 'Nummer vijf', $16\frac{1}{2}$ in (420 mm) across

Varieties

There are two Japanese varieties, one with small dark green sawtooth leaves (small-leaved) and another with broad oblong smooth leaves (large-leaved). There is also a double mixed variety, but this is usually sold for ornamental gardens.

Endive
(Cichorium endivia)
A rapid-growing plant, forming a broad flat rosette of leaves. It has a more or less filled head, tightly closed underneath, with a light-green to yellow heart. The two varieties, broad-leaf and curled, can be distinguished by leaf shape.
ORIGIN: Mediterranean area.
PRODUCTION: Italy, France, Spain, Greece, Netherlands.
SEASON: Endives grown under glass, November to June. In open ground, May to December.
USE: Cook on its own or with other vegetables, or raw in salads. Curled endive is especially suitable for salads and as a garnish.
STORAGE: Complete heads for about two weeks at 32 to 34°F (0 to 1°C) and in high humidity. Susceptible to drying out.
NUTRITIONAL VALUE: 8 kcal, 1 g carbohydrate, 1 g protein, 20 mg calcium, 1 mg iron, 1.2 mg vitamin A, 10 mg vitamin C per 100 g serving.
INDUSTRIAL PROCESSING: Deep-freezing, canning, bottling, making into endive à la crème (mixed with a sauce), drying.

Varieties

Nummer vijf A broad-leaf variety with a well-filled head and broad, shortish, soft green leaves. Grown in open ground and under glass.

△ Curled endive 'Wallone frisan', $14\frac{3}{4}$ in (374 mm) across ▽ Curled endive 'Pancalière' (cut through), $5\frac{3}{8}$ in (390 mm) across

Breedblad volhart winter A broad-leaf variety. The heart fills out only at a late stage. The leaves are quite long and narrow, dark green and rather stringy. Suitable for autumn and winter cultivation under glass.

Golda A rapid-growing broad-leaf variety with a rather loose head and long narrowish leaves, green to light green. Suitable for growing under glass.

Géante maraîchère A broad-leaf variety with a moderately filled head. The green leaves are quite long and broad.

Pancalière A very curly compact variety. The head is flat and well-filled. Not suitable for a cool moist climate.

Wallone frisan A strong-growing curled endive with fairly long, upward-pointing, indented green leaves. Can be grown in a cool moist climate. President is a popular selection of this variety.

Green-leaved chicory
(Cichorium intybus, var. foliosum)
Large loose leaves with a rather bitter taste. Leaves are green unless they have been forced in the dark, when they are virtually white. Depending on variety, leaves are smooth or indented or form heads like tulips. Green leaves from the chicory root *(C. intybus, var. sativum)* are sometimes sold loose, as are leaves from thickly-sown sugar loaf selections (see under sugar loaf).
ORIGIN: Mediterranean area.
PRODUCTION: Italy, France, Spain.
SEASON: After mid-June. In winter as well, with frost-resistant and blanched varieties.
USE: Mainly in salads. Often used with other types of lettuce because of its bitter taste.
STORAGE: A few days at 32 to 34°F (0 to 1°C) and in high humidity.
NUTRITIONAL VALUE: 20 kcal, 3.8 g carbohydrate, 1.8 g protein, 0.3 g fat, 86 mg calcium, 4 mg vitamin A, 22 mg vitamin C per 100 g serving.

Varieties

Catalogna Italian variety with long, very narrow and often sharply-indented green leaves. The plants are harvested with a piece of the root. Suitable for forcing in winter.

Grumolo A variety with dark green tulip-like heads harvested in winter from the fields in Italy.

△ Sugar loaf 'Zuckerhut', 17¾ in (450 mm) long

Sugar loaf
(Cichorium intybus, var. foliosum)
A plant forming an oblong, rather open head in autumn with quite a lot of loose surrounding leaves. Many sugar loaf selections are fairly sweet compared with other types of chicory.
ORIGIN: Mediterranean area.
PRODUCTION: On a limited scale in France, Switzerland, Austria, southern West Germany.
SEASON: September to December.
USE: Chop finely and use like endive.
STORAGE: Heads and surrounding leaves for a few weeks in a cool place. The surrounding leaves wither, and when they are removed whitish heads will be found underneath.
NUTRITIONAL VALUE: 15 kcal, 2 g carbohydrate, 2 g protein, 0.1 g fat, 20 mg calcium, 1 mg iron, 0.95 mg vitamin A, 15 mg vitamin C per 100 g serving.

Varieties

Sugar loaf An old variety with large oblong heads, quite an open heart, and a number of loose surrounding leaves. The varieties Gradina and Elmo have a rather wild growth.

Scarpia and **Poncho** Two new varieties with more compact growth. The oblong heads run to a point and have fewer surrounding leaves.

△ Sugar loaf 'Poncho', 11¾ in (300 mm) long ▽ Red-leaved chicory 'Rode van Treviso', 4¾ in (120 mm) across

Red-leaved chicory
(Cichorium intybus, var. foliosum)
Small, round, red-leaved heads with either dark or white leaf-veins. The leaf tastes rather bitter. Sometimes incorrectly called red lettuce.
ORIGIN: Mediterranean area.
PRODUCTION: Chiefly Italy.
SEASON: Autumn and winter.
USE: Eat raw with ordinary cabbage lettuce or crisphead lettuce. The heads can also be baked or grilled.
STORAGE: Peeled heads two to three weeks at 32 to 34°F (0 to 1°C) in high humidity.
NUTRITIONAL VALUE: As sugar loaf.

Varieties

Rode van Verona Oblong and upward-pointing green leaves with reddish veins. Leaves turn red in the autumn and then the roundish red heads develop in the heart. Harvested in winter.

Rode van Treviso Like the Rode van Verona this belongs to the Witloof type and has oblong leaves. The peeled heads are also oblong and rather loose.

Cecare A new Dutch variety with broad reddish leaves, shaped rather like a cabbage lettuce. It hearts early and so is suitable for summer and autumn harvesting in a cool climate.

Otello A Dutch variety of the cabbage lettuce type, suitable for late harvesting as it can withstand a certain amount of frost. Slower than Cecare to turn red and form a heart.

Robin A variety derived from a cross of red-leaved chicory and Witloof. Suitable for forcing in a cold frame with soil cover. This produces oblong whitish heads with red-edged leaves.

Chioggia A rosette-forming Italian variety of red-leaved chicory. The heads have a bitter taste and are available throughout the summer into autumn.

△ Red-leaved chicory 'Chioggia', $11\frac{1}{2}$ in (290 mm) long

Witloof chicory or **Brussels chicory**
(Cichorium intybus, var. foliosum
Oblong heads blanched white or yellowish-white. The plant is lifted in the autumn, the leaves are removed just above the neck, and it is then replanted to produce white heads. Formerly the roots were placed in a frame and covered with a layer of earth, but nowadays they are often forced in tanks of running water in dark, climate-controlled cells. If so, the roots are not covered.
ORIGIN: Mediterranean area.
PRODUCTION: France, Belgium, Netherlands.
SEASON: Mostly October to May, but when forced in running water, throughout the year.
USE: Boil the heads whole or cut up and mix with cheese and/or ham. Raw and finely-chopped heads can be used in vegetable salads, for instance mixed with beetroot and apples.
STORAGE: Heads for two to three weeks at 32 to 34°F (0 to 1°C) in high humidity.
NUTRITIONAL VALUE: 17 kcal, 3 g carbohydrate, 1 g protein, 0.1 g fat, 20 mg calcium, 0.5 mg iron, 5 mg vitamin C per 100 g serving.
INDUSTRIAL PROCESSING: Deep-freezing (raw or à la crème). Some bottling and canning.

Varieties

Mechelen extra early Quite short, oval heads with rather broad leaves, thickened leaf-veins and a fairly long core. This variety is quite bitter. Suitable for early forcing with soil covering.

Mechelen early Similar but grows more slowly.

Zoom A hybrid variety from France, with firm, well-closed heads and a relatively short core. Suitable for early forcing with or without soil covering.

Mechelen mid-early and **Mechelen late** Similar to other Mechelen varieties, but suitable for mid-early and late forcing with or without soil covering. On the market quite late, until May.

Dutch mid-early Rather long, narrow and elliptical heads. Leaf quite narrow with thickened leaf-veins. The core is short. Not very bitter. Suitable for mid-early and sometimes even for late forcing with soil covering.

△ Witloof chicory, mid-early Mechelen type, $6\frac{1}{2}$ in (163 mm) long

Cardoon
(Cynara cardunculus)

Large, heavily-leaved, thistle-like plants with heavy, fleshy leaf stems. In autumn the leaves are bound together and wrapped in black plastic sheets, and the tops of the plants are cut off. After about two weeks the plants are cut off at ground level, the fibrous outer leaf stalks are removed, and the blanched inner stems are suitable for eating.

ORIGIN: Mediterranean area.

PRODUCTION: Italy, Spain, France.

SEASON: September to November.

USE: Remove any remaining roots or green leaves from the blanched leaf stems, cut stems into pieces. Immerse at once in water with a dash of vinegar to prevent blackening. Needs to be cooked for a long time.

STORAGE: Blanched plants for a few weeks (at low temperature and high humidity). If the stems dry out they become very stringy.

NUTRITIONAL VALUE: 60 kcal, 19 g carbohydrate, 3 g protein, 40 mg calcium, 1 mg iron, 10 mg vitamin C per 100 g serving.

△ Cardoon, $20\frac{1}{2}$ in (520 mm) long

Varieties

Plein blanc inerme A sturdy species with sharply-indented, greyish-green leaves and light yellow leaf stems.

Blanc amélioré Very sturdy with coarse green leaves.

Vert inerme Sturdy plant with sharply-indented, fine, greyish-green leaves. Leaf stems remain green in the field and are difficult to blanch in autumn. Fairly resistant to frost.

△ Artichoke 'Camus de Bretagne', $5\frac{7}{8}$ in (150 mm) across ▽ Artichoke 'Violette', 10 in (254 mm) long

Artichoke
(Cynara scolymus)
Large thistle-like plants with spherical or slightly pointed greyish-green (sometimes violet) flower buds the size of a fist.
ORIGIN: Mediterranean area.
PRODUCTION: Italy, Spain, France, Israel, Egypt.
SEASON: July to November.
USE: Wash heads thoroughly, cut away the three or four lowest leaves, and the stalk as far as the leaf base. Cut off the top and trim the points of the scale-shaped leaves. Boil in plenty of salted water. Drain well. Pull off the cooked leaves one at a time and suck out the soft moist flesh. If you like you can dip the leaf in a sauce first. Finally remove the fibres at the base, and eat the heart. The hearts can also be made into a separate dish.
STORAGE: One to three weeks at freezing point in high humidity, covered with foil.
NUTRITIONAL VALUE: 70 kcal, 15 g carbohydrate, 3 g protein, 50 mg calcium, 1 mg iron, 5 mg vitamin C per 100 g serving.
INDUSTRIAL PROCESSING: Hearts are deep-frozen, bottled or canned. Also used in pickle and relish manufacture.

Varieties

Camus de Bretagne Tall plants, up to 4 ft 6 in (150 cm) with a broad thick heart. The stubby leaves are mainly green, with a violet colouring on the edges.

Groene van Laon Mid-early variety with broad thick heads and pointed leaves, green shading towards violet.

Violette or **Vroege paarse** Early variety with a narrow, deep heart and rather pointed leaves. When young the heads are green, but turn violet later.

△ Artichoke 'Groene van Laon', 8¼ in (210 mm) long ▽ Jerusalem artichoke 'Bianka', 4¾ in, (120 mm) across

Varieties

Bianka Early variety, on sale in October. The white tubers are quite regular in shape.

Topianka Mid-early variety, reasonably productive with attractive white tubers.

Rozo Late, less productive variety. Can be harvested in winter only. Tubers white and attractively shaped.

Waldspindel Late but very productive with oblong violet heads containing a great deal of inulin. This variety is mainly used for processing.

Jerusalem artichoke *(Helianthus tuberosus)*
Irregularly-shaped, fairly large, white or purplish tubers with a thin skin. Has a laxative effect.
ORIGIN: America.
PRODUCTION: America, France, West Germany, Netherlands.
SEASON: October to March.
USE: Boil the tubers for a short time and then bake or purée. Older tubers should be peeled thinly, but young tubers do not need peeling when cooked, and can also be eaten raw. Flavour similar to globe artichoke.
STORAGE: Tubers susceptible to drying out. Best kept in a frame or in a covered heap in the field. Will then keep till spring. If allowed to sprout, eating quality drops.
NUTRITIONAL VALUE: 74 kcal, 16 g carbohydrate, 2.5 g protein, 0.4 g fat, 10 mg calcium, 3.7 mg iron, 4 mg vitamin C per 100 g serving.
INDUSTRIAL PROCESSING: Used for extracting fructose (for distilling alcohol), and for making flour.

△ Stem lettuce or celtuce, 19¼ in (490 mm) long

Stem lettuce or **Celtuce**
(Lactuca sativa, var. angustana)
Non-heading variety of lettuce with stiff oblong leaves and a longish, thick, fleshy stalk or stem which is eaten. On the market since the 1970s, also called celtuce and asparagus lettuce.
ORIGIN: China.
PRODUCTION: Mainly Taiwan and China.
SEASON: In northern regions, summer and early autumn, but may be imported at other times as well.
USE: Remove the leaves from the stalk and peel it. Cut the pith into slices and use in mixed salads. The stem may also be boiled and used in hot or cold dishes. The leaf can also be cooked.
STORAGE: The bare stems can be kept for a few weeks at low temperature and high humidity.

Cabbage lettuce
(Lactuca sativa, var. capitata)
This plant forms a fairly closed head, light to dark green, sometimes with red edges, depending on variety. If grown in the greenhouse all the leaves can be eaten, but if cultivated in open ground the outer leaves should be removed.
ORIGIN: Europe
PRODUCTION: Italy, France, Spain, Britain and Benelux countries.
SEASON: Open ground May to November, under glass October to June.
USE: Remove the leaves from the head, discarding the outer leaves if necessary, and then wash thoroughly. Eat raw, in mixed salads with tomato, cucumber, onion. Also use to garnish other dishes.
STORAGE: Must be kept cool or it wilts and the edges discolour. Will keep for a few days in the refrigerator.
NUTRITIONAL VALUE: 12 kcal, 1 g carbohydrate, 2 g protein, 30 mg calcium, 0.4 mg iron, 10 mg vitamin C per 100 g serving.

Varieties

There is a large number of cabbage lettuce varieties. The most important difference between them is the cultivation period (spring, summer, autumn, winter), and the method of cultivation (open ground or under glass).

Spring — under glass

Baccarat Shiny green to yellowish-green leaves with well-filled head.

Marcia Smooth yellowish-green leaves, a well-filled head and compact growth.

Mir Smooth, thin-leaved, green variety with compact growth.

Pallas Small variety, rather open at the top, with smooth, dark green leaves. A compact type of lettuce with an open but firm head.

Spring — open ground

Mondian Mid-early variety with a fairly large, firm, light yellow to greyish-green, well-closed head. Also used for early summer cultivation in open ground.

Reskia Fairly large, firm, well-closed heads. Also suitable for open-ground cultivation in early summer.

Summer — under glass

Salina Leaves smooth and dark green. Head not very large, open at the top.

Sitonia Medium-sized with well-filled top. Leaves smooth, light- to mid-green.

△ Cabbage lettuce 'Mir', 11 in (280 mm) across ▽ Cabbage lettuce 'Reskia', $12\frac{5}{8}$ in (320 mm) across

△ Cabbage lettuce 'Bataviaanse roodrand', $14\frac{1}{2}$ in (370 mm) across ▽ Cabbage lettuce 'Wonder der vier jaargetijden', $12\frac{1}{4}$ in (310 mm) across

Summer — open ground

Bataviaanse roodrand Fairly large heads with lumpy, reddish, wavy-edged leaves. Resembles crisphead lettuce.

Benita Forms a fairly large, firm, light yellowish-green head, well closed at the top. Also suitable for autumn cultivation.

Cindy Forms quite a large, firm, green head, well-closed on the top. Can also be used for autumn cultivation.

Soraya Fairly large, firm, green heads, reasonably well closed on top.

Wonder der vier jaargetijden Medium-sized heads. Outside leaves are reddish-brown, inside leaves green with red edges. The lower the temperature, the slower the growth, and the more intense the red colouring.

Autumn — under glass

Pascal Smooth, greyish-green leaves, compact growth.

Panvit Fairly smooth, shiny, green leaves. Head is excessively loose if harvested too early. Can also be used for growing heavy lettuce in winter.

Autumn — open ground

Clarion forms fairly large, firm, greyish-green heads, well-closed at the top. Leaves rather thick.

Winter — under glass

Columbus Smooth leaves, dull dark green to greyish-green, with rather an open top. Heads can be very heavy.

△ Crisphead lettuce 'Calmar', $20\frac{7}{8}$ in (530 mm) across

Crisphead lettuce
(Lactuca sativa, var. capitata)
A sturdy type of cabbage lettuce with a large firm head like a small white cabbage. The thickish leaves are hard and crispy, the loose surrounding leaves are rather stiff and are not eaten.
ORIGIN: USA.
PRODUCTION: USA (California, Arizona), Spain, Israel, France, Netherlands.
SEASON: March to December.
USE: Eat raw like ordinary cabbage lettuce.
STORAGE: About two weeks at 32 to 34°F (0 to 1°C) in high humidity. Cut heads can be kept for a few days in the refrigerator.
NUTRITIONAL VALUE: 14 kcal, 2.4 g carbohydrate, 0.9 g protein. 0.1 g fat, 20 mg calcium, 0.5 mg iron, 0.33 mg vitamin A, 6 mg vitamin C per 100 g serving.

Varieties

Calmar Large, dark green, reasonably firm head.

Ithaca Great Lakes Mid-early variety with a moderately large, green, fairly firm head, rather oblong in shape.

Nabucco Mid-early to late variety with fairly large, light green, firmish head.

Saladin Mid-early variety with large, reasonably firm, dark greyish-green head.

△ Crisphead lettuce 'Ithaca Great Lakes', $5\frac{7}{8}$ in (150 mm) across

△ Loose-leaf lettuce 'Australian yellow', $13\frac{3}{8}$ in (340 mm) across ▽ Loose-leaf lettuce 'Lollo' (green), $8\frac{1}{4}$ in (210mm) across

Loose-leaf lettuce
(Lactuca sativa, var. crispa)
Non-heading type of lettuce with frizzy or sharply indented leaves, tinted red in some varieties with anthocyanin. This red-leaved variety is becoming more popular.
ORIGIN: As cabbage lettuce.
PRODUCTION: USA, France, Italy, Benelux countries.
SEASON Throughout the year.
USE: As cabbage lettuce.
STORAGE: As cabbage lettuce.
NUTRITIONAL VALUE: As cabbage lettuce.

Varieties

American red edge An old variety. Lightly-curled green leaves with red spots. Rarely on the market.

Australian yellow Another old variety. Yellowish-green leaves, delicately curled. Mainly grown by amateur gardeners, seldom on sale.

Salad bowl Curly-leaved lettuce with light green indented leaves, very soft in structure. Heads keep for only a short time, becoming flabby a few hours after harvesting.

Red salad bowl Curly lettuce with reddish indented leaves. Often called oakleaf lettuce because of the shape and colour of the leaves. Keeps better than salad bowl.

Lollo Very curly and complex lettuce from Italy. There is one type with yellowish-green leaves and others that contain anthocyanin and are therefore red.

△ Loose-leaf lettuce 'Red salad bowl', 9½ in (240 mm) long ▽ Loose-leaf lettuce 'Lollo (red), 8¼ in (210 mm) across

Shredding lettuce Various rapid-growing varieties of lettuce are used for cultivating shredding lettuce. They are sown thickly and cut off at ground level while young. People speak of white and black young lettuce according to the colour of the seed.

Misticanza Obtained from a seed mixture of various types of lettuce, often mixed with chicory, staghorn plantain and other rapid-growing leaf vegetables. It is sown and harvested like shredding lettuce.

△ Cos lettuce (young plant), 8¾ in (220 mm) long

Cos or **Romaine lettuce**
(Lactuca sativa, var. longifolia)
Oblong head fairly loose at the top. The leaf is rather stiff and not very suitable for eating raw. Cos lettuce has been a cooking vegetable from time immemorial.
ORIGIN: Mediterranean area, Iran, Egypt.
PRODUCTION: Southern Europe.
SEASON: April to June.
USE: Wash and cook the leaves.
STORAGE: As crisphead lettuce.
NUTRITIONAL VALUE: As cabbage lettuce.

Varieties

White self-closing A sturdy plant with a coarse green leaf. Heads somewhat open at the top. Inside the head the leaf is yellowish-green.

Paris white Almost the same but coarser.

Green cos lettuce A little less sturdy than the others, but hearts up rather better. A popular variety is barcarolle, with fairly narrow leaves and long, oval, well-closed heads.

△ Green cos lettuce 'Barcarolle', $10\frac{5}{8}$ in (270 mm) long

△ Scorzonera, $12\frac{5}{8}$ in (320 mm) long

Scorzonera
(Scorzonera hispanica)
Straight, white, fleshy roots with a brownish-black skin, about 16 inches (40 cm) long. They contain a lot of milky juice and inulin.
ORIGIN: Southern Europe, probably Spain.
PRODUCTION: Belgium, Netherlands, France.
SEASON: October to April.
USE: Peel and cut the roots into chunks of about $1\frac{1}{2}$ to 2 inches (4 to 5 cm). Immerse the pieces in water with a little vinegar to prevent them turning brown. Then boil, stew or bake. Alternatively, boil the roots until almost done, then rinse in cold water, strip off the skin and prepare further.
STORAGE: Roots that are not quite ripe can be stored for a long time if kept cool. Up to four months at 32 to 34°F (0 to 1°C) and high humidity.
NUTRITIONAL VALUE: 68 kcal, 15 g carbohydrate, 1 g protein, 0.5 g fat, 60 mg calcium, 1.5 mg iron, 5 mg vitamin C per 100 g serving.
INDUSTRIAL PROCESSING: Bottled or canned. Also deep-frozen to some extent.

Varieties

Improved giant non-shooters A cultivar with various selections, such as Belstar super, Maxima, Negro, Torpedo and Triplex. All have smooth, long and quite uniform roots.

Long John A very productive variety with a cylindrical or inverted conical root with a blunt point.

△ Dandelion (not blanched), $8\frac{3}{4}$ in (220 mm) long

Dandelion
(Taraxacum officinale)
The green or blanched leaflets of the dandelion or of its leafy cultivars. The blanched leaves are forced, just like Witloof chicory.
ORIGIN: Europe and western Asia.
PRODUCTION: France.
SEASON: March to December (green leaf). September to March (blanched leaf).
USE: Raw in salads.
STORAGE: A few days in the refrigerator.
NUTRITIONAL VALUE: 18 kcal, 4 g carbohydrate, 1.5 g protein, 0.2 g fat, 20 mg calcium, 0.7 mg iron, 7 mg vitamin C per 100 g serving.

Varieties

Improved volhart A leafy variant of the ordinary dandelion. Forms a heavy leaf rosette. Inside the heart the leaflets blanch without soil covering.

Vert de Montmagny amélioré Covered with soil in autumn for blanching.

Amélioré géant Cultivated in the same way as Witloof. Roots grown in the field are forced in the dark in winter.

Convolvulaceae

The Convolvulus family contains more than 1,500 varieties. Most of them are climbing plants or creepers: *Convolvere* in Latin means to wind around.

Although most *Convolvulaceae* grow in the tropics and subtropics, some are also to be found in temperate regions. In northern latitudes there is the field bindweed *(Convolvulus arvensis)*, the hedge bindweed *(C. sepium)*, the rarer sea bindweed *(C. soldanella)* and the parasitical plants, greater dodder and common dodder *(Cuscuta europaea* and *C. epithymum)*. These are also known as devil's sewing thread, contain no chlorophyll and live as parasites on other plants, such as the nettle.

Several well-known ornamental plants belong to the *Convolvulaceae* family, including the dwarf convolvulus *(Convolvulus tricolor)* and the morning glory *(Ipomoea purga)*. The genus *Ipomoea* provides two types of vegetable, the water spinach and the sweet potato. Water spinach is a herbaceous plant growing on river banks and in marshes, with light pink bell-shaped or beaker-shaped flowers. We do not know where it came from originally, but it can now be found in many tropical countries. In south-east Asia it is cultivated widely for its tasty leaves that have a laxative effect. Some botanists distinguish between two types, *Ipomoea aquatica*, mainly suitable for growing on flooded land, and *I. reptans*, more suited to dry ground. *I. reptans* is an important vegetable in Indonesia and Malaya. Water spinach seed can be bought for cultivation under glass in northern regions, but those on sale, in shops specializing in tropical food, are mostly imported.

The sweet potato or Batata is a perennial herbaceous plant with long creeping stems. It blooms with purplish to light red bell or trumpet-shaped flowers and forms tuberous thickened roots. These differ widely in shape and colour — there are white, light yellow, orange, violet and red tubers. All are rich in starch and sugar and good to eat, with a sweetish taste, and can be used in many dishes. In Indonesia the sweet potato is cut into chunks and cooked with sugar and coconut milk, or it may be sliced, dipped into paste and then baked in oil, or else it may be lightly cooked, mashed and moulded into balls, to be baked in coconut oil.

The sweet potato is an old species, and its origin is not known. It was first imported to Europe at the time of Columbus, but had been cultivated in Polynesia much earlier. What we do know is that botanically it is not even a distant relative of the potato itself, which belongs to the *Solanaceae* family. Of the 20 million acres (8 million hectares) of sweet potato grown today, over 12 (5) million are in China, over 16 (6.6) million in Asia altogether, 2 (0.8) million in Africa, and nearly one (0.4) million in North and South America.

△ Water spinach, 6¼ in (160 mm) long

Water spinach
(Ipomoea aquatica)
A leaf vegetable with oblong narrow leaves and hollow, juicy, cylindrical stems. The so-called Chinese type has long thin stems with lancet-shaped leaves.
ORIGIN: Not known. Probably east Asia.
PRODUCTION: China, Japan, Malaysia, Taiwan, Indonesia, Thailand, Vietnam.
SEASON: Throughout the year. The Chinese type can be grown in the greenhouse in northern regions, April to December.
USE: Wash the leaf, eat raw or cook like spinach. Has a mild flavour.
STORAGE: For a limited period in the salad compartment of the refrigerator.
NUTRITIONAL VALUE: 30 kcal, 2.7 g protein, 60 mg calcium, 2.5 mg iron, 2.9 mg vitamin A, 45 mg vitamin C per 100 g serving.

△ Sweet potato, about $6\frac{3}{4}$ in (170 mm) long

Sweet potato or **Batata**
(Ipomoea batatas)
Fleshy, thickened roots, often fantastically shaped, round, oval or oblong. Colour varies from white or light yellow to reddish-violet. Length up to 10 inches (25 cm), diameter up to $4\frac{3}{4}$ inches (12 cm).
ORIGIN: Not known.
PRODUCTION: Mainly China, but also Vietnam, Indonesia, Philippines, India, Uganda, Rwanda, Madagascar, Egypt. Also Italy and Spain.
SEASON: Throughout the year.
USE: Peel the tubers, cut into chunks or slices, wash and boil, bake or fry in batter. Or steam, purée, sweeten and shape into balls with flour, then bake balls in oil as a delicacy.
STORAGE: For a long time in a cool place (not in the refrigerator).
NUTRITIONAL VALUE: 42 kcal, 3.2 g protein, 85 mg calcium, 4.5 mg iron, 2.7 mg vitamin A, 20 mg vitamin C per 100 g serving.

Cruciferae

Of all flowering plant families the *Cruciferae* seem best able to withstand a cold climate. Although the 3,000 or so varieties are spread throughout the world including the tropics, *Cruciferae* have penetrated the far north, even towards the North Pole. They flourish in the north of Greenland, and of all the flowering plants in Spitsbergen, 20 per cent are members of this family.

The *Cruciferae* get their name from the crosswise growth of the four loose crown leaflets of the flowers. The pods, divided into two by a thin membrane, are called siliqua or silicle. The family includes a number of well-known ornamental plants, such as honesty, sweet-scented stock and wallflower, as well as wild plants like shepherd's purse *(Capsella bursa-pastoris)* and cuckoo flower *(Cardamine pratensis)*. As for vegetables, all known cabbage varieties belong to this family, as well as radish, turnip tops and broccoli. Yet another member of the *Cruciferae* family has a considerable reputation as a dye: this is the woad plant *(Isatis tinctoria)*. The dark blue dye obtained from this plant was mainly used for dyeing fabrics, but Julius Caesar reported that the British warriors painted themselves with *vitrum* to look even more terrifying than they already were. Woad was cultivated widely until it was replaced, first by indigo from the tropics, and later by synthetic dyes such as aniline.

Types of cabbage

The most important supplier of vegetables in the *Cruciferae* family is the genus *Brassica*. There is some confusion about the botanical names for the many cultivated species. The Latin names are often very long: curly kale, for instance, is called *Brassica oleracea, convar. acephala, var. sabellica*. A name like this is often shortened, and then gets confused with other related species with equally long names. To make it worse, many species and variety names have been altered and modernized without any general agreement.

The main group is the cabbage *(Brassica oleracea, convar. capitata)*, including white cabbage, red cabbage, yellow and green savoy cabbage. It is one of the oldest vegetable species, originating in Asia Minor and round the Mediterranean. In earlier times it was a rather loose-leaved cabbage — the type with firm, closed head dates from around 1800. Grown across an area of some 4 million acres (1.6 million hectares) mainly in Asia and Europe, the various species of cabbagehead are of great importance

Brussels sprouts, another *Brassica* variety, are only a few centuries old. The clearly recognizable straight varieties originated at the end of the eighteenth century in Belgium, hence the name. From Belgium they spread to Britain, the Netherlands and France, and after 1945 to North America. The old straight varieties have now been almost entirely replaced by hybrids. Pre-eighteenth century references to a multi-headed cabbage were probably a savoy type or else a primitive type of cabbage with smooth leaves and numerous loose shoots. This species is known as cloven cabbage or everlasting kale *(B. oleracea, convar. oleracea, var. ramosa)*.

Cauliflowers were grown as early as the sixth century BC in Turkey and Egypt. A description from Spain, dating from the twelfth century, mentions three varieties, all originating in Syria. In the *Herb Book of Dodonaeus* (1554) a cauliflower plant is depicted with a great deal of leaf and a small head. By selection, varieties have been produced with less leaf and more head. White cauliflower must not be exposed to sunlight while growing or the curds will turn yellow, so young cauliflowers are covered with a few leaves. Nowadays we can also buy the sunlight resistant green and the yellowish-green Romanesco, that do not have to be covered.

Kale is another old type of *Brassica*. The present form is more than 2,000 years old, and a number of varieties were developed by the Romans. It is close to the wild form of *Brassica oleracea*, and its origin is said to be the country of the Sabines, who used to live near Rome, but who have now disappeared.

Kohlrabi probably developed from marrow cabbage *(var. medullosa)*, an animal fodder species with a fleshy stalk. First reports of the kohlrabi date from the sixteenth century, but its popularity as a vegetable (especially in Germany) is relatively recent.

Little is known about the origins of the swede. In Scandinavia it is a popular vegetable, and it is sometimes called lemon of the north because of its high vitamin C content. Closely related to the swede are winter rapeseed and leaf cabbage (both *Brassica napus, var. napus* or *ssp. oleifera)*. Crossed leafy varieties of these are called shredding kale and used as an early leaf vegetable.

Broccoli originally came from Italy, but owes its present popularity to the United States, where it is a more important species than cauliflower. The original type was probably leafy and branching with a lot of small shoots and no clearly-defined main head, rather like the present-day winter broccoli, planted in summer and harvested early next spring. The newer summer broccoli (planted and harvested within the same year) has a large main head and is now the main source of supplies on the market.

There are eight other significant *Brassica* varieties: Chinese cabbage *(pe-tsai)*, a head-forming, oblong or short leafed broccoli from north China: the eating or May turnip: Chinese broccoli *(kailan)* from south China: *pak-choi* or *paksoi*, an open leaf cabbage with edible leaf stems; *choisum* or *tsoi-sum*, a tropical leaf cabbage from Asia; mustard greens or *amsoi*, a light green roughish leaf vegetable with a sharp taste; mustard spinach, a cross of various leafy varieties; and finally so-called turnip tops, grown from the seed of may tubers, Chinese cabbage or special crosses.

Other types of vegetable

As well as all the *Brassica* vegetables, the family provides a number of others: radish, black radish, the various types of cress, salad rocket, sea kale and horseradish. Some are classified as kitchen spices.

The radish and black radish were both eaten by the Egyptians in about 2000 BC. As well as the small, round and long varieties, the Romans knew of enormous, heavy types. In China, where they have been cultivated for thousands of years, there are varieties even now that can weigh as much as 45 lb (20 kg), and in Japan, too. Our present radish types are thought to have their origin in Asia Minor, while the black radish is believed to have come from China. Within the species there are three edible varieties: *var. mougri*, the snake radish from the region between Java and north-western India, with a very long thin fleshy white root; *var. niger*, the winter black radish as well as the white and pink summer black radish; and the *var. sativus (syn. radicula)* containing all ordinary radish varieties.

White cabbage forms a firm closed head, unlike cabbages from warmer regions. It is one of the oldest known vegetable plants

The rapid-growing garden cress is the best known of all the different cress types. This old cultivated species, appreciated by the Egyptians, Greeks and Romans, comes from the north and east of Africa. Watercress, originally a marsh plant from Europe and Asia, is a perennial species (unlike garden cress), and in some countries is a river weed. Winter cress is a biennial plant from the northern hemisphere, closely related to the Barbara cress. Both plants form flat rosettes with oblong leaves and they are difficult to tell apart. Yellow mustard is sometimes called mustard cress, and the young leaflets of this annual plant can be eaten as salad, just like garden cress. Yellow (or even white) mustard is cultivated for seed production or as fertilizer.

Salad rocket is an annual plant growing in an area from eastern Afghanistan to Britain and Norway, and in the United States too. The young leaf, with its crisp taste, has been marketed since 1981 as a new vegetable called rucola.

Seakale is a salt-loving perennial plant, growing wild along the Atlantic coasts of Britain and France. The sturdy plants have fleshy roots and open leaf rosettes. The roots can be forced in the dark in winter and early spring, just like witloof chicory, and then form long, yellowish-white leaf stems with a small leaf blade, that can be eaten as a vegetable.

The horseradish is a perennial plant from eastern Europe and western Asia. Dodonaeus regarded it as a wild radish. The roots have a sharp taste from mustard oil, and are used to season sauces.

On the following pages, various types of vegetable from the *Cruciferae* family are listed in alphabetical order of their Latin names.

△ Horse radish, $5\frac{7}{8}$ in (150 mm) long ▽ Winter cress, $\frac{5}{8}$ in (15 mm) long

Horseradish
(Armoracia rusticana)
Fairly thick, hard, yellowish to light brown roots with a roughish skin and white flesh, 12 to 16 inches (30 to 40 cm) long. Peeling or scraping releases the sharp mustard oil and makes your eyes water.
ORIGIN: Eastern Europe and western Asia.
PRODUCTION: Poland, Hungary, USSR.
SEASON: Late autumn and winter.
USE: Peel the roots and then grate them. Use in sauces or mix with grated apple. Rapidly discolours when grated, so mix in a little vinegar or lemon juice. Should not be cooked as the taste disappears.
STORAGE: A few months at 32 to 34°F (0 to 1°C) in high humidity.
NUTRITIONAL VALUE: 69 kcal, 15 g carbohydrate, 2 g protein, 0.3 g fat, 105 mg calcium, 1.4 mg iron, 114 mg vitamin C per 100 g serving.
INDUSTRIAL PROCESSING: Made into powder.

Winter cress
(Barbarea vulgaris)
Young leaf vegetable with a sharper taste than garden cress.
ORIGIN: South-west Europe.
PRODUCTION: France, North America.
SEASON: Throughout the year.
USE: The leaf can be eaten as a vegetable (raw or lightly cooked) or used as seasoning in salads and sauces.
STORAGE: Very limited.
NUTRITIONAL VALUE: 28 kcal, 4 g carbohydrate, 2 g protein, 0.3 g fat, 80 mg calcium, 2.5 mg iron, 50 mg vitamin C, 1 mg vitamin A per 100 g serving.

Chinese kale
(Brassica campestris, var. alboglara)
An open brassica plant with a fleshy stem and smallish, rather loose florets, rather like broccoli. The stem and the florets, some of the small leaves and even the single open white flower can be eaten.
ORIGIN: Southern China.
PRODUCTION: Thailand, southern China.
SEASON: Throughout the year.
USE: As broccoli.
STORAGE: As broccoli.
NUTRITIONAL VALUE: As broccoli.
INDUSTRIAL PROCESSING: None, but said to be suitable for freezing.

Pak-choi or **celery cabbage** *(Brassica campestris, var. chinensis)*
Open-leaved brassica, often with bare, white leaf stalks that can be eaten with the leaf.
ORIGIN: East Asia.
PRODUCTION: China, Japan, Korea, Taiwan, and now Europe.
SEASON: Throughout the year.
USE: Wash the leaves and stems, cut into pieces of $1\frac{1}{2}$ to 2 inches (4 to 5 cm) and lightly stew them. Can also be used in vegetable soup.
STORAGE: Three weeks at 32 to 34°F (0 to 1°C) in high humidity.
NUTRITIONAL VALUE: 14 kcal, 3 g carbohydrate, 1.2 g protein, 0.1 g fat, 43 mg calcium, 0.6 mg iron, 25 mg vitamin C per 100 g serving.
INDUSTRIAL PROCESSING: The coarse type is salted in Asia, just as white cabbage is processed to make sauerkraut.

Varieties

Japro Semi-long type with white leaf stalks and shiny, darkish green leaves.

Taisai Long type with long, bare, white leaf stalks and fairly light greyish-green leaves. This variety is used in Asia for salting.

△ Pak-choi 'Japro', $11\frac{3}{4}$ in (300 mm) long

△ Chinese cabbage 'Cantonner witkrop', $22\frac{3}{4}$ in (580 mm) long

Chinese cabbage or **Pe-tsai** *(Brassica campestris, var. pekinensis)*
Slender, oblong or broad, short-leaf brassica with a closed head. The outer leaves are yellowish-green to dark green according to variety, while the leaf veins are broad and white. The inner leaves are yellow to golden-yellow.
ORIGIN: Northern China, Korea.
PRODUCTION: Japan, China, Taiwan, Korea, Austria, Spain, Netherlands.
SEASON: Chiefly April to December.
USE: Remove outermost loose leaves. Chop up the rest of the cabbage. The Japanese type (broad and short) can be eaten raw; the pomegranate type (long and slim) is generally cooked.
STORAGE: About four weeks at 32 to 34°F (0 to 1°C) in high humidity.
NUTRITIONAL VALUE: 15 kcal, 2 g carbohydrate, 1 g protein, 0.3 g fat, 250 mg potassium, 125 mg calcium, 45 mg phosphorus, 10 mg sodium, 1 mg iron, 25 mg vitamin C per 100 g serving.
INDUSTRIAL PROCESSING: In Asia (particularly Korea) a kind of sauerkraut is made from the chopped cabbage.

Varieties

Cantonner witkrop An old variety with a slender, oblong head, about 20 inches (50 cm) long and $4\frac{3}{4}$ inches (12 cm) in diameter, dark green outer leaves with notched edges. This type is called grenade or torpedo according to the shape of the head. Can be stored for a short time only.

Chiko and **Granado** Two intermediate types, with shorter heads than cantonner witkrop. Chiko has green outer leaves, Granado's leaves are darker.

Regina (WR50) A very early Japanese hybrid with light green to green outer leaves. The head is about 9 inches (23 cm) long and 6 inches (15 cm) in diameter.

Kasumi Early Japanese hybrid with green outer leaves. Short and broad.

Osiris (WR60) Mid-early Japanese hybrid with a head about 11 inches (28 cm) long and 6 inches (15 cm) in diameter. Keeps well.

Mustard spinach
(Brassica campestris, var. perviridis)
Leafy plants, derived from crosses within the species *Brassica campestris*, for example *pak-choi* or Chinese cabbage crossed with garden turnips. The young green leaf is usually mild-flavoured, but can sometimes be sharp, like mustard.
ORIGIN: Japan, Taiwan, Korea.
PRODUCTION: Japan, China, Taiwan, Korea, USA.
SEASON: Throughout the year.
USE: Eat the leaf like spinach, but cook for about 10 minutes. You can use it in many cabbage and spinach recipes. For eating raw, only the very young leaves should be used. It has a marked cabbage taste and is sometimes rather sharp.
STORAGE: Very limited, only a few days at 32 to 34°F (0 to 1°C) in high humidity.
NUTRITIONAL VALUE: 22 kcal, 3.9 g carbohydrate, 2.2 g protein, 0.3 g fat, 2 g calcium, 1.5 mg iron, 9.9 mg vitamin A, 130 mg vitamin C per 100 g serving.

△ Chinese cabbage 'Osiris' 11½ in (290 mm) long

Varieties

The varieties of mustard spinach look very different, depending on the parent plants. Some tend to be like the mustard types and are used for cultivating mustard greens.

Komatsuma Large plants with smooth greyish-green leaves.

Tendergreen Similar to komatsuma, but the leaf lacks the mustard taste and is sometimes rather bitter. In Japan two hybrid varieties have been produced: all-top (oblong, grey-green leaf with green leaf stalks) and savanna (dark green shiny leaf, also with green stalks).

Green wave Sharply-curled darkish green leaf, with a strong flavour.

Florida broad leaf A mustard-type variety with light green leaf and a sharp mustard taste. Looks very like mustard greens.

△ Garden turnips. From left to right, 'Italian white redhead', 'Tokio market', and 'Des vertus marteau'

Garden turnip
(Brassica campestris, var. rapa)
Flat, round, semi-long to long, white-fleshed tubers or roots, sometimes with a coloured head. The young tubers in particular are mild-flavoured.
ORIGIN: Mediterranean, western Asia.
PRODUCTION: Japan, China, Italy, France, Britain.
SEASON: April to November.
USE: Peel the tubers, wash, cut into strips, slices or chunks and stew or eat raw.
STORAGE: A few weeks at 32 to 34°F (0 to 1°C) in high humidity.
NUTRITIONAL VALUE: 34 kcal, 8 g carbohydrate, 1 g protein, 0.1 g fat, 30 mg calcium, 0.4 mg iron, 25 mg vitamin C per 100 g serving.
INDUSTRIAL PROCESSING: None but said to be suitable for deep-freezing.

Varieties

Platte witte mei Flat, white, rather angular tubers with a green head, suitable for early cultivation.

Italian white redhead Round tubers with purplish-red head. Suitable for early cultivation under glass.

Tokyo market Pure white tuber. Can be cultivated in spring, summer and autumn.

Des vertus marteau Semi-long, white, spherical garden turnip.

Long dur d'hiver Longish, conical white root. Resistant to night frost and therefore comes on the market quite late.

Goudbal Develops round or top-shaped tubers with yellow flesh. These are also called sand turnips and should not be confused with the yellow swede.

△ Turnips tops 'Namenia', 5½ in (138 mm) high overall

Turnip tops or **Turnip greens** *(Brassica campestris spp.)* Young leaf vegetable. Several rapid-growing varieties are used. The entire plant is harvested and sold either tied in bunches or as loose leaves cut off at ground level, depending on variety.
ORIGIN: As Chinese cabbage and garden turnip.
PRODUCTION: Netherlands, West Germany.
SEASON: February to June.
USE: Wash the leaf and stew. Alternatively, chop up finely when raw and use in salads or in bubble-and-squeak.
STORAGE: About eight days at 32 to 34°F (0 to 1°C) in high humidity. At 35 to 41°F (2 to 5°C) it will keep for only two to three days.
NUTRITIONAL VALUE: 11 kcal, 0.5 g carbohydrate, 2 g protein, 0.1 g fat, 100 mg calcium, 3 mg iron, 1 mg iodine, 35 mg vitamin C, 2 mg vitamin A per 100 g serving.

Varieties

Gewone groene Cultivated from the seed of the garden turnip platte witte mei. Leaf green to dark green. Plants harvested whole and sold in bunches.

Gele malse Grown from seed of Chinese cabbage. Leaf soft and bluish-green. Susceptible to disease so availability limited.

Namenia Independent variety with long, green, indented leaves, rather similar to endive. Leaf not as stiff as gewone groene. Usually cut off at ground level and supplied loose in boxes.

Mustard greens or **Brown mustard** or **Sarepta mustard**
(Brassica juncea, ssp. juncea)
Light green leaves, rather rough to the touch, growing in the form of rosettes.
ORIGIN: Africa.
PRODUCTION: Taiwan, Thailand.
SEASON: Throughout the year.
USE: Leaves usually stewed. Young leaves, finely chopped, can be eaten like garden cress.
STORAGE: As turnip tops.
NUTRITIONAL VALUE: 24 kcal, 2.4 g protein, 160 mg calcium, 2.7 mg iron, 75 mg vitamin C, 1.8 mg vitamin A per 100 g serving.

Varieties

Florida broad leaf
Light green, rather rough leaves,

Tua choy A heading variety cultivated on a large scale in Thailand. In a temperate climate this type does not form a head but has light yellowish-green leaves.

Bau sin Also a heading mustard from Taiwan. When cultivated in a temperate climate it is very similar to tua choy.

△ Mustard greens, 14¼ in (360 mm) long

Swede
(Brassica napus, var. napobrassica)
Rather angular, tall, round turnips with yellow or white flesh. The yellow-fleshed varieties are mainly intended for eating fresh, while the white-fleshed are generally sent to the vegetable dryers for processing.
ORIGIN: Probably temperate Europe.
PRODUCTION: Scandinavia, West Germany, Netherlands, Canada, USA (California, Oregon).
SEASON: September to May.
USE: After peeling cut the swede into chips, boil and eat with a sauce. Or grate and use in uncooked dishes.
STORAGE: Uncut swedes 6 months at 32 to 34°F (0 to 1°C) in high humidity. If stored in drier conditions they rapidly become woolly.
NUTRITIONAL VALUE: 26 kcal, 5 g carbohydrate, 1 g protein, 0.2 g fat, 0.5 mg iron, 35 mg vitamin C per 100 g serving.
INDUSTRIAL PROCESSING: White-fleshed swedes are dried in blocks and used in dried and canned soups.

△ Swede 'Friese gele', $5\frac{7}{8}$ in (150 mm) across

Varieties

Friese gele Yellow-fleshed variety, often with purple or bronze head with no neck. Round to egg-shaped.

Hollandse roodkop Round, rather angular swede. Sometimes forms a neck. Upper part red to purplish.

△ Kohlrabi 'Blaro', $2\frac{1}{2}$ in (62 mm) across

Kohlrabi
(Brassica oleracea, convar. acephala, var. gongulodes)
Flat to oval tuber shows above ground due to thickening of the stem. Pale green or bluish-violet if anthocyanin is present.
ORIGIN: Probably north-west Europe.
PRODUCTION: Germany, Switzerland, Austria.
SEASON: March to November, in decreasing quantities.
USE: Both the tuber and the leaf of young plants (grown under glass) can be eaten, but mostly the tuber is used, stewed or in soup or chopped raw in salad.
STORAGE: About three weeks at 32 to 34°F (0 to 1°C) in high humidity.
NUTRITIONAL VALUE: 25 kcal, 4 g carbohydrate, 2 g protein, 0.1 g fat, 90 mg calcium, 1.2 mg iron, 60 mg vitamin C, 0.25 mg vitamin A, 0.4 mg vitamin PP per 100 g serving.
INDUSTRIAL PROCESSING: Deep-freezing.

Varieties

Trero Swiss variety with round white tubers.

Blaro Also Swiss, with round, bluish-violet tubers.

Azur-star Early variety from West Germany with round, azure blue tubers.

Superschmelz Giant kohlrabi, seldom on the market because the tubers are so large and heavy. Most suitable for deep-freezing, as the flesh retains its quality very well.

△ Kale 'Westlandse winter', 17¾ in (450 mm) long

Kale or **curly kale**
(Brassica oleracea, convar. acephela, var. sabellica)
Large plants with largish oblong leaves forming an open leaf rosette. Leaves are curled, and the colour and curliness of the leaf depends on the variety. Early varieties usually have light green, finely-curled leaves. Later varieties have dark green leaves only slightly curled to start with, and the curliness increases through the winter. Generally the leaves are on sale, but sometimes leaves and leaf stalks are sold in bunches.
ORIGIN: Probably the Atlantic coast of Britain and France.
PRODUCTION: Netherlands, Britain, West Germany.
SEASON: September to March.
USE: Pull the curly leaf away from the stem, chop up finely and use with mashed potatoes and cabbage, like bubble-and-squeak.
STORAGE: About 4 weeks at 32 to 34°F (0 to 1°C) in high humidity.
NUTRITIONAL VALUE: 40 kcal, 4 g carbohydrate, 4 g protein, 0.9 g fat, 200 mg calcium, 1 mg iron, 100 mg vitamin C, 5.3 mg vitamin A, 1.5 mg vitamin PP, 0.225 mg vitamin B6 per 100 g serving.
INDUSTRIAL PROCESSING: Deep-freezing, canning or bottling, drying.

Varieties

For the fresh vegetable market, varieties of medium height are mostly cultivated, for industry low-growing varieties are used as they are easier to harvest by machine.

Westlandse herfst A variety of medium height with green, finely-curled leaves, forming a tight head. Harvested before winter sets in.

Westlandse winter A variety of medium height with a green leaf, coarsely curled in autumn. Leaves become more finely curled through the winter. Fairly resistant to frost.

Lerchenzungen Medium-height variety with long, narrow, sharply-curled leaves, dark greyish-green. Harvested before the onset of frost.

Lage fijngekrulde or **Moskrul** Short-stemmed variety with upturned, bright green, finely-curled leaves. Harvested before winter.

△ Kale 'Lerchenzungen', 10¼ in (260 mm) across ▽ Cauliflower 'Mechelse', 7½ in (190 mm) across (described on page 74)

Cauliflower

(Brassica oleracea, convar. botrytis, var. botrytis)
A firm spherical brassica made up of short stems with florets. Nowadays there are green and yellowish-green cauliflowers as well as white ones.

ORIGIN: Mediterranean and Atlantic coast of Europe.

PRODUCTION: France, Italy, Britain, Netherlands, Belgium, Poland, India, China.

SEASON: Throughout the year: 'greenhouse cauliflower' March to June.

USE: Remove any remaining leaves. Wash the curd or the separated florets thoroughly. Boil in salted water. Can be covered with a sauce or baked *au gratin*. Finely-chopped florets can also be used in vegetable soup or salads.

STORAGE: Three to six weeks at 32 to 34°F (0 to 1°C) in high humidity.

NUTRITIONAL VALUE: 20 kcal, 3 g carbohydrate, 2 g protein, 20 mg calcium, 0.5 g iron, 80 mg vitamin C, 0.6 mg vitamin PP, 0.2 mg vitamin B6 per 100 g serving.

INDUSTRIAL PROCESSING: Deep-freezing, drying (for soups), salting (for pickles), sterilizing.

△ Cauliflower 'Purple Cape', (young), $5\frac{1}{8}$ in (130 mm) across

▽ Cauliflower 'Romanesco', $9\frac{1}{4}$ in (250 mm) across

△ Cauliflower 'Alverda' (young), $6\frac{1}{4}$ in (160 mm) across

Varieties

Mechelse An early variety, forming a chunky, white, fine-grained curd.

Alpha Early variety with a spherical, firm, white curd, rather coarse-grained.

Walcheren winter Quite firm, spherical, chunky cauliflower, planted in August and harvested in the spring.

Alverda Green cauliflower with a fairly strong taste, on the market between September and December.

Romanesco Very decorative, yellowish-green cauliflower, made up of tightly-packed, small 'turrets'. September to December. Cooks quickly and has a mild taste.

Purple cape winter cauliflower with purple stalks and a very good flavour.

△ Sprouting broccoli 'Corvet', rosette 7⅞ in (200 mm) across

Sprouting broccoli or **Calabrese**
(Brassica oleracea, convar. botrytis, var. italica)
Quite short, fleshy flower stems with fully-developed green flower buds, forming a firm, single head by harvest time. The flower buds are generally green, but there are some varieties with a purplish tint.
ORIGIN: Italy.
PRODUCTION: North America, Britain, Italy, Spain, and some other west European countries on a small scale.
SEASON: April to December.
USE: Peel the thick, fleshy flower stems and then boil with the green flower buds. Small rosettes can also be used in soups and salads.
STORAGE: One to two weeks at 32 to 34°F (0 to 1°C) in high humidity. Protect against drying out by covering or wrapping with cling-film (saran wrap)
NUTRITIONAL VALUE: 36 kcal, 5 g protein, 3 g carbohydrate, 0.4 g fat, 24 mg calcium, 3 mg iron, 114 mg vitamin C, 1.3 mg vitamin B5, 1.9 mg vitamin A, 1 mg vitamin PP per 100 g serving.
INDUSTRIAL PROCESSING: Deep-freezing.

Varieties

Corvet Mid-early hybrid variety with a firm, light greyish-green main head.

Southern comet Early hybrid from Japan, with a rather flat, reasonably firm main head, bluish-grey to green.

Skiff Fairly late hybrid with a tall, rounded, firm and heavy main head.

White cabbage, including **pointed cabbage** and **spring greens**
(Brassica oleracea, convar. capitata, var. alba)
A cabbage with smooth green outer leaves and a flat, round or pointed, closed, firm head. The pointed type is often regarded as a separate variety (pointed cabbage), but botanically it belongs with the white cabbage. The best white cabbage varieties for later cultivation are firm and keep well.
ORIGIN: Mediterranean, Asia Minor.
PRODUCTION: Soviet Union, Poland, Yugoslavia, Britain, Greece, Italy, Germany, Netherlands, China, Japan.
SEASON: Pointed cabbage, April to December. Early white, June to December. Autumn white, September to December. Storage white November to June.
USE: Pointed cabbage is mainly boiled. Early white cabbage can be boiled or eaten raw in salads. Autumn white cabbage mainly for sauerkraut. Stored white cabbage for salads.
STORAGE: At 32 to 34°F (0 to 1°C) in high humidity, pointed cabbage one to two weeks, early white four weeks, autumn white two months, storage white six months.
NUTRITIONAL VALUE: 26 kcal, 4 g carbohydrate, 2 g protein, 0.2 g fat, 50 mg calcium, 0.5 mg iron, 40 mg vitamin C, 0.3 mg vitamin PP per 100 g serving.
INDUSTRIAL PROCESSING: White cabbage is made into sauerkraut and also dried.

△ Pointed cabbage 'Eersteling', 10⅝ in (270 mm) long

Varieties

Eersteling or **Express** Straight, pointed cabbage variety for early cultivation. Fairly firm, green head, pointed to blunt. Good selections are raket and spiko.

Prospera Pointed cabbage hybrid with well-closed, pointed, smooth-leaved head. Suitable for winter cultivation and spring harvesting.

Cape Horn Japanese pointed cabbage hybrid for summer and autumn cultivation. Head closes well, has a blunted point, and darkish green, smooth leaves.

△ White cabbage 'Langedijker bewaarwitte', 6¼ in (160 mm) across ▽ White cabbage 'Langedijker herfstwitte', 13¾ in (350 mm) across

Langedijker vroege witte Early variety with firm, round head, and few surrounding leaves. This old, straight variety has been displaced by early hybrid varieties of the same type, also used for summer cultivation, such as balbro, quickstep, predena and minicole. The last two are firmer than the others.

Langedijker herfstwitte The old, straight selections of early and late herftswitte and modern hybrid varieties of the same type such as krautpacker, krautprinz, erdeno, hidena, and strukton are used almost exclusively for producing sauerkraut. They all have a lot of outer leaf and large, round to conical heads.

Langedijker bewaarwitte and **deense witte** are chiefly suitable for storage. Head round to conical, abundant outer leaf is green, often with a wavy edge. Popular hybrids of this type are Bartole, Bison, Lennox and Polinius.

Red cabbage
(Brassica oleracea, convar. capitata, var. rubra)
Closed-head type with smooth, green and red surrounding leaves, and a firm, round to conical, closed, red head. The red colour is caused by the presence of anthocyanin, and varies in intensity according to variety and type.
ORIGIN: Mediterranean area, Asia Minor.
PRODUCTION: West Germany, Netherlands, Scandinavia, Poland.
SEASON: Throughout the year. Early red appears in June, autumn red in September. The first storage reds appear on the market in October and are on sale well into spring as they keep for months under refrigeration.
USE: Mainly boiled, but also finely chopped and used in salads.
STORAGE: At 32 to 34°F (0 to 1°C) in high humidity, early red one month, autumn red two months, storage red six months. At 31°F (−0.5°C), storage red cabbage can be kept for eight months.
NUTRITIONAL VALUE: 26 kcal, 4 g carbohydrate, 2 g protein, 0.2 g fat, 50 mg calcium, 0.5 mg iron, 60 mg vitamin C, 20 mg vitamin PP, 0.125 mg vitamin B6 per 100 g serving.
INDUSTRIAL PROCESSING: Deep-freezing, canning or bottling.

△ Red cabbage 'Langedijker allervroegste', $7\frac{1}{4}$ in (185 mm) across

Varieties

Langedijker allervroegste and **Langedijker vroege** are early varieties with round to conical heads and little surrounding leaf. Rapid growth, light red or light purple, short cooking-time, easily digestible. Good selections of this type are the Preko (very early) and Norma (early — leaf and head covered with a thick layer of wax).

Langedijker herfst Robust variety with plenty of large surrounding leaves and a thin layer of wax. Large, red to dark red head is round to conical. Cooks quickly and is easy to digest. Good selections are Volga and Roodsnit and a hybrid, Autoro.

Langedijker bewaar Robust species with long-stemmed leaves, often with notched or crinkled edges. Dark purple head is round to inverted egg-shape. There are tender and tough selections. The tough is darker, keeps for longer, and is less digestible. Good selections are Dorota and the new hybrids Extaro and Roxy.

△ Red cabbage 'Langedijker herfst' (without surrounding leaves), $6\frac{1}{4}$ in (156 mm) across

△ Red cabbage 'Langedijker bewaar' (without surrounding leaves), 7½ in (190 mm) long

△ Savoy cabbage 'Langedijker bewaargele', 13⅜ in (340 mm) long

Savoy cabbage
(Brassica oleracea, convar. capitata, var. sabauda)
Crinkled and deeply-veined leaves, classified as green or yellow by the leaf colour. The green type varies from greyish-green to very dark green outside, and golden-yellow inside. The yellow type is light-green to bluish-green outside and creamy-white to golden-yellow inside.
ORIGIN: Mediterranean area.
PRODUCTION: West Germany, Netherlands, France, Britain, East Germany, Poland, Soviet Union.
SEASON: Throughout the year.
USE: Chop finely and boil.
STORAGE: Yellow savoy cabbage has the same keeping quality as white or red cabbage. Green savoy is stored with the surrounding leaves and will keep for one to three weeks (early types) or two to four weeks (late types) at 32 to 34°F (0 to 1°C) in high humidity.
NUTRITIONAL VALUE: 34 kcal, 4 g carbohydrate, 3 g protein, 0.7 g fat, 30 mg calcium, 1 mg iron, 80 mg vitamin C, 1 mg vitamin A, 0.3 mg vitamin PP per 100 g serving.
INDUSTRIAL PROCESSING: Drying (on a limited scale).

△ Savoy cabbage 'Winterkoning', $18\frac{7}{8}$ in (480 mm) long ▽ Savoy cabbage 'Hammer', $10\frac{1}{2}$ in (265 mm) across

Varieties

Vroege groene spitse A small variety with coarsely-wrinkled, greyish-green surrounding leaves and a pointed head.

Novum Available July to October with strongly-wrinkled, dark green surrounding leaves and a round, firmish, moderately wrinkled green head. A good hybrid of this type is Novusa.

Hammer Later variety (mid-October to December) with a lot of finely-wrinkled, greyish-green surrounding leaves, and a flattish-round, firm, green to light green head. Good hybrid varieties are Icebridge, Ice Queen, Saria and Taler.

Putjes There are two forms: the Bredase putjes, an autumn type with a flattish-round, moderately-wrinkled, light green head, and the Late putjes, with a round to conical, green to dark green head.

Winterkoning Winter-hardy variety, harvested from the field in winter. The greyish-green surrounding leaves are very finely wrinkled, with a flat-round, moderately firm head. Good hybrid varieties are Tarvoy, Wirosa and Wivoy.

Langedijker vroege gele Round to conical, firm but tender, very tasty head. Few surrounding leaves are basin-shaped, finely wrinkled and yellowish-green.

Langedijker herfstgele Robust variety with plenty of moderately-wrinkled, yellowish-green to green surrounding leaves. Large, firm, round to conical head.

Langedijker bewaargele Robust variety with lots of coarsely-wrinkled surrounding leaves, yellowish-green to greyish-green. Firm, yellowish-green head is round to inverted egg-shaped. Darsa is a good hybrid.

Bloemendaalse gele An old variety that winters out in the field and provides a golden-yellow head in spring.

△ Savoy cabbage 'Bloemendaalse gele', 13⅜ in (340 mm) long

Seakale
(Crambe maritima)
Open-leaf cabbage with long, bare, leaf stalks and wavy bluish-green leaves. The juicy stems are eaten and are blanched by earthing up the plants (like asparagus) or by placing the roots in a dark climatic cell. These blanched stems have a pleasant cabbage taste.
ORIGIN: Atlantic coast of Britain and France.
PRODUCTION: Britain.
SEASON: December to April.
USE: Lightly cook blanched stems or eat raw.
STORAGE: About one week in the refrigerator.
NUTRITIONAL VALUE: 25 kcal, 4 g carbohydrate, 2 g protein, 0.2 g fat, 60 mg calcium, 0.14 mg iron, 30 mg vitamin C per 100 g serving.

Salad rocket
(Eruca vesicaria, ssp. sativa; syn. E. sativa)
Fine leaf vegetable with a good flavour when harvested young. Old leaves are bitter and tough.
ORIGIN: Mediterranean area.
PRODUCTION: Italy, France.
SEASON: Throughout the year.
USE: Wash the leaf and boil for about 10 minutes. Can also be eaten raw in salads.
STORAGE: Two days at 32 to 34°F (0 to 1°C) in high humidity.
NUTRITIONAL VALUE: Probably the same as turnip tops.

△ Brussels sprouts 'Perfect line' (cylindrical sprout formation) and 'Acropolis' (pyramid sprout formation), 23¼ in (590 mm) high

Brussels sprouts
(Brassica oleracea, convar. oleracea, var. gemmifera)
Sprouts are very small cabbages growing in the leaf axils of erect, long-stemmed plants. There are few differences in shape or colour. After picking they are normally classified in four sizes by diameter: A, $\frac{7}{8}$ to $1\frac{5}{16}$ inch (23 to 33 mm); B, $1\frac{5}{16}$ to $1\frac{11}{16}$ inches (33 to 43 mm); C, over $1\frac{11}{16}$ inches (43 mm); D, $\frac{5}{8}$ to $\frac{7}{8}$ inch (16 to 23 mm).
ORIGIN: Belgium.
PRODUCTION: Britain, Netherlands, France, Belgium.
SEASON: August to March.
USE: Peel off loose leaves, cut away stems, wash well and boil.
STORAGE: Three to four weeks at 30°F (−1°C) in high humidity.
NUTRITIONAL VALUE: 41 kcal, 5 g carbohydrate, 4 g protein, 0.5 g fat, 30 mg calcium, 1 mg iron, 150 mg vitamin C, 1 mg vitamin A, 0.5 mg vitamin PP per 100 g serving.
INDUSTRIAL PROCESSING: Chiefly deep-freezing.

▽ Salad rocket, $3\frac{1}{2}$ in (90 mm) long △ Sea kale, $19\frac{3}{4}$ in (500 mm) high ▽ Garden cress, $5\frac{1}{8}$ in (130 mm) high

Garden cress
(Lepidium sativum)
Very young plants are sold growing in small boxes. Each consists of a small stem with two cotyledons.
ORIGIN: Eastern north Africa and south-west Asia.
PRODUCTION: France, Britain, Netherlands, Scandinavia.
SEASON: Throughout the year, particularly February to July.
USE: Wash carefully, drain well and eat raw with meat or fish. Can also be made into soup.
STORAGE: The growth of the plants can be slowed down at 32 to 34°F (0 to 1°C), and they can be kept for about two weeks in their boxes.
NUTRITIONAL VALUE: 12 kcal, 0.3 g carbohydrate, 2 g protein, 0.3 g fat, 250 mg calcium, 2.5 mg iron, 50 mg vitamin C, 2 mg vitamin A, 1 mg vitamin PP per 100 g serving.
INDUSTRIAL PROCESSING: Dried soups.

Varieties

Ordinary garden cress A rapid-growing variety with slightly indented leaves. Used for forcing in boxes, as is the Cressida variety (with paler leaves).

Grootbladige Has coarsely indented leaf edges. Not forced in boxes, but harvested from the garden. Includes the selections Groka and Brevet.

Fijne gekrulde or **Moskrul** A rapid-growing variety with deeply indented leaf edges. Cultivated less than before.

Watercress
(Nasturtium officinale)
A water plant with longish stalks and dark green, rounded leaves. White roots form on the leaf buds.
ORIGIN: Western Asia, southern Europe.
PRODUCTION: Britain, France.
SEASON: Throughout the year.
USE: Eat raw or boil quickly.
STORAGE: A few days at 32 to 34°F (0 to 1°C) in high humidity.
NUTRITIONAL VALUE: 28 kcal, 4 g carbohydrate, 2 g protein, 0.3 g fat, 80 mg calcium, 2.5 mg iron, 50 mg vitamin C per 100 g serving.

△ Watercress, leaf 1½ in (40 mm) long ▽ Black radish 'Rex', 11¾ in (300 mm) long

Black radish
(Raphanus sativus, var. niger)
Used to be thought of as a shortish or round, black-skinned root, but now the demand is mainly for types with long white roots.
ORIGIN: Probably east Asia.
PRODUCTION: China, Japan, West Germany, Austria, Italy, France, Netherlands.
SEASON: Throughout the year.
USE: Peel or wash the roots and slice or grate. Can be eaten raw on bread or in salads.
STORAGE: Winter black radish, four months at 32 to 34°F (0 to 1°C) in high humidity. Summer black radish does not keep so well and soon becomes woolly. Will keep for about two weeks with the leaf.
NUTRITIONAL VALUE: 30 kcal, 5 g carbohydrate, 2 g protein, 0.2 g fat, 400 mg potassium, 120 mg calcium, 2 mg iron, 30 mg vitamin C, 0.4 mg vitamin PP per 100 g serving.

△ Black radish 'Ronde zwarte winter', with leaves 15⅜ in (390 mm) long

Varieties

Rex A German summer variety with a pointed, smooth, white root and quite a sharp taste. Tends to become woolly.

Unus treib Another German summer variety with a pointed, white root, somewhat shorter and more irregular in shape than the rex. Also tends to become woolly.

Minowase Various Japanese hybrid types are marketed under this name. The smooth, white roots are usually very long and cylindrical. They keep well in winter without becoming woolly.

Munchener bier An old variety with a round white root. Keeps quite well without becoming woolly.

Ronde zwarte winter An old variety with a round black root. Keeps well without becoming woolly.

Lange zwarte winter Old variety with a shortish, black, blunt-tipped root. Keeps well without becoming woolly.

△ Black radish 'Minowase', 17 in (430 mm) long

Radish
(Raphanus sativus, var. sativus; syn. radicula)
A herbaceous species with a thickened tap root. The best known is the round, red, bulbous type, but there are also bi-coloured and white radishes with longish, blunt or pointed roots.
ORIGIN: Probably China.
PRODUCTION: France, Italy, Netherlands, Spain, USA.
SEASON: March to August, mainly in bunches with leaves. Throughout the year, packed in bags without leaves.
USE: Slice or grate, and eat on bread, or as a garnish, or in salads. Old roots lose their taste.
STORAGE: With leaves, about eight days at 32 to 34°F (0 to 1°C) in high humidity.
NUTRITIONAL VALUE: 14 kcal, 2 g carbohydrate, 1 g protein, 0.2 g fat, 30 mg calcium, 2 mg iron, 20 mg vitamin C, 0.2 mg vitamin PP per 100 g serving.

△ Radish 'Icicle', $6\frac{1}{4}$ in (160 mm) long ▽ Radish 'Ronde rode broei', $1\frac{1}{8}$ in (28 mm) across

Varieties

Ronde rode broei and **Ronde rode vollegrond** Principal variety for growing both under glass and in open ground. Leaf sometimes quite long, roots spherical and bright scarlet. Some selections, such as Scharo and Revosa, do not become woolly as quickly as others.

Cherry belle Variety with fairly long leaf and good-sized spherical root. Colour varies from bright scarlet to pinkish.

Ronde rode groot witpunt Old variety with spherical roots, purplish-red on top and white underneath. Not widely grown.

Ronde rode klein witpunt Another old variety. Spherical roots are purplish-red with a white tip. This variety has been superseded by the round red varieties.

Halflange rood/witpunt A variety with slender, oblong, blunt radishes. The tops are red and the undersides white. Flamboyant and Pernot have a small white tip, French breakfast lanquette a large white tip.

Icicle A longish, pointed, white radish. Tastes quite sharp.

Cucurbitaceae

The thousand or so species of the *Cucurbitaceae* family are mainly climbing plants from the warmer parts of the world. Most of them have coarse, bristly leaves and attach themselves to plants or other objects with their corkscrewing tendrils. One wild member of the family is the bryony *(Bryonica dioica),* whose greenish-yellow flowers ripen into poisonous red berries in autumn. The squirting cucumber *(Ecballium elaterium)* grows in the Mediterranean area. When ripe this fruit develops a pressure of about 30 atmospheres, springs away from the stem and expels its slimy seeds with considerable force.

Fruit varieties of this family include the melon, watermelon and chayote, and internationally-known vegetable species (in order of economic importance) are the cucumber and gherkin, pumpkin, courgette (zucchini), custard marrow, vegetable spaghetti, sinkwa, wax gourd and balsam pear.

The gherkin and the cucumber may have come from north India, and probably developed from the wild *Cucumis sativus, ssp. agrestis.* They were known in India some 3,000 years ago and were also enjoyed in Egypt and other Mediterranean countries. The Romans brought them to France, and from there they spread across Europe. They made their debut in the New World in the fifteenth century, when Columbus sowed the first gherkin and cucumber seeds on Haiti. About two million acres (800,000 hectares) are given over to gherkins and cucumbers at present, half in Asia and about 320,000 (130,000) in Europe (mainly Poland, Romania, Yugoslavia and Hungary). The Soviet Union grows about 430,000 acres (175,000 hectares).

Both gherkins and cucumbers are rapidly-recovering varieties: when the fruits are picked new young fruits grow in their place, but if they are not picked no new fruits develop. Modern varieties of the cucumber carry mostly female flowers that ripen into fruit without fertilization, but in order to produce a gherkin, the female flower must be fertilized with pollen from the male flower.

In some countries people prefer the more bitter prickly gherkins and the slightly bitter field cucumbers, while in other places the blander smooth-skinned cucumbers and gherkins are more popular. Besides green cucumbers there are also white and yellow as well as prickly varieties.

The pumpkin, courgette, custard marrow and vegetable spaghetti all belong to the genus *Cucurbita,* which contains a wide range of plant types and fruit shapes. The parent is thought to be *C. lundelliana,* indigenous to south Mexico, Guatemala and Honduras. The pumpkin is cultivated internationally over an area of some 1.37 million acres (550,000 hectares). The most important species are *C. maxima,* with enormous fruits and soft, round stems thickened by a cork-like tissue, and *C. moschata,* with smaller fruits and a hard stem, only slightly swollen at the joint, growing mainly in hot countries.

Courgettes, when very young and still bearing the flower petals, are known as 'courgette-fleur'. As a delicacy, the flower is filled with minced meat and is then lightly baked

The courgette, the custard marrow and the remarkable vegetable spaghetti all belong to the same genus and grow mainly in cooler climates. The fruits are usually harvested while they are still young and unripe, and do not keep very well.

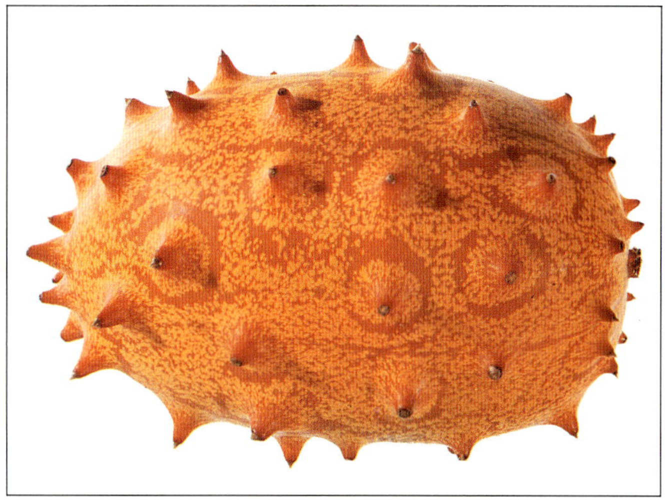

A new vegetable from the cucumber family is the kiwano, developed and grown in New Zealand. The spiked fruit body, about 4 in (10 cm) long, is orange in colour when ripe. The inside is bright green and has a taste half way between that of banana and lemon, with an aftertaste of passion fruit.

The sinkwa is believed to come from India and is mainly grown in China and Japan. The club-shaped, ribbed fruit is used as a vegetable and as a medicine in India. A very strong laxative can be made by boiling the fruit.

A versatile relative of the sinkwa, the sponge calabash *(Luffa aegyptiaca, syn. L. cylindrica)*, is eaten when young, but has other uses as well. After washing and drying the fibrous flesh, it is used as a vegetable sponge and as packing material.

The bitter cucumber came from the tropics of Asia and Africa, but has now spread over the whole tropical belt. The ripe fruit are orange on the outside and blood-red on the inside. They are best eaten before they get too ripe.

The young fruits and young leaves of the bottle gourd *(Lagenaria siceraria)* can be eaten, although they are not usually exported as food. The fruits are varied in shape (spherical, club-shaped, oblong), and are used in many tropical countries as pitchers, or else are made into spoons, dishes, bottles and jars, often painted and attractively decorated.

△ Rough-skinned gherkin, $2\frac{1}{2}$ in (65 mm) long

△ Prickly gherkin, $6\frac{1}{4}$ in (160 mm) including stem

Wax gourd or **white gourd** *(Benincasa hispida)*
Large, ovoid or spherical, dark green to bluish-green fruits with a chalk-white wax layer. The flesh is pure white and juicy, and quickly becomes spongy in the centre. Half-ripe fruit are best for eating. Resistant to soil diseases and therefore also useful as a stock for grafting melons.
ORIGIN: South-east Asia, Indonesia.
PRODUCTION: India, China, Japan, Malaysia, Australia.
SEASON: August to September.
USE: Peel the half-ripe fruits, then cut into strips and boil. In Indonesia the fruit is candied and eaten with tea or coffee or used in cakes and biscuits like sugar.
STORAGE: Half-ripe fruit can be kept for four to six weeks (not in the refrigerator).
NUTRITIONAL VALUE: 36 kcal, 8 g carbohydrate, 1 g protein, 0.9 g fat, 20 mg calcium, 0.5 mg iron, 16 mg vitamin C per 100 g serving.

△ Smooth-skinned gherkin, 4¼ in (110 mm) across

Gherkin

(Cucumis sativus)

Small, oblong, green fruits with a smooth or thorny skin, according to variety. They vary in length from 2⅜ to 8 inches (6 to 20 cm). The prickly varieties generally have a bitter taste.

ORIGIN: India.

PRODUCTION: Poland, Hungary, Romania, Italy, France, Belgium, Netherlands, USA.

SEASON: May to October, with a peak in August.

USE: Mainly pickled, and then eaten straight from the bottle or used as a garnish or with appetizers, such as rollmops.

STORAGE: Fresh gherkins only for a short time as they are sensitive to low-temperature decay, yellow discoloration and mildew. Pickled gherkins can be kept for a long time, even in opened jars (in the refrigerator).

NUTRITIONAL VALUE: Sweet pickle 12 kcal, pickle 6 kcal per 100 g serving. Quite a lot of sodium from the added salt. Few vitamins.

INDUSTRIAL PROCESSING: Salting for pickle manufacture, or pasteurizing to make a sweet-sour product.

△ Prickly cucumber (fruit and tendril with leaf, flower and young fruit), 11¾ in (300 mm) long

Cucumber

(Cucumis sativus)

Long, fleshy, berry fruits with a smooth, ribbed or knobbly skin. Green, yellow or white. A good specimen has a small core of jelly-like texture containing the seed-pods, a thick wall of firm, greenish-white flesh, and around it the skin. Length up to 18 inches (45 cm).

ORIGIN: Probably India. Possibly Africa too.

PRODUCTION: Italy, Spain, Canary Islands, France, Netherlands, Belguim.

SEASON: Throughout the year.

USE: Peel if necessary, then eat raw as cucumber salad, or with lettuce and tomato. Also use in soups, sweet pickle, or stuffed.

STORAGE: About a week in a cool place. Two to three weeks if packed in cling-film.

NUTRITIONAL VALUE: 6 kcal, 1 g carbohydrate, 0.5 g protein, 20 mg calcium, 0.5 mg iron, 10 mg vitamin C per 100 g serving.

INDUSTRIAL PROCESSING: Pickling.

△ Cucumber 'Gele tros', $15\frac{3}{4}$ in (400 mm) long

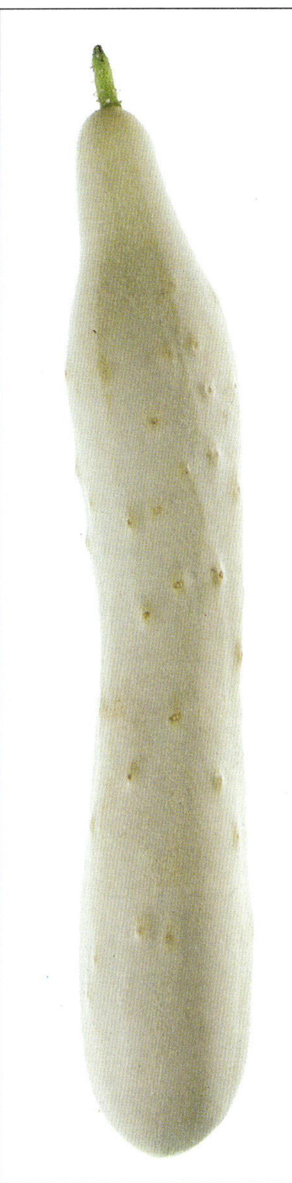

△ Cucumber 'Bianco lungo', $5\frac{5}{8}$ in (142 mm) long

△ Pumpkins. From left to right, 'Golden debut', $7\frac{1}{2}$ in (190 mm) across, 'Butterball', $5\frac{7}{8}$ in (150 mm) across, and 'Gold nugget', 5 in (125 mm) across

Varieties

Corona Long, heavily-ribbed, slightly knobby, quite a dark green. Not bitter.

Petita Mini-cucumber with a smooth green fruit, 6 to 8 inches (15 to 20 cm) long.

Burpless tasty green A variety with longish, knobby, green fruits.

Marketmore Knobby fruits about 8 inches (20 cm) long. Not bitter.

Gele tros An old variety, only suitable for growing in open ground. Slightly knobby, yellow fruits are sometimes bitter and often form seeds.

Bianco lungo Another old variety with long white fruits, often bitter, containing seeds.

△ Pumpkin 'Table king', $12\frac{1}{4}$ in (310 mm) across

Pumpkin or **wintersquash** *(Cucurbita maxima* and *C. moschata)*
Large to very large fruits with many different shapes and colours. The flesh is neutral or slightly scented in taste, and white, yellow or orange.
ORIGIN: Central and South America.
PRODUCTION: China, Turkey, Japan, Egypt, Argentina, Mexico, Romania, Spain, France.
SEASON: Throughout the year.
USE: Peel, cut into slices, chunks or strips, and stew, bake or use in salads. Can also be used for compote, sweet pickle, piccalilly and jam.
STORAGE: Fully-grown, sound fruits for a few months if not kept too cold. Best kept at about 54°F (12°C). May dry out and become spongy.
NUTRITIONAL VALUE: 24 kcal, 5.5 g carbohydrate, 1 g protein, 0.4 g fat, 20 mg calcium, 0.8 mg iron, 2 mg vitamin A, 9 mg vitamin C per 100 g serving.
INDUSTRIAL PROCESSING: Jam, compote, sweet pickle.

△ Pumpkin 'Gele reuzen', 12¼ in (310 mm) across

Varieties

Gele reuzen Large, round fruit with yellow to orange skin and yellow, rather insipid flesh. Can weigh over 90 lb (40 kg). Flesh quickly becomes woolly.

Golden debut Japanese hybrid variety with round orange fruit with firm, yellowish flesh. Fruit weigh 2 to 3 lb (1 to 1.5 kg). This is one of the varieties called Kokkaido pumpkin as they came from that island.

Butterball Japanese hybrid with flattish-round fruits, about 4 inches (10 cm) tall and 6¾ inches (17 cm) in diameter. Ochre flesh, skin green, but becoming orange as it ripens. After boiling for a short time, can be used to make an excellent purée, rather like chestnut purée in colour and taste.

Lunga di Napoli Large, oblong, slightly club-shaped, green fruits. Flesh yellow, becoming orange on ripening. The long end is made up of solid flesh, the club-shaped end contains a small core with seeds. Widely grown in Italy.

Ponca Yellow, rather oblong, spherical on the underside. Weighs about 2 lb (1 kg) and is very good for eating.

Gold nugget Small round winter pumpkin, yellow with very hard flesh. Well-developed fruits should weigh about 2 lb (1 kg), but are often sold when still too small.

Table king A variety with pomegranate-shaped, yellow, sharply-ribbed fruits weighing 1 to 2 lb (0.5 to 1 kg).

Vegetable spaghetti
(Cucurbita pepo)
Smooth, oval to round fruit, green at first, turning yellow. When cooked the stringy flesh looks very much like spaghetti.
ORIGIN: Northern Mexico and the southern USA.
PRODUCTION: Limited to countries with a temperate climate. Mainly popular with amateur gardeners.
SEASON: August to September.
USE: Boil the whole fruit for about 20 minutes, cut open, remove the seed core, and dig out the stringy flesh with a fork. This 'spaghetti' can be eaten warm or cold with a spicy sauce.
STORAGE: One to two months at 54°F (12°C).
NUTRITIONAL VALUE: 21 kcal, 12.4 g carbohydrate, 1.4 g protein, 0.3 g fat, 22 mg calcium, 0.6 mg iron, 3.7 mg vitamin A, 13 mg vitamin C per 100 g serving.

△ Vegetable spaghetti, 8¾ in (220 mm) across ▽ Courgette 'Tondo di Piacenza', 6¾ in (170 mm) long

△ Courgette 'Elite', $4\frac{1}{4}$ in (108 mm) long

△ Courgette 'Gold rush', $5\frac{3}{8}$ in (137 mm) long

△ Courgette 'Blackini', $5\frac{1}{2}$ in (139 mm) long

△ Courgette 'Greyzini', $5\frac{1}{4}$ in (132 mm) long

Courgette or **zucchini**
(Cucurbita pepo)
Pulpy berry-fruits, usually harvested in a young and unripe stage. Shape varies from round to oblong, colour from creamy-white to dark green, often with grey speckles.
PRODUCTION: Italy, France, Spain, Israel, Britain, Netherlands.
SEASON: Throughout the year.
USE: Boil, bake or stew without peeling, or use raw in salads. Fully-grown fruits are usually peeled, cut into chunks and made into sweet pickle.
STORAGE: Young fruits about one week at 53 to 55°F (12 to 13°C). Fully-grown fruits, one to two months at the same temperature.
NUTRITIONAL VALUE; 16 kcal, 4 g carbohydrate, 0.6 g protein, 0.1 g fat, 15 mg calcium, 0.4 mg iron, 0.2 mg vitamin A, 17 mg vitamin C per 100 g serving.

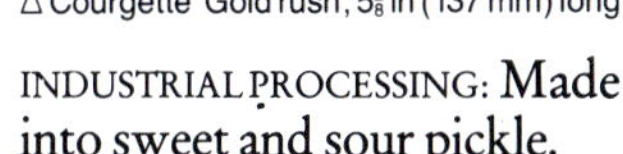

INDUSTRIAL PROCESSING: Made into sweet and sour pickle.

Varieties

Elite A hybrid with oblong, greyish-green speckled fruits, much in demand.

Blackini Hybrid variety with oblong, shiny, dark green fruits. Sometimes dark green on top and light green underneath.

Kussa An old variety with oblong, creamy-white fruits.

Clarita Hybrid variety with pear-shaped, very light green fruits.

Tondo di Piacenza Old Italian variety. Fruits almost spherical, green with greyish-green spots or stripes.

Greyzini Hybrid variety with oblong, bottle-shaped, greyish-green striped fruits.

Eldorado Old variety with oblong, bottle-shaped, yellow fruits that quickly become woolly.

Gold rush Hybrid with attractive, oblong, yellow fruits.

Custard marrow or **crown gourd**
(Cucurbita pepo)
Saucer-shaped fruits, often with lobed edges, harvested when young. Most are white, but some are light green or yellow.
ORIGIN: As courgettes.
PRODUCTION: France, Britain, USA.
SEASON: July to October.
USE: As courgettes. Small fruits 3 to 4 inches (8 to 10 cm) in diameter can be stuffed.
STORAGE: As courgettes.
NUTRITIONAL VALUE: As courgettes.

Varieties

Patty pan Late variety with white fruits. **White bush** is similar but earlier.

Peter Pan Early American variety with light green fruits.

Custard yellow Quite late English variety with yellow fruits, sometimes striped yellowish-green.

Sunburst New American hybrid with yellow fruits.

△ Custard marrows: white 'Patty Pan': green 'Peter Pan': yellow 'Custard', about 5¾ in (145 mm) across

Sinkwa
(Luffa acutangula)
Club-shaped fruits of a climbing plant with a strong and unpleasant smell. The green fruits are up to 24 inches (60 cm) long with ten sharp longitudinal ribs.
ORIGIN: Probably India.
PRODUCTION: China, Japan, Suriname, Thailand.
SEASON: Throughout the year.
USE: Boil or stew the young fruit and eat as a vegetable.
STORAGE: Young fruits two to three weeks at 53 to 55°F (12 to 13°C).

Balsam pear or **bitter gourd** or **bitter cucumber**
(Momordica charantia)
Greyish-green fruits with a warty skin, becoming orange when ripe. The blood-red flesh of the ripe fruits is slightly sweet in taste.
PRODUCTION: Many tropical countries.
SEASON: Autumn and winter.
USE: Choose fruits that are fully grown but not too ripe. Peel, slice, then boil or steam. Alternatively, hollow out the fruits and stuff.
STORAGE: Two to three weeks at 53 to 55°F (12 to 13°C) (not in the refrigerator).
NUTRITIONAL VALUE: 44 kcal, 5.6 g protein, 290 mg calcium, 5 mg iron, 5.1 mg vitamin A, 170 mg vitamin C per 100 g serving.

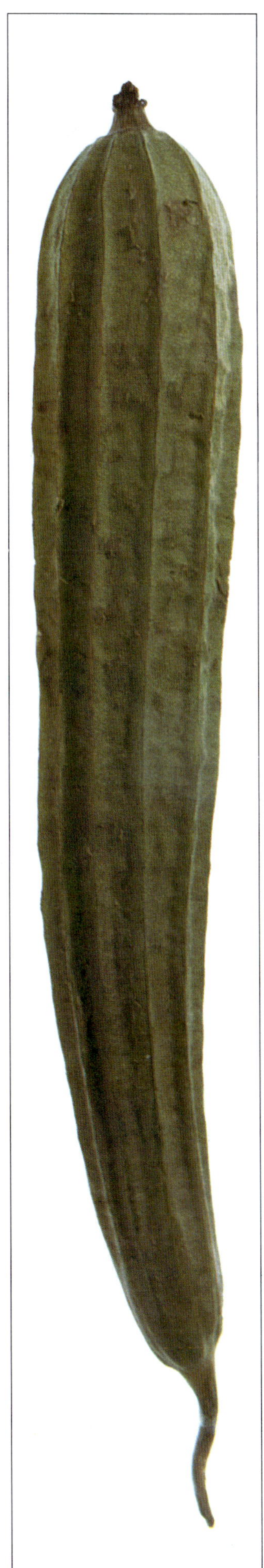

△ Sinkwa, 13½ (345 mm) long

△ Bitterkomkommer, 340 mm lang

Cyperaceae

The sedge family *(Cyperaceae)* includes a number of rush-like plants that grow in clumps with creeping rootstocks. They mostly grow in marshes or on river banks. In northern latitudes, for instance, there are the various types of sedge *(Carex spp.)*, the cotton grass *(Eriophorum vaginatum)*, and the bulrush *(Scirpus lacustris)*, formerly used for weaving mats and chair seats.

Some of the *Cyperaceae* form edible tubers at the roots, for instance the salt marsh club-rush *(S. maritimus)*, often found near salt water in northern regions. Similar tubers grow on the roots of the chufa *(Cyperus esculentus)*, introduced to southern Europe by the Arabs, and probably originating in the White Nile area. The annual form of the chufa has chestnut-brown to black tubers $\frac{3}{8}$ to $\frac{3}{4}$ inch (10 to 20 mm) long, that can be eaten raw, boiled or roasted. They are often known as earth almonds, having a fine, almondy taste, and give off a coffee-like aroma when roasted, as the sugars caramelize. The perennial form of the chufa, however, is a rampant weed, a menace to gardeners and farmers, as its creeping, winter-hardy rootstocks rapidly form dense clumps. One plant can spread far in one season, choking all other vegetation. The threat is so serious that gardeners are discouraged from growing any earth almonds at all.

The water chestnut is another member of the *Cyperaceae* family with edible tubers. There are probably two types, *Eleocharis dulcis*, said to have originated in west Africa, and now to be found in Madagascar, India and tropical east Asia, and *E. tuberosa* from eastern India, China and Japan, known among the Chinese as *pi-tsi*. Some botanists regard these two as a single species. Fresh tubers can occasionally be bought in shops specializing in tropical products.

The water caltrop *(Trapa natans)* is often called water chestnut but this produces a nut, not a tuber. It is eaten in northern Italy (boiled or baked), and from archaeological excavations in Switzerland and southern Sweden, we know that it used to be eaten there in the late Stone Age. Today the shells of these nuts are used to make beads and rosaries. The water caltrop is not a member of the *Cyperaceae*, but belongs to the small family of the *Trapaceae*.

△ Water chestnut (peeled), $1\frac{1}{2}$ in (40 mm) across

Water chestnut
(Eleocharis dulcis)
Flattish-round, tuberous rootstocks, brown to dark brown, and yellowish-white inside. Flavour crisp and sweet.
ORIGIN: Western Africa.
PRODUCTION: Eastern Africa, southern China, Japan, Philippines.
SEASON: Sporadic.
USE: Peel and use in Oriental recipes, soups and other dishes. Alternatively boil, remove skin, and eat or bake.
STORAGE: Limited. Fresh tubers a few days in the refrigerator. Canned chestnuts, after opening, may be kept in the refrigerator in a glass jar of water. If the water is changed daily, the chestnuts will keep for a month.
NUTRITIONAL VALUE: 19 g carbohydrate, 1.4 g protein, 0.2 g fat, 0.6 mg iron, 4 mg vitamin C per 100 g serving.
INDUSTRIAL PROCESSING: Canning.

Dioscoreaceae

There are about 600 species in the family of the *Dioscoreaceae,* but the genus *Dioscorea* is by far the most important, since the ten other genera put together include no more than 35 species. In northern latitudes the family has only one representative, the black bryony *(Tamus communis),* growing in woods and under hedges.

The family is mainly known for the many varieties of yams; the edible tubers of these tropical creepers can be formed both below and above ground. Yams are cultivated over 6.2 million acres (2.5 million hectares) worldwide, and of these 5.7 million (2.3 million) are in Africa. Central America with 136,000 acres (55,000 hectares), South America with 99,000 (40,000), and Asia with 40,000 (16,000) lag far behind.

Yams originated in Africa and Asia, and have spread over the entire tropical belt, as far as the islands of the Pacific. They are even grown in the south of the United States, although not a major crop. It is difficult for the consumer to differentiate yams, as the differences are only visible in the growing plants, the tubers seen looking very similar. To confuse the issue still further, some sweet potato varieties *(Ipomoea sp.)* are imported under the name of yam and some yams as sweet potatoes.

There are two varieties know as the Chinese yam. From time to time amateur gardeners can buy small tubers of one of these *D. batatas,* called igname de Chine. Planted in the hothouse during mid-May, they produce 16-inch (40 cm) tubers in November, that can be stored like potatoes. Possibly yams bought in the shops could be treated the same way.

From west Africa and Central America we get *D. cayennensis* (known as yellow yam, Guinea yam, twelve-month yam, cut yam or come yam), from India and Malaysia we get *D. esculenta* (Chinese yam or lesser yam), from west Africa comes *D. rotundata* (white yam), from central Africa there is *D. dumentorum* (bitter yam, cluster yam).

△ Potato yam *D. bulbifera*, 1¼ in (185 mm) long

Asiatic yam or **winged yam**
(Dioscorea alata)
Lobed or branched, fleshy tubers, varying in shape but resembling dahlia tubers.
ORIGIN: South-east Asia.
PRODUCTION: India, Philippines, Polynesia.
SEASON: Throughout the year.
USE: Raw in salads or sliced and baked in oil.
STORAGE: Short. Tends to deteriorate at low temperatures.
NUTRITIONAL VALUE: 23 g carbohydrate, 2 g protein, 0.2 g fat, 10 mg calcium, 0.3 mg iron, 10 mg vitamin C per 100 g serving.

Chinese yam
(Dioscorea batatas)
Oblong, white tubers, about 16 inches (40 cm) long.
ORIGIN: China.
PRODUCTION: China, Korea, Japan, Taiwan.
SEASON: November to April.
USE: Slice and bake in oil.
STORAGE: A few months in a dry, cool place (not in the refrigerator).
NUTRITIONAL VALUE: 131 kcal, 32.4 g carbohydrate, 2 g protein, 0.2 g fat, 10 mg calcium, 0.3 mg iron, 10 mg vitamin C per 100 g serving.

Potato yam or **aerial yam**
(Dioscorea bulbifera)
Spherical or fan-shaped, lobed tubers with a reddish-brown skin and white flesh. After boiling, the flesh changes colour to a dirty greenish-yellow, and is tender with a rather bitter flavour. Ripe tubers taste best.
ORIGIN: Tropical Africa and Asia.
PRODUCTION: Philippines, Malaysia.
SEASON: Irregular.
USE: Peel, cut into pieces and boil.
STORAGE: A few months in a cool dry place (not the refrigerator).
NUTRITIONAL VALUE: 131 kcal, 32.4 g carbohydrate, 2 g protein, 0.2 g fat, 10 mg vitamin C per 100 g serving.

Euphorbiaceae

The spurge family *(Euphorbiaceae)* is one of the larger families in the plant kingdom. About 6,500 species are included in its 300 genera. Most are tropical, but a few grow in temperate regions, for instance the annual mercury *(Mercurialis annua)*, and a number of species of spurge *(Euphorbia spp.)*, with their milky juice. This juice is poisonous, in some tropical varieties fatally so.

Poisonous plants often have curative properties as well, and this is true of many *Euphorbiaceae*. The name comes from the scholar Euphorbes, who was physician to King Juba II of Numidia in the first century BC. According to tradition he discovered the medicinal effect of one of the native spurges. Many spurge species have a good reputation as medicines, although they are often dangerously potent. For example, sixteenth-century Portuguese explorers brought some seeds of *Croton tiglium* to Europe from south-east Asia, one of the most powerful laxatives in nature, so powerful that in some recorded cases just two seeds killed the patient. These seeds were used by the Indonesians to poison the wells of enemies and rivals, a horribly effective form of secret weapon.

A similar but less drastic effect can be achieved with castor oil, pressed from the seeds of the long-cultivated castor oil plant *(Ricinus communis)*. In its unpurified form the oil is poisonous, and is often used as lamp oil or lubricating oil, but after heating it can safely be used as a laxative.

The most important plant in this family economically is *Hevea*, with its rubber-producing sap. The principal variety nowadays is *H. brasiliensis*. Many cultivars have been developed from it, some growing to over 65 feet (20 m) high in ten years.

Although a number of *Euphorbiaceae* supply edible fruits or seeds, there is only one significant internationally-grown species, the cassava or manioc. This plant comes from South America, and was brought to Spain in the sixteenth century. From Spain it was taken to Africa and from Africa on to Asia, where it was popular by the nineteenth century. The two types of cassava, the sweet and the bitter, are now planted over 37 million acres (15 million hectares) worldwide, about 20 million acres (8 million hectares) in Africa alone. The young leaves and stem tops of the shrub or tree are eaten as vegetables, especially in Sierra Leone, Zaïre and Indonesia. The really important parts of the plant are the heavily swollen tubers, rich in starch. These can be ground into flour (tapioca) by a process of grating, rinsing, soaking and drying. This flour can then be used in many different ways, for making flat cakes, or crackers, or as a binding agent.

△ Cassava, 9 in (230 mm) long

Cassava
(Manihot esculenta)
Thick, irregularly-shaped roots, rich in starch, brownish or dirty-white. There are sweet and bitter varieties.
ORIGIN: South America.
PRODUCTION: Zaïre, Tanzania, Nigeria, Brazil, Indonesia, Thailand.
SEASON: Throughout the year.
USE: Peel the tubers and boil, cut into strips or chunks and then bake or fry. Alternatively, dry the peeled tubers and grate, then allow the starch to seep out in water. From the dried precipitate, make flat cakes and bake them in oil.
STORAGE: For a long time.
NUTRITIONAL VALUE: 60 kcal, 6.9 g protein, 145 mg calcium, 2.8 mg iron, 8.3 mg vitamin A, 2.8 mg vitamin C per 100 g serving.
INDUSTRIAL PROCESSING: Cracker manufacture (on a very small scale).

Gramineae

The grass family *(Gramineae)*, with about 8,000 species, is possibly the most important food supplier in the world. All the significant grain species (rice, wheat, rye, barley, maize) belong to this family, providing food for people, animals and poultry.

There are not many vegetables among the *Gramineae*. There are the sprouts that can be grown by soaking grains in water and then allowing them to germinate at a high temperature. These apart, the grass family provides only three internationally-prized vegetables, bamboo shoots, sweetcorn and lemon grass *(Cymbopogon citratus, syn. Andropogon citratus)*. Lemon grass is known mainly as a spicy herb, though its young growing tips are eaten as a vegetable in Asia.

Young bamboo shoots, growing above ground or under ground, are very tender and sweet. The various kinds belong to a number of different genera, all from Asia, and it is usually impossible to tell from the fresh or canned imports what species they are.

Maize comes originally from Central America, and grows best in a warm dry climate, particularly the starch maize, with its dry, smooth grains used for making flour, cornflakes or cornflour (cornstarch). In cooler climates the starch maize hardly ever ripens, and the yield is disappointing. Hybrids are grown as cutting maize. This is harvested when still green, then finely chopped, and stored for animal fodder. Sometimes the cobs of these plants are harvested and sold as a vegetable, but the grains are floury, not sweet, and tasteless.

The varieties and hybrids of sweetcorn, a co-variety of the starch maize, especially the newer ones in the United States, have a high sugar content and are sweet. They are harvested when the silk threads of the cob are brown and dry: the grains are then yellow, and slight pressure with a fingernail produces a milky-white juice. Grains harvested too early do not have the right colour or flavour, and those harvested too late are wrinkled and indented.

Sugar cane *(Saccharum officinarum)* also belongs to this family. From south-east Asia originally, its juice contains about ten per cent cane sugar. Pieces of the jointed stems are often sold as a delicacy in shops specializing in tropical products.

△ Bamboo shoot, 11 in (280 mm) long

Bamboo
(Bambusa sp.; also other genera*)*
Short, tapering, herbaceous, with leaves like scales.
ORIGIN: Tropical Asia.
PRODUCTION: China, Japan, Indonesia, Philippines, Thailand, India.
SEASON: Throughout the year.
USE: As a cooked vegetable, or in pickles.
STORAGE: Keeps well, particularly under water in the refrigerator.
NUTRITIONAL VALUE: 32 kcal, 6 g carbohydrate, 2.5 g protein, 0.3 g fat, 33 mg calcium, 0.5 mg iron, 4 mg vitamin C per 100 g serving.
INDUSTRIAL PROCESSING: Canning and bottling.

Sweetcorn
(Zea mays, convar. saccharata)
Ears with soft, smooth, yellow grains, tasting juicy and sweet if harvested at the right time. Ears often sold in pairs, with leaves removed.
ORIGIN: Central America, Mexico.
PRODUCTION: USA, Israel, Spain, Netherlands.
SEASON: Throughout the year.
USE: Remove leaves and silk from cob, and boil or grill the cobs. Grains can also be eaten raw.
STORAGE: Only limited in the refrigerator. Grains rapidly lose their crispness and flavour, and become wrinkled.
NUTRITIONAL VALUE: 101 kcal, 20 g carbohydrate, 3 g protein, 1 g fat, 6 mg calcium, 0.5 mg iron, 12 mg vitamin C, 0.35 mg vitamin A per 100 g serving.
INDUSTRIAL PROCESSING: Loose grains are deep-frozen, canned or bottled. For pickling mini-cobs another type of maize is used.

△ Sweetcorn 'Tasty sweet', 8¾ in (220 mm) long ▽ Sweetcorn 'Early extra sweet', 5¾ in (145 mm) long

Varieties

Preference is given to extra-sweet hybrid varieties with a higher sugar content, from the USA.
Early extra sweet An extra-sweet, early hybrid with fairly large, thickish cobs. Tops of cobs have only a few grains. High sugar content, good flavour.
Tasty sweet An extra-sweet, quite early hybrid with thick, heavy cobs. Again, the tops are not packed with grains. Sugar content very high, good flavour.

Labiatae

The *Labiatae* family includes about 3,000 species, and is known for its herbs, both culinary and pharmaceutical. Basil, savory, hyssop, marjoram, mint, balm, rosemary, sage and thyme are all members, and so is the dead nettle *(Lamium)*, formerly regarded as a powerful styptic, helping to stop bleeding. Most *Labiatae* contain a pleasantly scented oil, used in the manufacture of spiced liqueurs, perfumes, lotions, mouth washes and soaps. Around the Mediterranean, where many *Labiatae* grow on the warm, dry mountain slopes, their nectar contributes to some delicious sorts of honey.

They feature in sagas, legends and folklore. The rosemary was regarded for centuries throughout Europe as a symbol of love, life, fertility and death. In some parts of Belgium, children are not brought by the stork or found under a gooseberry bush, but appear from sweet-smelling rosemary bushes.

There are not many real vegetables in this family. In England, country people used to eat the tubers that grow on the roots of the marsh woundwort *(Stachys palustris)*. Indonesians eat the fleshy leaves and stems, and the round black tubers of *Coleus tuberosus; syn C. edulis* and *C. parviflorus*, calling it Java potato.

In some restaurants you may find Japanese potato, the small, ring-like tubers that grow on the roots of the Japanese artichoke. These tubers used to be grown on a large scale near the French village of Crosnes, until about a century ago, and are sometimes still known as *crosnes*.

Japanese artichoke or **Chinese artichoke** or **crosne**
(Stachys sieboldii, syn. S. affinus)
Small, oblong, ring-like white tubers without skin.
ORIGIN: Central and northern China.
PRODUCTION: China, Japan, France, Belgium.
SEASON: October to March.
USE: Wash and scrub the tubers, use raw in salads or boil for a short time and then fry or bake them.
STORAGE: A few months in moist sand, at 32 to 36°F (0 to 2°C). Take care not to let them dry out. Tubers will sprout easily at about 41°F (5°C) in March.

△ Japanese artichoke, max. $2\frac{1}{2}$ in (65 mm) long

Leguminosae

The family of the pulses or *Leguminosae* is one of the largest in the plant kingdom. There are at least 15,000 species world-wide. Botanists have been struggling for many years to organize this vast number. Some prefer to regard the *Leguminosae* as an order rather than a family, and call it *Fabales.* They then subdivide this order into three families, the *Fabaceae* or *Papilionaceae,* the *Caesalpiniaceae,* and the *Mimosaceae.* Others (and we support their view), regard the *Leguminosae* family as a principal classification, and divide it into three sub-families, the *Papilionaceae* or butterfly flowers, the *Caesalpiniaceae* or Christ's thorns, and the *Mimosaceae* or mimosas.

Nevertheless, all members of this family have in common that after flowering, they develop pods to carry their seeds. A pod is actually a fruit leaf, where the right and left sides have grown together, forming a sheath for the developing seeds, each attached to the seam by a thin joint. This form can be found in all pulses, though sometimes it is hard to recognize. An unshelled peanut does not look much like a pod, but it is. After blooming, the peanut flower droops to the earth, and the pod (the peanut shell) develops underground in the soil.

The *Mimosaceae* have no edible parts, but the *Caesalpiniaceae* produce edible seeds, used in the manufacture of drinks and syrup, as well as being delicacies in their own right.

The sub-family of butterfly flowers or *Papilionaceae* is the major vegetable supplier in this family. All the pulses are in this sub-family, snap beans, slicing beans, green peas, sugar peas, broad beans, soya beans and the many varieties of peas and beans that play such an important part in the diet of people all over the world. Pulses are also important as animal fodder and fertilizer, for example, clover, alfalfa, lupin and vetch. These, working together with tuber bacteria, fix free nitrogen from the air, and so enrich the soil.

All pulses are rich in proteins, fats, carbohydrates, minerals and vitamins. Indeed the protein in beans can be an alternative to animal protein, which is important for millions of people world-wide who have limited access to meat and is useful to vegetarians. Some types of *Papilionaceae,* for instance soya beans and peanuts, have a high fat content, others have a particularly high vitamin content, especially the B-complex. Pulses are also useful in other ways, for example the blue dye indigo has been prepared from the pulses of the genus *Isatis* for thousands of years. Indigo has been largely replaced in the modern dye industry by synthetic dyes, but is still used, especially in the Arab world. The nomadic Tuareg from the African desert are called blue men because the indigo from their clothing stains their skins. The crushed leaves of the pulse *Tephrosia vogelii* from tropical Africa are placed in a pool or dammed section of river, and these stun the fish, so that they can easily be caught. The leaves contain the poison tephrosine, so potent that it is still effective at a dilution of 1 part to 50 million. The woody roots of *Glycyrrhiza glabra* from the Mediterranean area are pleasanter to eat — as licorice.

Pulses are eaten as vegetables in four ways: the whole pod is eaten, as with snap and slicing beans; only the green seeds are used, where the pod is too tough to eat, like green peas and marrowfat peas; the dried seeds are eaten, like many beans and peas and some types are germinated at high temperatures in the dark and the seeds eaten as sprouts, like mung beans and alfalfa.

In the following pages we have classified the various types of vegetable from the sub-family of the *Papilionaceae* in order of their economic significance for western Europe. The descriptions of the species that follow are in alphabetical order of their Latin names.

Snap beans and related species

Snap beans and slicing beans, as well as brown, white, black and other coloured beans, all belong to one species of international importance, *Phaseolus vulgaris.* They are probably descended from the wild form *Ph. aborigineus,* growing to the north-west of Argentina in the Andes mountains. All the present-day cultivars that grow in temperate climates were developed from this primitive type of bean during centuries of selection and improvement.

There is a wide range of types. To start with, we can distinguish between the dwarf beans and the climbing types. A second important characteristic is a parchment-like membrane in the pod wall. We can eat the pods of varieties where this membrane does not form at all, or forms only at a late stage, like the snap and slicing beans, those with green pods as well as those with yellow or purple pods. The varieties that do form this membrane early must be harvested very young if they are to be eaten whole, or they become too tough. This applies to haricots verts and one variety of slicing bean.

Brown, white, black and lemon beans all have this stiff membrane, so only the dried seeds are eaten. These beans can be stored for a long time after drying, and when they are needed they are soaked and then boiled. The flageolet is also a hard-skinned type, but the seeds are often eaten fresh. It is therefore a sort of pod bean, rather like a green pea.

Worldwide dried beans are a much more important product than green beans. Only 940,000 acres (380,000 hectares) are used across the world for the cultivation of green bean types, while the dried beans are grown over 58 million acres (23.5 million hectares), half in Asia and 11.8 million (4.7 million) in South America.

Other *Phaseolus* species to be found in the shops mostly in the dried form include the small red adzuki bean

Dried beans and peas. From top to bottom: chick-peas, soya beans, flageolets, adzuki beans, lima beans, broad beans

Dried beans. From top to bottom: mung bean (green), mung bean (red), black-moon bean (split), black-eye bean, lentil (green), lentil (red)

Dried peas. From top to bottom: green pea, split pea (green), split pea (yellow), marrowfat pea, raisin pea

Right: *the remarkable stink bean or peteh bean from East Asia, mainly used to make sauces*

from East Asia; the small oval mung bean from southern Asia, that may be green, golden-yellow or black; the equally small, green or brownish-yellow rice bean from the Himalaya region, said to be very nutritious; the large and small lima bean from Central and South America, usually white but sometimes coloured, that needs to be boiled for a long time (especially the coloured types) because the seed coat is not entirely free from prussic acid; and lastly the runner bean. This bean originally from Mexico and Guatemala, flourishes in northern regions too. When harvested young, the long, fairly broad pods can be eaten like slicing beans. The purple-grained seeds bloom red, the white ones produce white flowers.

Sugar peas, green peas and marrowfat peas

These are all forms of one species, *Pisum sativum.* As a cultivated species it has a considerable history. In archaeological excavations in Switzerland, peas have been found among human settlements 5,000 years old. The parent is probably the wild form *P. sativum, var. elatius,* still to be found in the eastern Mediterranean area, and in Iran and Afghanistan.

Like the beans, the degree of parchment-like membrane in the pod decides the way they are to be used. If there is a strong membrane, only the seeds, the peas, are eaten, either unripe or as dried peas (especially in soups). If the membrane is absent or late-developing, then the pods can be eaten, as with the sugar peas. These are a luxury vegetable, available only in limited quantities because of labour-intensive harvesting. In northern Europe the small-podded varieties are grown, while the large-podded types are cultivated in southern Europe and north Africa. A new phenomenon is the string pea from the United States, a type with a fleshy pod wall and no parchment-like membrane. The pods are harvested when the seeds are well developed. They are pleasantly sweet in taste, and can be eaten whole or shredded.

The cultivation of green peas dates from around 1600, like the sugar peas. Before that time the pea was used only in a dried form, in soups and stews. The peas are taken out of the pod before cooking. There are three types of green pea: the wrinkled pea, with rather a sweet flavour and a furrowed, wrinkled skin; the round pea, that stays smooth, both green and dried, with a distinctive, rather acid taste; and a variety including the marrowfat peas and the purple-podded kidney beans. Marrowfat peas are sold dried as well as fresh.

The cultivation of peas for drying has a long history and is still important internationally. World-wide, about 18 million acres (8 million hectares) are grown, about 12.3 million (5 million) of these in the Soviet Union. Dried peas include the round yellow pea, the marrowfat pea, the raisin or grey pea, and the round green pea that is processed to produce the split pea (the two seed halves without the seed coat). Dried peas must be soaked before cooking.

The broad bean and the cowpea

The pulses of the species *Vicia faba* originate in south-west Asia and are one of the oldest cultivated species.

Small-seeded species like the horse bean, the tick bean and the seaweed bean form the group of field beans, used as animal fodder. Large-seeded varieties from the broad bean group are grown for human consumption. Until the end of the Middle Ages the broad bean was a very important vegetable. The dried seeds were boiled in water after soaking or ground into flour to make bread, biscuits and cakes. After the discovery of America, and the arrival in Europe of beans of the genus *Phaseolus* as well as the potato, broad beans became less important, and now they are mostly eaten fresh.

Raw broad beans contain toxic substances that cause clotting of the blood or even breakdown of the red blood corpuscles, or they may have a negative effect on protein metabolism. These substances break down at high temperatures and occur chiefly in the multicoloured flowering varieties. These varieties produce brown beans with a distinctive acid taste, caused by the presence of tannic acid. The white-flowering varieties do not contain any tannic acid, and the beans remain white or green after boiling, with a milder flavour.

Closely related to the broad bean is the cowpea, originating in western Africa, and now established in tropical America and Asia. There are three species: the yardlong bean, with very long, ribbon-like, greyish-green pods; the peanut bean *(Vigna unguiculata, spp. cylindrica)* cultivated in the tropics as animal fodder; and the cowpea itself *(V. unguiculata, ssp. unguiculata),* mainly grown in the tropics for drying, when it has a small dark ring round the hilum, but sometimes eaten young.

Other pulses

A number of other pulses are to be found on the market, often as dried beans, though supplies are often irregular and limited. The most important are:

The **pigeon pea** from the tropical regions of Africa and Asia, with seeds that can be white, yellow reddish-brown or black. The young pods can be eaten as a vegetable, and the young seeds can be used raw in many different dishes. Raw seeds contain a completely harmless soporific substance. Ripe seeds are baked in oil or used to make vegetable sprouts.

The **chick-pea** originates from the Himalayas and south-western Asia. Chick-peas vary widely in colour from yellowish-white to black and in size from $3\frac{1}{2}$ to $12\frac{1}{2}$ oz (100 to 350 g) per 1,000 seeds. They are an old cultivated species, still grown on a large scale for eating, usually dried.

The **soya bean,** cultivated in China as early as 2700 BC, found its way to North America at the beginning of the nineteenth century. Soya beans form a very important source of vegetable protein and may in future play an increasingly important role in world food supply. At the moment the total area (worldwide) devoted to soya beans is 125 million acres (50 million hectares), half in the United States and 25 million (10 million) in Asia. The beans, green, reddish, or creamy-white, are also used for producing oil and artificial meat.

The **lentil** is another old cultivated species from eastern Mediterranean countries as far as Afghanistan. The round, flat, lens-shaped seeds are white or light-brown to reddish and grow in small, flat pods. Lentils are still cultivated on a fairly large scale, over 5 million acres (2 million hectares). The large-seed species come chiefly from the Mediterranean region, the small-seed species from further east.

The **asparagus pea** is a relatively unknown pulse from the Mediterranean area. The young stem shoots without leaves can be eaten just like asparagus, and the young pods are also edible.

Alfalfa or lucerne *(Medicago sativa)* has been fed to animals from time immemorial but is now also used to produce a sprouting vegetable. The young blanched seedlings can be eaten raw.

The **yam bean**, originating in South and Central America and now cultivated in Thailand, Indonesia, and southern China, is mainly known for its heavy, flattish-round tubers, often weighing 22 lb (10 kg), but both pods and seeds may be eaten too. Although some sources report that the leaves and pods are poisonous, the young tubers are particularly good when roasted.

Growing vegetable sprouts

It is quite easy to produce sprouts from various dried pulses. The beans are first soaked in water and then kept in the dark at quite a high temperature. After a few days they germinate, mostly producing a white stem with two cotyledons. All vegetable sprouts can be eaten raw, used in salads or in oriental dishes. They are delicious and easily digestible. Species used for this germination process are pigeon peas, adzuki beans, mung beans, peanut beans, rice beans and alfalfa. It is easy to experiment with other dried pulses, and with many types of grain.

Stages in the growth of sprouting vegetables

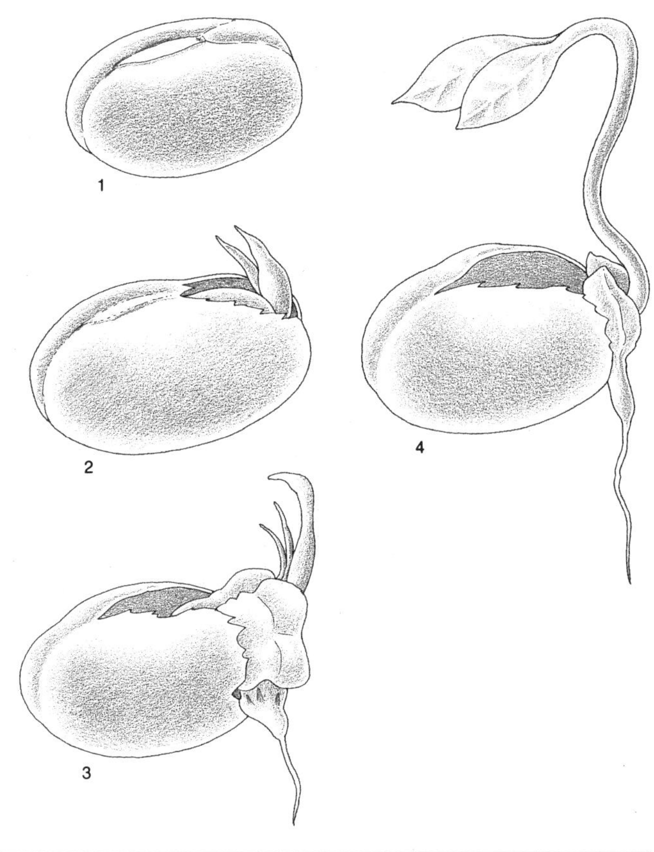

Pigeon pea or **cajan pea**
(Cajanus cajan)
Dry pulse, with seeds similar to peas. Colour varies from white or yellow to reddish-brown and black.
ORIGIN: Tropical Africa.
PRODUCTION: Tropical Africa and Asia.
SEASON: Throughout the year.
USE: Dry seeds in pulse dishes or for vegetable sprouts. The dry seeds are difficult to cook thoroughly. They are more easily digested as split peas, without the seed coat.
STORAGE: Keep for a long time in a cool, dry place.
NUTRITIONAL VALUE: 58 g carbohydrate, 20 g protein, 1.3 g fat per 100 g serving.

△ Asparagus pea (pods, leaf and flower), longest pod $3\frac{3}{4}$ in (95 mm)

Chick-pea or **gram**
(Cicer arietinum)
Dry pulse, mostly with a whitish or light-yellow seed coat. The seeds are rather large and sharply indented, but there are varieties with small seeds.
ORIGIN: Probably south-west Asia or the Himalayas.
PRODUCTION: India, Pakistan, Turkey, Ethiopia, Spain.
SEASON: Throughout the year.
USE: Roast the dry seed or soak and use in various dishes. If fresh can be eaten raw.
STORAGE: Dry seed for a long time in a cool, dry place.
NUTRITIONAL VALUE: 163 kcal, 8 g protein, 3 g fat, 26 g carbohydrate, 58 mg calcium, 3 mg iron per 100 g serving.
INDUSTRIAL PROCESSING: Canning.

Varieties

Album Yellowish-white lightly-indented seeds weighing 12 to 13 oz (350 to 370 g) per 1,000 seeds. The best type for human consumption.

Rhytidospermum Round, smooth, reddish-brown to dark red seeds, weighing 10 to 12 oz (280 to 350 g) per 1,000 seeds.

Vulgare Black seeds, sharply indented at the hilum, weighing 11 to 12 oz (320 to 350 g) per 1,000 seeds. Used for animal fodder.

Asparagus or **winged pea**
(Lotus edulis)
Winged, light-green pods, developing from red flowers. Can be eaten as a vegetable when young. They have an almond flavour.
ORIGIN: Round Mediterranean.
PRODUCTION: Throughout western Europe, mainly by amateur gardeners.
SEASON: June to October.
USE: Boil for a very short time, use in vegetable dishes or in mixed vegetable soups.
STORAGE: Very limited (in the refrigerator). Pods soon become flabby and tough.

Yam bean
(Pachyrrhizus erosus)
Edible thickened roots shaped like a beet or swede.
ORIGIN: South and Central America.
PRODUCTION: Various tropical countries.
SEASON: May to October.
USE: Raw in salads (shredded). Young tubers roasted or in soup. Older tubers may be dried and finely chopped to produce starch.
STORAGE: For a few weeks in the refrigerator.
NUTRITIONAL VALUE: 41 kcal, 1 g protein, 0.1 g fat, 9 g carbohydrate, 15 mg calcium, 0.5 mg iron, 20 mg vitamin C per 100 g serving.

Adzuki bean
(Phaseolus angularis)
Dried pulse with rather fine, red seeds.
ORIGIN: East Asia.
PRODUCTION: China, Korea, Japan.
SEASON: Throughout the year.
USE: In bean soup or soak and then boil. Also for bean sprouts.
STORAGE: Dried beans for a long time in a cool, dry place.

△ Yam bean, 3¾ in (97 mm) across

Soya bean
(Glycine max)
Dry pulse, rather fine, oval to round. Generally creamy-white, but there are also green and red-seeded varieties.
ORIGIN: East Asia.
PRODUCTION: USA, Brazil, Argentina, China, Romania, Soviet Union.
SEASON: Throughout the year. When grown in northern regions pods appear in August and September. The pods are covered with short, matted, woolly hairs.
USE: Dry soya beans should be soaked in water and then boiled. During soaking, the water should be changed once. Fresh soya beans can be shelled like peas and then boiled.
STORAGE: Dry seed, for over a year in a cool, dry place. Fresh pods for a few days in the refrigerator.
NUTRITIONAL VALUE: 33 g protein, 17 g fat, 30 g carbohydrate per 100 g serving.
INDUSTRIAL PROCESSING: Soya oil, artificial meat.

Lentil
(Lens culinaris, syn. esculentus)
Dry pulse, with round, flat, lens-shaped seeds, either white or light brown to red. There are large-seed and small-seed varieties. The small seeds have a better taste and are marbled light brown or red.
ORIGIN: Probably eastern Mediterranean and further east.
PRODUCTION: India, Turkey, Yugoslavia.
SEASON: Throughout the year.
USE: Soak for only a short time before boiling, or not at all. Eat with herbs or make into lentil soup.
STORAGE: For a long time. The older the seed, the longer the soaking time needed.
NUTRITIONAL VALUE: Dry seed 286 kcal, 47 g carbohydrate, 21 g protein, 1.5 g fat, 80 mg calcium, 5 mg iron per 100 g serving.
INDUSTRIAL PROCESSING: Canning with herbs and meat, soups.

Mung bean or **green gram**
(Phaseolus aureus, syn. mungo)
Small bean, may be green, brown, yellow or black. Green ones mainly used for bean sprouts.
ORIGIN: Southern Asia.
PRODUCTION: Seeds from Asia or Africa.
SEASON: Throughout the year.
USE: Sprouts in salads or in oriental dishes. Dried beans can be boiled.
STORAGE: Beans keep for a very long time (if dry and cool). Sprouts soon become flabby and tough, and can only be kept for a few days in a polythene bag in the refrigerator.
NUTRITIONAL VALUE: Sprouts 40 kcal, 3 g carbohydrate, 5 g protein, 0.9 g fat, 38 mg calcium, 1 mg iron, 14 mg vitamin C, a relatively large amount of vitamin B1 per 100 g serving.
INDUSTRIAL PROCESSING: Sprouts, canning and bottling.

Δ Runner bean (red-flowering), longest pod 10⅝ in (270 mm), described on page 110

Δ Sprouting green katjoeng idjoe (below)

Rice bean
(Phaseolus calcaratus)
Small-seeded, tropical pulse with wide variations in colour. Varieties with greenish-yellow or brownish-yellow seeds are the most nourishing.
ORIGIN: Himalayas, India.
PRODUCTION: India and central China.
SEASON: Throughout the year.
USE: In soups and in pulse dishes (soaked first). Can also be used for bean sprouts.
STORAGE: Very long if kept cool and dry.
NUTRITIONAL VALUE: Dry seed 324 kcal, 22 g protein, 1 g fat, 57 g carbohydrate, 100 mg calcium, 8 mg iron, no vitamins per 100 g serving.

Runner bean or **scarlet runner** *(Phaseolus coccineus, syn. multiflorus)*
Long, fairly narrow, flattish-oval, green pods with a rather rough skin. A string forms on the front and back seams as the pods get older. The pod wall produces a parchment-like membrane quite early on. Red or white flowers. The pods of the red-flowering varieties are generally more stringy than those of the white-flowering varieties, and the beans are darker coloured after boiling.
ORIGIN: Mexico and Guatemala.
PRODUCTION: Britain, Spain, Netherlands.
SEASON: July to December/ January.
USE: Remove strings if necessary from young pods and slice. Older pods unsuitable for eating.
STORAGE: Unsliced, about four days at 41 to 43°F (5 to 6°C). Can deteriorate in the refrigerator.
NUTRITIONAL VALUE: 25 kcal, 3 g carbohydrate, 3 g protein, 0.3 g fat, 40 mg calcium, 0.8 mg iron, 15 mg vitamin C per 100 g serving.
INDUSTRIAL PROCESSING: Freezing, canning and bottling.

Varieties

Emergo White-flowering with straight, narrow, fleshy, green pods with a string, 10 to 11½ inches (25 to 29 cm) long.

Prizewinner Red-flowering with straight, narrow, fleshy, rather rough, dark green pods with a string, 10½ to 12 inches (27 to 30 cm) long.

△ Runner bean (white-flowering), longest pod 10¼ in (260 mm)

Lima bean or **sieva bean** or **butter bean** *(Phaseolus lunatus)*
A tropical pulse of varied shape. Dried, large, flat, white seeds mostly available. Pods are broad and flat.
ORIGIN: South America (Andes and Amazon region).
PRODUCTION: Southern USA, Central and South America.
SEASON: Dried beans throughout the year. Fresh pods occasionally.
USE: Soak and boil the dried beans. Fresh pods should be shelled and the beans used like broad beans. Varieties with coloured beans contain prussic acid and must be boiled thoroughly with several water changes.
STORAGE: Dried beans for a very long time if kept cool and dry.
NUTRITIONAL VALUE: 123 kcal, 22.1 g carbohydrate, 8.4 g protein, 0.5 g fat, 52 mg calcium, 2.8 mg iron, 29 mg vitamin C per 100 g serving.
INDUSTRIAL PROCESSING: Deep-freezing and canning.

Dwarf and pole snapbean *(Phaseolus vulgaris)*
Fairly long pods usually green, but sometimes purple or butter-yellow, depending on variety. In cross-section they are round, oval or flat. The most modern varieties have no string on either side. There are white-seed and coloured-seed varieties.
ORIGIN: South America.
PRODUCTION: Italy, France, Spain, Romania, Britain, Netherlands, Belgium, USA, Egypt, some African countries.
SEASON: Throughout the year, from over 30 countries.
USE: If necessary string the pods, break into pieces if preferred, and boil.
STORAGE: Will keep for four to five days in a cool place. Do not keep in the refrigerator.
NUTRITIONAL VALUE: 36 kcal, 5 g carbohydrate, 3 g protein, 0.4 g fat, 40 mg calcium, 1 mg iron, 10 mg vitamin C per 100 g serving.
INDUSTRIAL PROCESSING: Freezing, canning, bottling. Also salting and drying.

△ Snap beans. From left to right, 'Fran-toccata', 4¾ in (123 mm), 'Flageolet', 6¼ in (160 mm), 'Purple queen', 4½ in (116 mm)

△ Snap bean 'Contender', 6⅛ in (155 mm) long

Varieties

There are a great many varieties, and we distinguish the following types on the basis of pod shape and colour.

Single snap bean, green Rather small, flat pods, with clearly visible seed nuclei. Very good for eating, but grown less and less by professional gardeners. Rentegevers and Mechelse tros are varieties, Amateur and Perfecto are dwarf varieties.

Double snap bean, green Pods are rounder and more fleshy, seed nuclei are barely visible from the outside or not at all. This is the main type on sale. Dwarf varieties are Centrum, Impala, Prelude and Gran-toccata. Pole varieties are Aromata, Chantal, Largo and Situla.

Chinese beans, green Small-pod varieties. Pods can be eaten whole. Pods not membranous, but turn yellow and then become tough. Mainly for processing industry.

Haricot vert French type of pole bean with long, straight, thin, flattish-oval pods. They are harvested when young, as they are not suitable for eating when fully grown.

Contender An American variety with coarse, fleshy pods and an insipid flavour.

Processor Also an American variety with coarse, insipid-tasting pods.

Wax pod The terms wax pod and butter bean refer to varieties with golden-yellow pods. Insipid flavour. More recent varieties are Constanza, Dorina and Goldfish. Older varieties are Wachs mont d'or and Brittle wax.

△ Dwarf slicing bean 'Admires', $7\frac{7}{8}$ in (200 mm) long

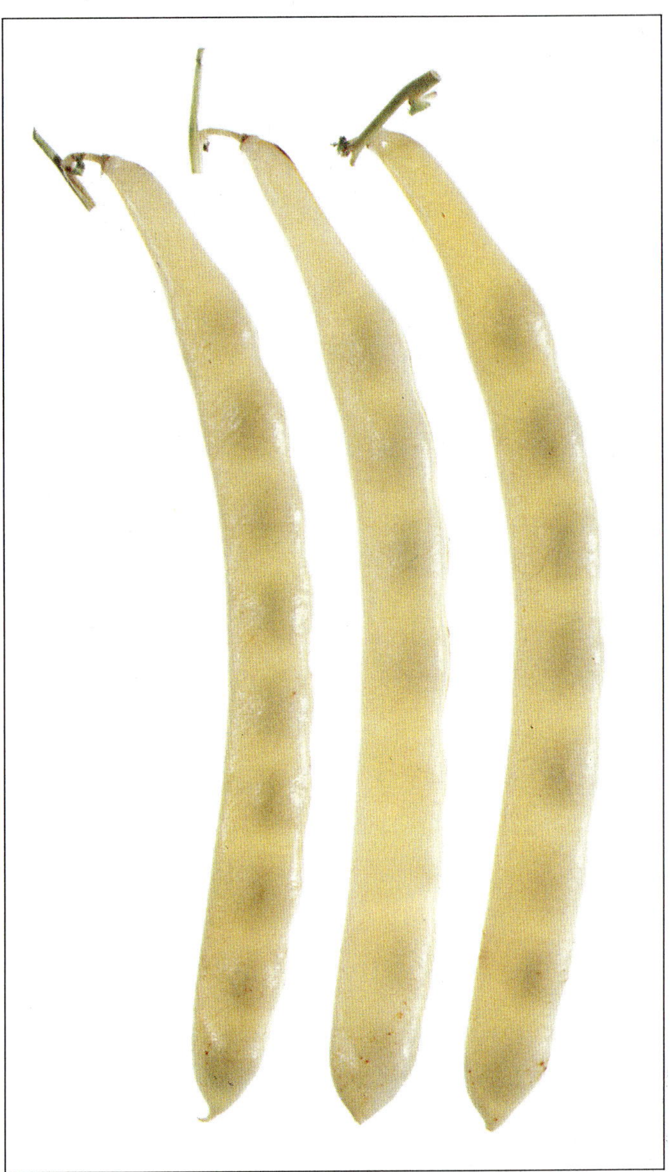

△ Pole slicing bean 'Reingold', $9\frac{1}{2}$ in (240 mm) long ▽ Pole snap bean 'Largo', $5\frac{1}{2}$ in (140 mm) long

Purple queen A dwarf snap bean with purple pods that turn green when boiled. Excellent to eat.

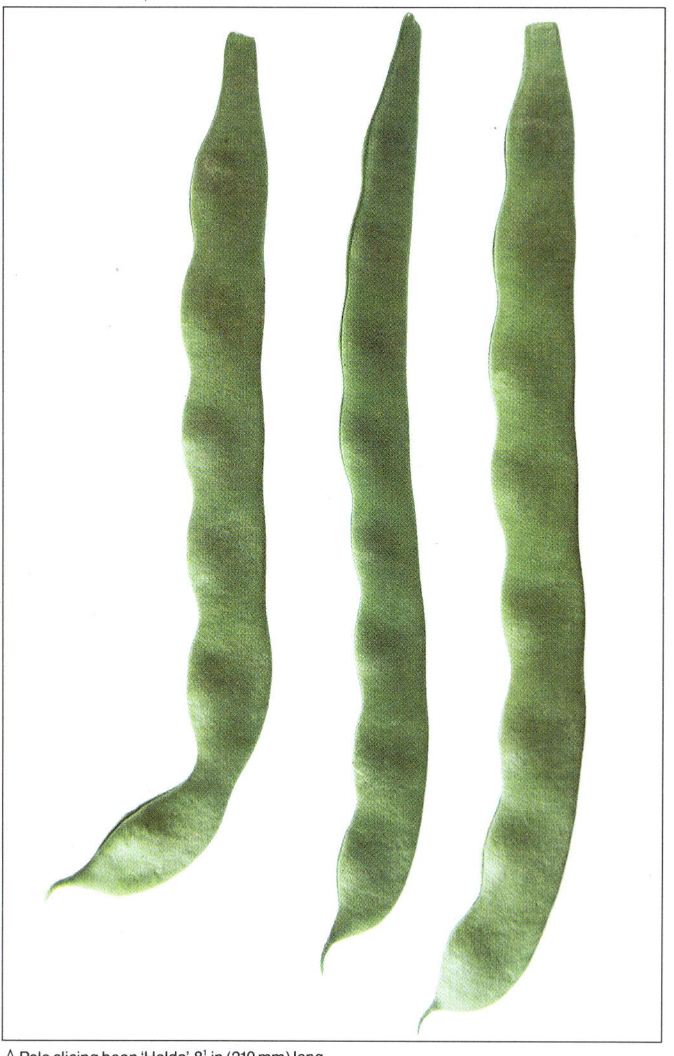

△ Pole slicing bean 'Helda', $8\frac{1}{4}$ in (210 mm) long

Slicing bean (dwarf and pole)
(Phaseolus vulgaris)
There are various types: the true slicing bean with long, flat, broad pods and its distinctive flavour; the bacon bean (long, oval-round pods, sweeter in taste); the runner bean and also cut, coarse, snapbeans.
ORIGIN: As snap bean.
PRODUCTION: True slicing beans, Netherlands, Belgium and some African countries; bacon beans, West Germany; runner beans, Britain.
SEASON: Throughout the year from various countries.
USE: Cut the fresh pods into pieces or shred and boil.
STORAGE: As snap bean.
NUTRITIONAL VALUE: 33 kcal, 5 g carbohydrate, 2.2 g fat, 0.3 g protein, 51 mg calcium, 0.8 mg iron, 19.5 mg vitamin C per 100 g serving.
INDUSTRIAL PROCESSING: Canning, bottling or deep-freezing.

Varieties

Dwarf slicing beans
Low-growing, mainly for the amateur gardener. Best-known variety is Admires with stringless green pods, about 6 inches (15 cm) long and $\frac{3}{4}$ inch (2 cm) wide. Very good when harvested young.

Pole slicing beans Mostly white-seed varieties with stringless green pods that only form a parchmenty membrane at a late stage. Popular varieties: Helda, light-green, $8\frac{3}{4}$ to $10\frac{1}{4}$ inches (22 to 26 cm) long and just over $\frac{3}{4}$ inch wide (20 to 22 mm); Precores, green, the same size; and Superia, green. $8\frac{3}{4}$ to $9\frac{7}{8}$ inches (22 to 25 cm) long and about $\frac{3}{4}$ inch (19 to 21 mm) wide; Reingold is a stringless slicing bean with long, broad, golden-yellow pods.

△ Bacon bean 'Blauwschedige spek', 9 in (230 mm) long

Bacon bean Generally white-seeded variety with green stringless pods lacking any membrane, but some varieties have yellow or purple pods. Popular varieties are Necores, long, curved, mid-green and oval in cross-section; Neckargold, long, golden-yellow, stringless, round in cross-section; and Blauwschedige spek, with curved, purple pods about $7\frac{1}{2}$ inches (19 cm) long.

Kidney bean or **French bean**
(Phaseolus vulgaris)
Dried beans, not eaten fresh because of their hard skin, tough string, and parchmenty membrane in the pod. There are a few exceptions, like flageolets, that are harvested, shelled, and eaten fresh. Dried types include white beans, brown beans, lemon beans, plover beans, black Mexican or Brazilian beans, red kidney beans and pinto beans.
ORIGIN: As snap bean.
PRODUCTION: Southern USA, South America, Asia, Africa.
SEASON: Throughout the year. Fresh flageolets August and September.
USE: Soak in water and boil (the older the bean, the longer the time needed for both soaking and boiling).
STORAGE: One to two years.
NUTRITIONAL VALUE: 282 kcal, 47 g carbohydrate, 20 g protein, 1.5 g fat, 80 mg calcium, 3 mg iron per 100 g serving.
INDUSTRIAL PROCESSING: Canning or bottling. Sometimes in sauces or with other beans.

Sugar pea
(Pisum sativum, convar. axiphium)
Flat pods. The older type is light green with poorly developed seeds, harvested very young. A newer type, the string pea, has thick-walled light and dark green pods with well-developed seeds. Taste sweet, but a little more acid if harvested when young.
ORIGIN: East of Mediterranean.
PRODUCTION: Thailand, Morocco, Spain, France and Kenya.
SEASON: Larger types December to May, smaller types June to September.
USE: After removing the string on each side, wash and boil quickly, adding sugar if preferred. The older type is boiled whole, the newer type, the string pea, is often shredded before boiling.
STORAGE: Limited, about four days in the refrigerator at 36 to 41°F (2 to 5°C).
NUTRITIONAL VALUE: 31 kcal, 5 g carbohydrate, 2.5 g protein, 0.1 g fat, 40 mg calcium, 0.5 mg iron, 70 mg vitamin C, 0.6 mg vitamin PP per 100 g serving.
INDUSTRIAL PROCESSING: Deep-freezing.

△ Sugar pea 'Early snap', $3\frac{3}{4}$ in (95 mm) long

Varieties

Can be divided into three groups, small- and large-podded (both *var. saccharatum* from the old type) and the string pea *(var. macrocarpum)* with a pod like a green pea. Small-podded varieties — the most important are **Agio-kortstro**, stubby, light-green, about 4 inches (10 cm) long and $\frac{3}{4}$ inch (20 mm) wide; **Norli-kortstro**, stubby, light green, about $3\frac{1}{8}$ inches (8 cm) long and $\frac{5}{8}$ inch (15 mm) wide; and **Record-langstro** smooth, light green, about $3\frac{1}{2}$ inches (9 cm) long and $\frac{5}{8}$ inch (15 mm) wide.
Large-podded varieties — the best known are **Reuzensuiker**, straight, green, about 4 inches (10 cm) long and 1 inch (25 cm) wide; and **Zwitserse reuzen**, light green, undulating, about $4\frac{3}{4}$ inches (12 cm) long and $1\frac{1}{4}$ inches (33 mm) wide.
String pea varieties form pods with a thick, crisp pod wall and sweet, green, fairly large peas. The new American varieties include **Early snap**, dark green pods shaped rather like those of the kidney bean, about $3\frac{1}{8}$ inches (8 cm) long and oval in cross-section; **Sugar snap**, with identical pods; and **Sweet snap**, light green, rather curved pods, round in cross-section, about $3\frac{1}{8}$ inches (8 cm) long, and very sweet.

△ Rice pea, round-seeded, 'Vlijmse krombek', 4 in (100 mm) long

Green pea
(Pisum sativum, convar. medullare and *sativum)*
Thick bulbous pods, green except for the purple-podded marrowfat pea. Only the fresh seeds are eaten. The round-seed varieties have the distinctive, slightly acid pea flavour, the wrinkled-seed varieties have a sweet taste.
ORIGIN: As sugar peas.
PRODUCTION: Britain, France, Italy, Belgium, Netherlands, Greece, USA, India, and eastern Europe.
SEASON: Fresh green peas January to October from various countries.
USE: Remove peas from pod and boil.
STORAGE: Very limited. In the pod for five days, shelled peas for one day in the refrigerator.
NUTRITIONAL VALUE: 61 kcal, 10 g carbohydrate, 4 g protein, 0.5 g fat, 20 mg calcium, 2 mg iron, 50 mg vitamin C, 2.7 mg vitamin PP, 0.4 mg vitamin A per 100 g serving.
INDUSTRIAL PROCESSING: Deep-freezing, canning or bottling.

Varieties

The development of new varieties has resulted in a number of types with very small peas, so now a small pea is not necessarily a tastier pea as it was in the days when the small peas were the youngest.

Round, yellow-seeded Still cultivated by amateur gardeners. Important varieties are Early May (straight, stubby pods), and Vlijmse krombek (sharply curved, pointed pods).

Round, light green-seeded Important varieties are Marzia (small, light-green peas), and Lisette, Arno, Barette and Evi (all with extra small light green peas).

Wrinkled, light green-seeded The most important varieties are Mini (extra small light green peas), Cisca (light green peas, small to very small), Sol (moderately small light green peas), Starlette (very small light green peas), and Otex (small light green peas).

Wrinkled, dark green-seeded Chiefly grown by amateur gardeners, most important varieties are Kelvedon wonder, Triton and Vitalis (all with coarse peas).

△ Marrowfat pea (Blauwschokker), with leaf and flower, pod 4 in (100 mm) long

Marrowfat peas Important varieties are Imposant (green pods and light green, coarse peas), Purple-podded (blue pods) and Desiree (blue pods).

Pea
(Pisum sativum, convar. speciosum)
Dried peas, including green peas, yellow peas, marrowfat peas, raisin or grey peas.
ORIGIN: As sugar peas.
PRODUCTION: Soviet Union, China, India, Ethiopia, France, Hungary, Germany, Netherlands, Britain.
SEASON: Throughout the year.
USE: Marrowfat and raisin peas should be soaked in water and boiled, the other peas are mostly used in soups.
STORAGE: For a long time, if kept in a cool dry place.
NUTRITIONAL VALUE: 282 kcal, 47 g carbohydrate, 20 g protein, 1.5 g fat, 80 mg calcium, 5 mg iron per 100 g serving.
INDUSTRIAL PROCESSING: Split peas in soups, marrowfat and raisin peas are soaked and then canned or bottled.

Varieties

Finale Round green pea, quite large, with a tendency to burst.

Miranda Large round yellow pea, mainly suitable for using in soup.

Maro Quite large green pea, light green with a good flavour. Green peas are normally used whole.

Imposant Marrowfat pea, large, angular, light brown to greenish.

Gastro Raisin or grey pea, large and angular, marbled brown.

Broad bean
(Vicia faba)
Large, green, woolly pods with two to five thick, flat, oblong to elliptical seeds, soft and greenish. The beans are eaten; during cooking they become brown, white or green, depending on variety.
ORIGIN: South-west Asia (small-seeded wild beans) and Mediterranean (large-seeded broad beans).
PRODUCTION: Italy, Spain, France, Britain, Germany, Netherlands, Turkey, Morocco.
SEASON: January to September.
USE: Remove the fresh beans from the pod and boil. The pod is sometimes boiled and eaten if picked very young, before the seed nucleus has formed. Broad beans should never be eaten raw because of toxic substances.
STORAGE: In the pod one to two weeks at 32 to 34°F (0 to 1°C) in high humidity. Shelled broad beans for a maximum of one day in the refrigerator.
NUTRITIONAL VALUE: 39 kcal, 4 g carbohydrate, 5 g protein, 0.3 g fat, 20 mg calcium, 1 mg iron, 80 mg vitamin C, 0.16 mg vitamin A per 100 g serving.
INDUSTRIAL PROCESSING: Canning, bottling or deep-freezing.

△ Broad bean 'Rato', 7½ in (190 mm) long

Varieties

The varieties can be subdivided into three groups depending on the colour of the cooked bean, those that turn brown, those that stay white and those that remain green. The ones that turn brown when cooked have thinner skins, and the typical, slightly bitter broad bean flavour. They are mainly intended for eating fresh or deep-freezing and have white/black flowers. The beans that stay white or green when cooked have a milder taste and are mainly used for canning or bottling. These are white-flowering.

Witkiem Large, broad pods, 6¾ to 7½ inches (17 to 19 cm) long, with three to four quite large beans that turn brown when cooked. Good selections are Major, Heerenveense, Ezetha's Witiem, Bonus, Futura and Rato.

Express Long, slender pods, over 8 inches (20 cm) in length, with four to five beans that turn brown when cooked. Only suitable for eating fresh. Good selections are con amore and trio.

Lange hangers Old variety with black beans and long to very long pods. Still occasionally grown for eating fresh.

Statissa Pods of 4¾ to 5⅛ inches (12 to 13 cm) long with four to five coarse beans, turning brown when cooked.

Propix Pods 6 to 6¼ inches (15 to 16 cm) long with four to five fairly large beans that turn brown when cooked.

Minica Pods 5⅛ to 5½ inches (13 to 14 cm) long with four to five moderately small beans that turn brown when cooked.

Brunette Pods of 4¼ to 4¾ inches (11 to 12 cm) long with three to four small beans. They turn brown when cooked.

Driemaal wit An old variety with a white hilum and beans that stay white. The narrow pods are about $6\frac{1}{4}$ inches (16 cm) long and contain four to five coarse beans. By selection varieties with smaller beans have been obtained, such as Bianka, Eureka, Medes, Metissa and (even smaller) Optica.

Rowena and **Ité Beryl** are crosses of field beans and broad beans, with very fine beans, that look more like brown beans than broad beans.

Cowpea or **yardlong bean** *(Vigna unguiculata ssp. sesquipedalis)*
Very long ribbon-like greyish-green pods that can grow to over a yard (metre) long in a warm climate.
ORIGIN: West Africa.
PRODUCTION: Suriname, USA (California), south-east Asia.
SEASON: Most of the year.
USE: Cut the pods into short lengths and boil.
STORAGE: As snapbean. Pods from Thailand can be kept longer than those from Suriname.
NUTRITIONAL VALUE: 34 kcal, 4.2 g protein, 110 mg calcium, 4.7 mg iron, 2.4 mg vitamin A, 35 mg vitamin C per 100 g serving.

△ Cowpea, $24\frac{1}{2}$ in (620 mm) long

Liliaceae

A few years ago the lily family or *Liliaceae* was twice the size it is today. This is not the result of an environmental catastrophe, but botanists deciding to remove a number of plant genera from the family and place them elsewhere. That happened to the onion family, now promoted to a family of its own, the *Alliaceae* (see page 14).

Even so, there are still 2,000 *Liliaceae* species throughout the world. The family has not lost its economic importance, as it still includes a number of bulb species, like tulips, hyacinths and lilies. There are plenty of wild *Liliaceae* too. Some are fairly common, like the Solomon's seal *(Polygonatum odoratum)* and the lily of the valley *(Convallaria majalis)*. Others are rarer, like the fritillary *(Fritillaria meleagris)*, the stars of Bethlehem *(Ornithogalum sp.)*, and the gageas *(Gagea sp)*.

Practically all *Liliaceae* have an underground tuber, bulb or rootstock, including the family's single vegetable species, the asparagus. It is not the rootstock of the asparagus that is eaten, however, but the tender young stems that shoot up from the root and can be harvested three years after planting.

Normally the stem is green and in North America and many other countries green asparagus is on sale. White asparagus is produced by earthing up the asparagus beds in spring, so that the stems grow in the dark, or by forcing it in a dark cell, like witloof chicory. Green asparagus is less fibrous than white, has more flavour and considerably more vitamins, as long as the stems can grow rapidly. This is not possible in temperate climates, so the quality of green asparagus grown in northern regions leaves much to be desired.

The genus *Asparagus* includes about ten species. There are paintings of asparagus plants in Egyptian tombs 5,000 years old. The Greeks cultivated the species *Asparagus acutifolius,* with hard, shiny needles and sharp-tasting green stems. This species, now growing wild, used to be gathered in the countryside and fetched very good prices.

Around 1100 a new species of asparagus is mentioned, less sharp in flavour and available in the spring. This is probably our true asparagus, *Asparagus officinalis.* It originated on the salt steppes of eastern Europe and came from there via Asia Minor to the rest of Asia, the Mediterranean countries and later North America. The cultivated form developed from it *(var. altilis)* is also called upright asparagus, though there is a recumbent form *(var. prostratus)* with bluish-grey stems, bent at the foot.

As well as white and green asparagus, there are also violet-coloured varieties.

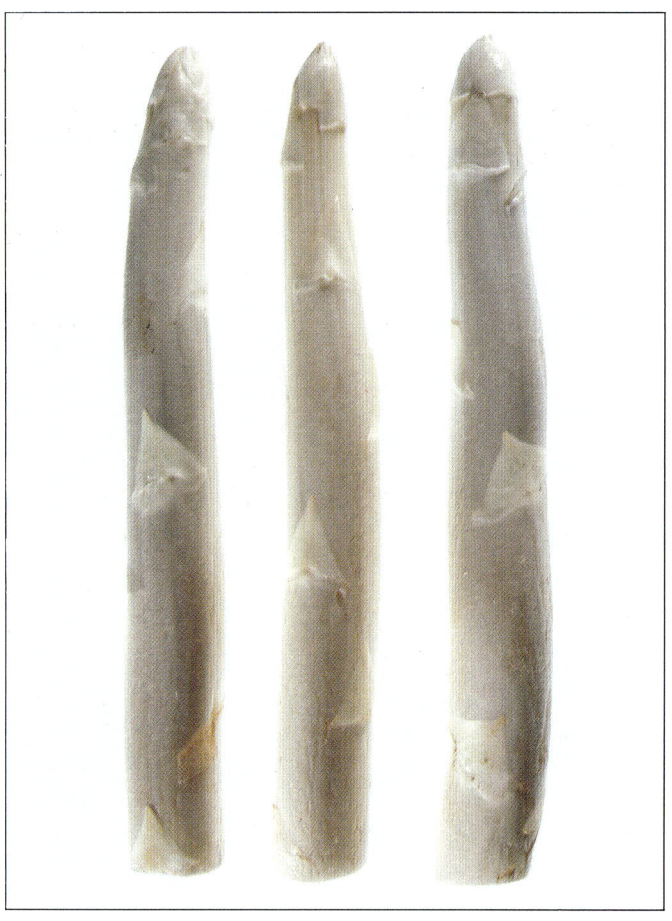

△ Asparagus 'Limbras 26', 8¾ in (220 mm) long

Asparagus
(Asparagus officinalis, var. altilis)
White, violet or green, straight stems of even length, non-fibrous, with a well-closed head. The stems, 4¾ to 8¾ inches (12 to 22 cm) long and ¼ to 1⅛ inches (8 to 28 mm) thick, are graded after harvesting by length and thickness.
ORIGIN: Eastern Europe.
PRODUCTION: France, Spain, Italy, Germany, Netherlands, Taiwan, South Africa, USA.
SEASON: April to the end of June.
USE: Peel stem thinly and boil. Use the less attractive stems and the left-over ends to make asparagus soup. Eat cooked asparagus with ham, clarified butter and hard-boiled eggs. Steamed asparagus can be used in salads if allowed to cool first.
STORAGE: About one week at 36 to 41°F (2 to 5°C) in the refrigerator. Sensitive to drying out.
NUTRITIONAL VALUE: White asparagus 21 kcal, 3 g carbohydrate, 2 g protein, 0.1 g fat, 20 mg calcium, 1 mg iron, 20 mg vitamin C, 0.6 mg vitamin PP per 100 g serving. Green asparagus contains twice as much vitamin C and a great deal of vitamin A.
INDUSTRIAL PROCESSING: Drying, canning or bottling. deep-freezing. Dried as an ingredient in soups.

△ White asparagus, $7\frac{7}{8}$ in (200 mm) long ▽ Green asparagus, $7\frac{7}{8}$ in (200 mm) long

△ Asparagus 'Roem van Brunswijk', $8\frac{7}{8}$ in (225 mm) long

Varieties

Backlim Quite a late hybrid, with very thick, white stems. Few hollow stems and loose heads.

Boonlim Mid-early hybrid with very thick, grooved, white stems.

Gijnlim Very early hybrid with fairly thick, white stems. No hollow stems or loose heads.

Lucullus Quite early hybrid with fairly thick stems.

Argenteuil Old, early French variety with rather heavy stems and heads that are pink to start with, but turn violet later.

Mary grand and **Mary green** Two green varieties, similar to the old American variety Mary Washington, which can produce both white and green stems.

Malvaceae

The mallow family *(Malvaceae)* owes its economic significance to just one plant genus, *Gossypium.* This includes all the 40 species of the cotton plant, which has been used for textiles for at least 2,500 years. This is said to have started in India, where many cotton plant species originate. Another group comes from the South Pacific, and there too people discovered the usefulness of cotton very early on. Apart from cotton, this family gives us some popular garden plants like the hollyhock and the hibiscus, a few medicinal herbs such as the large and small mallows *(Malva sylvestris* and *M. neglecta),* and three tropical fruit vegetables. Only two of these are ever exported.

The best known of these tropical vegetable species is the okra or lady's finger. It originates from north-east Africa or India, and slaves took it with them to America. it has now made itself at home in practically all tropical regions. Oblong and heavily grooved capsules develop in the leaf axils of the flowers (yellow with a red centre). These capsules are harvested for eating when very young. They are then as long as a finger, hence the name. When fully developed the pods, containing a great number of seeds, can be 4 to 10 inches (10 to 25 cm) long.

The roselle is much less well known. It is an annual plant, probably from Angola, and has two varieties. One, with upright green stems and small blunt capsules, is not really suitable for eating and is mainly used for fibre. The other is a dwarf, branching plant whose calyx and calycle become fleshy after flowering and divide up into red, pointed capsules, also called Florida cranberries. In earlier times sorrel syrup was prepared from these fruits. The young tops and leaves, both red, are also edible.

Okra or **lady's finger**
(Abelmoschus esculentus, syn. Hibiscus esculentus)
Green longitudinally-grooved many-seeded capsules. Fully-grown fruits are hard and fibrous. The unripe fruits contain a milky secretion and have a crisp taste.
ORIGIN: Tropical Africa.
PRODUCTION: Thailand, Kenya, Ethiopia, USA.
SEASON: Throughout the year.
USE: Raw and cooked, in salads, soups, and with other vegetables.
STORAGE: Three to ten days (depending on the producing country) at 44 to 50°F (7 to 10°C). Susceptible to low-temperature deterioration, so do not store in the refrigerator.
NUTRITIONAL VALUE: 33 kcal, 7.6 g carbohydrate, 2.4 g protein, 0.3 g fat, 70 mg calcium, 1 mg iron, 31 mg vitamin C, 0.32 mg vitamin A, 0.17 mg vitamin B1, 0.21 mg vitamin B2 per 100 g serving.
INDUSTRIAL PROCESSING: Canning.

△ Okra, 5½ in (140 mm) long

Roselle or **Jamaica sorrel** or **Guinea sorrel**
(Hibiscus sabdariffa)
A fibrous plant with red stems and pointed fleshy capsules. Capsules may be red and very acid.
ORIGIN: Angola.
PRODUCTION: Tropics of Africa, America and Asia.
SEASON: Irregular.
USE: Unripe red fruits for making sorrel syrup, sorrel beer and sorrel jam.
STORAGE: Limited.
NUTRITIONAL VALUE: 44 kcal, 1.9 g protein, 115 mg calcium, 1.5 mg iron, 7.6 mg vitamin A, 35 mg vitamin C per 100 g serving.

Moraceae

Botanists have argued for decades over the correct position of the hop in the plant kingdom. Some include it in the stinging nettle family *(Urticaceae)* and regard it as belonging with plant genera such as the mulberry, the fig tree and the hemp. Others are convinced that the hop, like the hemp, belongs to the *Cannabaceae* family and place the mulberry and the fig in the mulberry family *Moraceae*. Others again agree as far as the mulberry and fig are concerned, but include the hop and the hemp in the *Moraceae* too. For the time being, we go along with this last opinion, but it must be admitted the hop does not contain any white latex, as the other *Moraceae* do.

The hop is a perennial climber that can grow over 20 feet (6 m) high. It can be found growing wild in damp woods, and in coppices. It is dioecious: with the male and female flowers appearing on different plants. The significance of the hop lies in the female plant. After the flowering period this develops the hop cone, groups of light-green bracteoles shaped like a small fir-cone. At the base of the bracteoles there are small, yellow resin glands that contain the bitter lupilin, a substance composed of humulon and lupilon among other things. These glands are detached from the hop cones by shaking and screening. As hop flour they are used for brewing beer and preparing medicines.

Until the beginning of this century the cones of the wild hop were collected mainly for the local breweries. The medicinal value of hop flour, now used in the preparation of a mild opiate, became known after observing the drowsiness of the hop-pickers after a few days' work. At present the demand for hop flour, from breweries and the pharmaceutical industry, is met by cultivating particular cultivars of the female plant, particularly in England, France, Belgium and Bavaria. Hop cultivation in Bavaria is very old: there is a ninth-century report of a hop garden in the monastery of Fresingen.

In winter the hop plant dies down to near ground level. The root stem produces young shoots in the spring, which can be eaten. In the eighteenth and nineteenth centuries these hop shoots were quite a popular vegetable. After a period of neglect, they now seem to have come into fashion again.

Hops
(Humulus lupulus)
Thin white shoots that spring up from the underground roots of the hop plant in spring. Generally sold loose or in bunches.
ORIGIN: Temperate regions of Europe, Asia and America.
PRODUCTION: Belgium, West Germany, France, Britain.
SEASON: From December to the beginning of April in climate-controlled cells, from the end of March in open ground. The shoots of the open-ground harvest rapidly become too long and green.
USE: Eat raw in mixed salads or boil.
STORAGE: Very limited.

△ Hop root with shoots, longest shoot 4¼ in (110 mm)

Musaceae

In the jungles of Madagascar a giant plant, called the traveller's tree grows to as much as 100 feet (30 m) tall. It's scientific name is *Ravenala madagascariensis* and it belongs to the *Musaceae* or banana family. It is not a true tree, because all members of this family lack one of the most important characteristics of a tree — the trunk. What serves as a trunk among the banana family is in fact a stem, formed by the broad leaf stalks that lie on top of each other. The plant owes its common name to the tradition that the enormous leaves always lie in a north/south direction, and can therefore guide lost travellers. The leaves are not really arranged so helpfully, as anyone can tell from seeing two or more trees growing close together. The wandering traveller could indeed use the plant, but not as a compass. In the space between the leaf walls about a third of a gallon (1.5 litres) of moisture quickly collects, and can be easily reached by making a hole in the stem, so providing the thirsty traveller with excellent drinking water.

A better-known member of the family is the bird of paradise flower *(Strelitzia reginae)*, grown for cutting in South Africa and the Canary Islands. Of the four known *Strelitzia* species the bird of paradise flower is certainly the most striking. It has an attractive, boat-shaped protective leaf lying horizontally on the flower stem, and from this two vivid orange sepals and two purplish-blue crown leaves grow.

The *Musaceae* species that gives the family its economic significance is the banana. Bananas are divided into dessert and cooking types. The fruits are produced by female flowers that develop on the underside of a thick, often downward-curved, flower stem. At the tip of this stem the male flowers also grow. They lie closed up in a strong spadix, often more than 20 inches (50 cm) long, surrounded by a few red or purplish-red leaves.

This remarkable banana flower is widely eaten in Asia as a vegetable, especially in Indonesia. In recent years it has also been exported and can sometimes be found in shops that specialize in tropical products. One of these Indonesian dishes is called *getjok*, where the spadix is first boiled or roasted in hot ashes and eaten with or without a hot spicy sauce of coconut milk, onions, salt, cayenne and spices.

△ Banana flower (male), $10\frac{1}{2}$ in (265 mm) long

Banana flower
(Musa sp.)
A spadix, shaped like a maize ear, up to 2 feet (60 cm) long, with a reddish-brown to purplish-red protective leaf. The spadix contains the stamens and a quantity of yellowish-white flesh.

ORIGIN: South-east Asia.
PRODUCTION: South-east Asia, Africa, Central and South America.
SEASON: Generally at the end of summer.
USE: Boil or roast, grated or chopped if necessary.
STORAGE: About two weeks.

Plantaginaceae

There are some differences of opinion about the small plantain family *(Plantaginaceae)*, which includes fewer than 250 species world-wide. The plantain genus *(Plantago)* is particularly controversial. Farmers and gardeners curse the plantain as a common weed, but herbalists and gourmets sing the praises of the medicinal qualities, the flavour and vitamin content of various plantain species.

Both of them are partly right. The plantain can be a pernicious weed, especially the greater plantain *(Plantago major)*, spread by the Europeans over a large part of the world, and picturesquely called 'the footprint of the palefaces' by the North American Indians. This very same greater plantain, however, has a valuable medicinal effect. The vitamin C content is high, giving protection against all kinds of infectious diseases, and plantain tea or juice helps against such different complaints as tuberculosis, bronchitis, asthma, constipation, stomach ailments and open wounds.

The plantain is also valued as a vegetable, particularly the buckshorn plantain, that grows wild in central and southern Europe, north Africa and the eastern Mediterranean, and is now also cultivated elsewhere. It is much liked as a leaf vegetable in Italy, and can be found there under the names *minutina* or *erba stella*.

The tropical fruit (sometimes classed as a vegetable) known as the plantain is a member of the banana family and has no connections with the *Plantaginaceae*.

Buckshorn plantain
(Plantago coronopus)
A fine leaf vegetable, when young, with tender, oblong, grass-like leaves. Later the leaf becomes sharply indented and is tough and fibrous.
ORIGIN: Coastal region of central and southern Europe.
PRODUCTION: Mainly Italy.
SEASON: From May to October.
USE: Boiled or raw in mixed salads.
STORAGE: In the refrigerator, one to two days at most. Leaf soon becomes limp.

△ Buckshorn plantain, $15\frac{3}{8}$ in (390 mm) long

Polygonaceae

Buckwheat used to be an important food plant but is now mainly grown for the pharmaceutical industry

The knotweed family *(Polygonaceae)* gets its name from the stems of many of its members, which are often clearly jointed, with conspicuous thickened knots. Another frequent characteristic is a membranous petiole on the joints on the stem where a leaf is attached. The group is not very large: a mere 900 species, spread throughout the world and found particularly in places with poor soil.

One member of this family that thrives on poor soil is the old cultivated species of buckwheat *(Fagopyrum)*. This plant played an important role in Europe's food supply for centuries. The seeds resemble those of the beech tree (called *boc* in Old English and can be ground into flour just like wheat. Our ancestors cooked them in many different ways: there was buckwheat porridge as well as pancakes made from buckwheat flour. The flowers of the plant contain an aromatic nectar, and were therefore very popular with beekeepers. Cultivation of buckwheat has fallen drastically in this century, because it is unsuitable for modern mechanized farming methods.

By contrast, the cultivation of rhubarb has increased. This started in Europe at the beginning of the seventeenth century, but has been of any importance only in the last 50 years or so. The rhubarb originally grew in the southern Siberian Volga region, and was probably grown some 5,000 years BC in China, Mongolia and Tibet. At that time the dried roots were used as an effective laxative. Anthraquinone, a bitter substance, is probably responsible. It is still used in some medicines and in the manufacture of some liqueurs.

Later, when some species came to Europe via the Red Sea and Italy, they were called *rha barbarum* — the rha of the barbarians, as *rha* was the Greek name for the plant. The leaf stems were then eaten for the first time. Their pleasantly acid taste derives from malic, oxalic and citric acids. Malic acid has a blood-cleaning effect, but oxalic acid is not so good for the health, and is often neutralized during cooking by the addition of a little powdered chalk.

Another plant in the knotweed family that has found its way to our kitchens is the dock. 150 species of this genus are known, and some ten or so are indigenous in northern latitudes, such as the curled dock *(Rumex crispus)* and the common sorrel *(R. acetosa)*. The sorrel, often growing among grasses, can colour whole meadows red in the summer months with the hundreds of fruitlets on each plant, surrounded by the coloured parts of the flower.

The wild species of sorrel are difficult to tell apart, and they are easily crossed, so there is a confusing number of varieties. Although most of them can be used in the kitchen for making soups and as a flavouring in sauces, salads and boiled vegetables, the cultivated form is the one to be found in the shops, with sturdier leaves than most of its wild relatives.

A third knotweed species that can be used as a vegetable is the patience dock, a plant from south-eastern Europe, sometimes eaten in Britain as a boiled vegetable. The leaf contains a great deal of iron and has rather a strong flavour.

The genus *Polygonum*, represented in northern latitudes by some 14 species including the bistort *(P. bistorta)* and the amphibious bistort *(P. amphibium)*, supplies a few edible types of vegetable in the Far East, in Japan and on Java, but these are hardly ever exported.

△ Rhubarb. From left to right, 'Sutton's seedless', $24\frac{3}{4}$ in (630 mm), 'Versteeg', $24\frac{3}{4}$ in (630 mm), Holsteiner bloed', $18\frac{1}{2}$ in (470 mm)

Rhubarb
(Rheum rhabarbarum)
Long, juicy leaf stems, concave in cross-section, green or red depending on the variety and the method of cultivation. The thickness of the stem and the acid content change with age and variety. As they get older they become more acid and more fibrous. Early rhubarb, forced in the dark, has light-red stems that cook easily and are less acid than rhubarb grown in the open.

ORIGIN: Siberia.

PRODUCTION: Britain, West Germany, Netherlands, North America.

SEASON: Forced rhubarb December to March, open ground from the end of March to September.

USE: Cut the leaf stems into pieces to make stewed fruit, jam or compote. Adding a little chalk neutralizes the oxalic acid.

STORAGE: Two to three weeks at 32 to 34°F (0 to 1°C) in high humidity. Wrapping in polythene helps to prevent drying out.

NUTRITIONAL VALUE: 11 kcal, 2 g carbohydrate, 0.5 g protein, 0.1 g fat, 40 mg calcium, 0.5 mg iron, 10 mg vitamin C per 100 g serving.

INDUSTRIAL PROCESSING: Bottling (stewed), deep-freezing.

Varieties

Goliath A late variety with thick stems shaped rather like spouts. If forced, light red with a white foot. If grown in the open, green and sharply acid.

Frambozen rood or **Champagne rood** Mid-early variety with red outsides to the stems and a red foot. Forced stems are red inside too, but those grown in the open are green inside.

Timperley early Very early, English variety with thin, curved stems, light red if forced and green if grown in the open.

Sutton's seedless A rather late British variety with thick straight stems and a pink foot. Red inside and outside.

Versteeg Late variety with long, thick, green stems and a white foot. Mainly used by processing industry.

Holsteiner bloed Old, mid-early variety from Germany with curved, blood-red stems. Has a very high oxalic acid content.

△ Sorrell 'Breedbladige nobel', 5⅛ in (130 mm) long

Sorrel

(Rumex acetosa,. var. hortensis)
Broad, oblong, green leaves with a rather acid taste.
ORIGIN: Europe.
PRODUCTION: France, Belgium, Netherlands.
SEASON: April to November.
USE: Leaves can be used for soup, sauces and salads, and for flavouring boiled vegetables such as spinach, orache, seakale and spinach beet.
STORAGE: One to two days in the refrigerator: the leaf wilts rapidly.
NUTRITIONAL VALUE: 22 kcal, 3.5 g carbohydrate, 2 g protein, 0.4 g fat, 54 mg calcium, 8.4 g iron, 3.5 mg vitamin A, 47 mg vitamin C per 100 g serving.

Varieties

Breedbladige nobel
Winter-hardy with a green leaf.

Reuzen van Belleville
Broad-leaved variety, with light-green leaves.

Lyonse grootbladige gele
Broad-leaved variety with round, light-green leaves.

Patience dock

(Rumex patientia)
Fairly narrow, oblong, green leaves, rather tough, with a bitter taste. Not to be eaten raw.
ORIGIN: South-east Europe.
PRODUCTION: Britain.
SEASON: Throughout the year, if the winter is mild.
USE: Boiled, with other leaf vegetables.
STORAGE: A few days in the refrigerator.
NUTRITIONAL VALUE: Similar to sorrel.

Portulaceae

At the time of the Pharaohs the Egyptians ate a vegetable that was almost certainly the same as the present-day summer purslane, though we know little about the origins of this member of the purslane family *(Portulaceae)*. The present-day locations of the wild species lead us to suspect that it used to grow across an area stretching from Greece via southern Russia as far as the western foothills of the Himalayas. It is a fast-growing annual plant and needs a moist, warm climate. In northern regions it is cultivated mainly under glass, and bears rather acid-flavoured leaflets on thick, fleshy stems. Winter purslane belongs to the same family as summer purslane, but is in another genus. This plant originated in North America, but now grows wild in western Europe. On its thin stems it forms green leaflets, diamond or saucer shaped, rich in vitamins. When grown as a vegetable, winter purslane is sown quite thickly in late summer and harvested in winter when still quite young.

Waterleaf or Suriname spinach belongs to yet another genus. This plant, originating in Central and South America, and perhaps in Africa too, is rather slimy and contains a great deal of oxalic acid. At the beginning of the twentieth century seed from this Suriname purslane was taken to Java, where it quickly became more popular in colonial European kitchens than the summer purslane.

All three species of purslane are of only marginal interest to the vegetable trade. At one time winter purslane practically disappeared as a cultivated species, but recently there has been a renewed demand from consumers and amateur gardeners.

The purslane (Portulaca grandiflora) *is a free-flowering ground-cover plant belonging to the Portulaceae family*

△ Winter purslane, leaf ¾ in (20 mm) across

Winter purslane
(Montia perfoliata, syn. Claytonia perfoliata)
Thin green stems with green diamond-shaped or saucer-shaped leaves.
ORIGIN: North America.
PRODUCTION: Britain, France, West Germany, Belgium, Netherlands.
SEASON: November to April. Sometimes in spring and autumn from plants grown outside.
USE: Raw in salads or very lightly boiled like spinach.
STORAGE: One to two days in the refrigerator.
NUTRITIONAL VALUE: 10 kcal, 1 g carbohydrate, 1 g protein, 0.2 g fat, 130 mg calcium, 3 mg iron, 1.7 mg vitamin A, 20 mg vitamin C per 100 g serving.

Purslane
(Portulaca oleracea, ssp.)
Rapid-growing leaf vegetable with fleshy, reddish stems and green or yellowish leaves. The stems must be firm and have a diameter of about $\frac{1}{12}$ inch (2 mm).
ORIGIN: From Greece to the western Himalayas.
PRODUCTION: Netherlands, Britain, France, Belgium, West Germany.
SEASON: March to October.
USE: Raw in salads or with mashed potatoes. Very lightly boiled or in a casserole.
STORAGE: Three to five days at 32 to 34°F (0 to 1°C) in high humidity.
NUTRITIONAL VALUE: 10 kcal, 1 g carbohydrate, 1 g protein, 0.2 g fat, 130 mg calcium, 3 mg iron, 20 mg vitamin C, 1.7 mg vitamin A per 100 g serving. Oxalic acid content 0.9 per cent.

Varieties

Gewone groene Most widely cultivated variety, with narrow, dull green leaves.

Gele Shiny, yellowish-green leaves, more tender than Gewone groene. There is also a Gele breedbladige, with larger leaves.

△ Purslane 'Gewone groene', leaf $1\frac{1}{4}$ in (30 mm) across

Waterleaf
(Talinum triangulare)
Long, spatula-shaped leaves with hardly any stem. Leaf rather slimy when cooked, with a lot of oxalic acid.
ORIGIN: Central and South America or Africa.
PRODUCTION: West Africa, Brazil.
SEASON: June to October under glass.
USE: Boiled.
STORAGE: As purslane.
NUTRITIONAL VALUE: 23 kcal, 1.9 g protein, 90 mg calcium, 4.8 g iron, 3 g vitamin A, 60 mg vitamin C per 100 g serving.

△ Purslane 'Gele', leaf 1 in (25 mm) long

Solanaceae

The tobacco plant *(Nicotiana sp.)* is an excellent example of the controversy surrounding its family as a whole, the nightshade family or *Solanaceae*.

Jean Nicot de Villemain, French ambassador to Portugal in the mid-sixteenth century, sent a few leaves of this newly-arrived American plant back to France. Use of the treated leaves quickly became all the rage — first as snuff, then for smoking. Sniffing or sucking tobacco became a popular craze, but not everyone was pleased. The Puritans were quick to criticize the sinful self-indulgence of the tobacco craze, and forbade or taxed the cultivation of the plant as far as they could. Anti-smoking crusaders now continually stress the proven carcinogenic properties of tobacco, and the authorities tax tobacco highly and restrict its public use.

A curse or a blessing? We may ask this question about many members of the nightshade family. A blessing, certainly, when we think of all the different vegetable plants from the family, the tomato, paprika, peppers, aubergine and, most important, the potato. Also a blessing are the various curative substances than can be extracted from nightshade species, such as atropine and hyoscine. These very same substances are simultaneously the curse of the family, because they are so poisonous. The valuable tubers of the potato are harmless but all other parts of the plant contain poisonous substances which may not always be fatal but are certainly very harmful. Even unripe tomatoes contain the poison solanine, though in very small quantities.

Other nightshade species are fatally poisonous if their fruits or leaves are eaten. This is true of plants like the deadly nightshade *(Atropa belladonna)*, the henbane *(Hyoscyamus niger)* and the thornapple *(Datura stramonium)*. Even in the Middle Ages people were aware that many of these plants could have a hallucinogenic effect. Their juices were an important ingredient in the 'witch's ointment'. Anyone who rubbed this thoroughly into their skin experienced such vivid visions that they were quite certain, after the 'trip', that they had flown through the air, taken part in a witches' sabbath, and had a delightfully sinful time. If the experiment is tried today, the visions turn out rather differently, but we may attribute this to our different world-view rather than to any changes in the toxin's molecular structure.

Due to its toxicity, hallucinogenic effect, and the activities of quacks, poisoners and black magicians, a number of colourful and mysterious superstitions grew up about the nightshade family. Maybe these have not died out completely, and even now, on moonless nights, someone still goes out to dig for the mandrake root. This forked root of the *Mandragora*, after a little trimming and decoration, does really look like a small human figure, and has long been regarded as a powerful talisman.

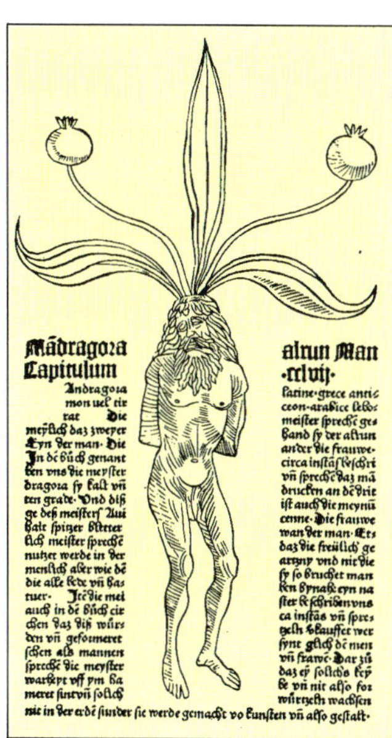

If you use a little imagination you can see the shape of a human body in the mandrake root (left). In the Middle Ages it was thought to have magical powers, particularly after it had been trimmed a little (right)

Edible nightshade species

Some of the edible nightshade species are classified as fruit and some as vegetables, of which we are only dealing with the vegetables.

The **paprika** and various **peppers** belong to the genus *Capsicum*, from tropical America, and became known in Europe only after the voyages of Columbus and his contemporaries. The plants bear a few juicy berry fruits, of many different colours, shapes and flavours, used mainly for seasoning.

Consumers have shown a preference for thick, rather chunky, oblong, green peppers, turning red as they ripen. There are other varieties with yellow, white, brown or purple fruits. Some are slightly pointed and sweeter than the green/red variety. All peppers are hollow berries with a fleshy pericarp.

The Spanish pepper is a sharp species, green or red, and mostly long, slender, slightly curved and pointed. Cayenne pepper is a variety with shorter, straighter fruits than the Spanish peppers, but there are also fruits shaped like a strawberry that have come to be know as cayenne pepper. The difference between sweet and sharp peppers depends on the capsaicin content, which is very high in the tabasco peppers, the small, shiny, blood-red, orange or yellowish-white fruitlets of a tropical plant. They are used in the preparation of sharp pickles and are sold dried, too.

The **tomato** also comes from the New World and the name is derived from the Aztec word *tomatl*. For over a hundred years Europeans thought it safer to treat this foreign Indian plant as purely ornamental. Only in the mid-eighteenth century do we find reports of tomatoes being used in soups, and later, at the beginning of the nineteenth century, the first tomatoes were grown in Sicily for the markets of Naples and Rome. Serious cultivation in northern Europe goes back only to the beginning of this century.

There are about 6.2 million acres (2.5 million hectares) throughout the world planted with tomatoes, of which 1.85 million acres (750,000 hectares) are in Asia, 1.23 million (500,000) in Europe (some under glass or plastic), 950,000 acres (385,000 hectares) in Africa, 740,000 (300,000) in North and Central America, and only 320,000 acres (130,000 hectares) in the region of origin, South America.

The tomato is a juicy berry with two or more segments, not only red, but also pink, yellow or white when ripe. As well as round varieties, there are also flattish-round, ribbed, pear-shaped and bottle-shaped tomatoes, and varieties with very small red or yellow fruits, the so-called cherry tomatoes, that still grow wild in Mexico. Some botanists assume that this cultivar developed from the red currant tomato (*Lycopersicon pimpinellifolium),* and that ultimately the large-fruited red tomatoes (*L. lycopersicum)* developed from it. The marmande tomatoes also belong to this group.

The deadly nightshade, a member of the Solanaceae family, really is deadly if eaten. The juice of the berry was sometimes used as eye-drops to expand the pupils and make the eye look larger

The most important vegetable plant of the genus *Solanum* is the **potato**, growing wild in the north of South America, and Mexico. The potato was also unknown to the rest of the world before the voyages of discovery, and its reception in Europe was rather similar to that of the tomato — it took a long time for people to trust it. There was a good reason for their caution: many small farmers suffered from eating the poisonous berries and leaves of the new plant instead of the tubers. By the eighteenth century people had got used to the potato, and it had become an important popular food. The tubers develop underground on stems, and the plant's reserve of food is stored in them in the form of starch. Normally a new plant develops out of the 'eyes' of these tubers. The total area laid down to potato cultivation worldwide is now around 50 million acres (20 million hectares). In recent years the potato has become an important raw material for products like crisps and pre-baked chips.

The **sweet potato** or **batata** is not a member of the *Solanaceae* and is one of the misnomers of the vegetable world. In fact it has usurped the name **batata,** by which the potato was known when first imported to Europe in the fifteenth century.

The **aubergine** is a relation of the potato, a member of the same genus from tropical Asia. The earliest information dates from the fifth century BC, from China. The plant presumably spread to Europe via Africa: there is no mention of it in Greek or Roman sources, so it was probably brought to Europe after the Roman period by the Arabs, although it is just possible that the Portuguese brought it directly from Asia.

As with peppers and the tomato, there are many different colours and shapes of aubergine. The oblong or pear-shaped, purple fruit is probably best known, but people are also familiar with the white, egg-shaped variety, hence the name 'eggplant'.

The so-called African aubergine is a related species. It comes from east Africa and is spherical. When ripe it is orange-yellow or brownish-yellow, with a crackled surface, although it is often sold unripe and greenish-white when exported.

Paprika or **sweet pepper**
(Capsicum annuum)
Hollow fruit berry with a thick pericarp and a leathery skin. There are several different shapes, rectangular and chunky, or tapering to a point, and many different colours, green (turning red when ripe), yellow, white, brown and purple. The flavour ranges from spicy-sweet to very sharp, depending on the capsaicin content. The riper the fruit, the higher the content of vitamins and minerals.
ORIGIN: Tropical America.
PRODUCTION: Italy, Greece, France, Yugoslavia, Spain, Romania, Bulgaria, Netherlands, and many Asian and African countries.
SEASON: Throughout the year.
USE: Raw, boiled or baked. Green peppers are good for stuffing with meat or fish, the red ones are mainly for salads.
STORAGE: Two weeks at 44 to 46°F (7 to 8°C) in high humidity. Sensitive to low temperature deterioration.
NUTRITIONAL VALUE: Very varied. The riper the fruit, the more nourishing. Red paprika 28 kcal, 6 g carbohydrate, 1 g protein, 15 mg calcium, 0.5 mg iron, 150 mg vitamin C per 100 g serving. Green paprika 16 kcal, 3 g carbohydrate, 1 g protein, 15 mg calcium, 0.5 mg iron, 70 mg vitamin C per 100 g serving.
INDUSTRIAL PROCESSING: In pickles or dried and ground into powder.

△ Pepper, red chequered type, $4\frac{1}{2}$ in (115 mm) long

△ Pepper, green chequered type, $4\frac{1}{2}$ in (115 mm) long ▽ Pepper, yellow chequered type, $4\frac{1}{2}$ in (115 mm) long

△ Pepper, purple chequered type, $2\frac{1}{2}$ in (65 mm) long ▽ Pepper, light yellow chequered pointed (Hungarian) type, $6\frac{1}{2}$ in, (165 mm) long

Varieties

Propa A cross with chunky, but slightly pointed fruits. Green, ripening to red.

Zoete westlandse Quite large, chunky fruits, dark green ripening to light red.

Golden boy Chunky fruits with a thick wall, green ripening to yellow. **Goldstar** is practically identical. Both have a sweet taste.

Tomato paprika
Flattish-round, ribbed fruits, very similar shape to marmande tomatoes. Ripen from green to dark red, with a high vitamin content.

Midal Sweet, white paprika from the Hungarian pointed type. Fruits are 4 to 6 inches (10 to 15 cm) long and $1\frac{1}{2}$ to $2\frac{3}{8}$ inches (4 to 6 cm) wide at the top, tapering to a point. Unripe fruits are creamy coloured to very light yellow, ripening to orange-red.

Violetta Occasionally on sale. Purple fruit, chunky, short, triangular or square.

Pusztagold Chunky yellow fruits, ripening to red. A comparable variety is the American **golden bell.**

Capsicum
(Capsicum annuum)
Long, slender and pointed, rather curved fruits, green changing to red, sharp taste due to capsaicin. This alkaloid is most highly concentrated around the seeds, and the pericarp is not so strongly flavoured.
ORIGIN: As paprika.
PRODUCTION: Asia, Africa, east and southern Europe.
SEASON: Throughout the year.
USE: Use with or without seeds for seasoning.
STORAGE: As paprika.
NUTRITIONAL VALUE: As paprika.
INDUSTRIAL PROCESSING: As paprika.

Varieties

Westlandse lange rode Oblong, conical, pointed fruits, about $4\frac{3}{4}$ inches (12 cm) long. Green, ripening to a shiny light to dark red.

Vurino Hybrid variety with long, conical, pointed fruits, about $4\frac{3}{4}$ to $5\frac{1}{2}$ inches (12 to 14 cm) in length, ripening from green to light or dark red. Quite sharp, but not so strong as the preceding variety.

Cayenne Shorter fruits than the other varieties, and less curved. Taste is very strong.

Madame Jeanette or **Madam Janet** Yellow, rather chunky peppers, pointed with a dent on the side.

△ Westlandse pepper (unripe), $7\frac{3}{4}$ in (195 mm) long ▽ Chilli, average 5 in (128 mm) long

△ Westlandse pepper (ripe, $7\frac{3}{4}$ in (195 mm) long

▽ Chilli, about $1\frac{1}{2}$ in (40 mm) long

△ Westlandse pepper, yellow (ripe), $5\frac{1}{4}$ in (133 mm) long

Chilli

(Capsicum frutescens)

Small, very sharp fruitlets, $\frac{1}{4}$ to 1 inch (7 to 25 mm) long, shiny blood-red, orange or yellowish-white. Also available dried.

ORIGIN: Tropical America.

PRODUCTION: South and eastern Europe.

SEASON: Throughout the year.

USE: Seasoning.

STORAGE: As paprika. When dried, for a very long time.

NUTRITIONAL VALUE: 291 kcal, 15 g protein, 11 g fat, 33 g carbohydrate, 150 mg calcium, 9 mg rion, 1 mg vitamin A (red higher), 10 mg vitamin C per 100 g serving.

INDUSTRIAL PROCESSING: In pickles, drying, grinding into powder.

Tomato
(Lycopersicon lycopersicum syn. L. esculentum)
Juicy fruit that can be round, pear-shaped, angular or ribbed. Has two or more segments. In most round tomatoes the seeds are embedded in a jelly-like substance. Large round fruits are generally more fleshy. The most fleshy is the larger, ribbed, Marmande tomato. The intensity of the red colouring depends on the temperature during ripening. May also be yellow, pink or white.
ORIGIN: Peru, Chile and Ecuador.
PRODUCTION: China, Turkey, Italy, Romania, Spain, Greece, Yugoslavia, Poland, Bulgaria, Netherlands.
SEASON: Throughout the year, including production under glass.
USE: Raw in sandwiches or in salads, boiled or baked. Also in soups, and as purée or ketchup.
STORAGE: About two weeks at 55°F (13°C) in fairly high humidity. At lower temperatures deteriorates. Unripe fruits do not reach their full colour below 55°F (13°C).
NUTRITIONAL VALUE: 18 kcal, 3 g carbohydrate, 1 g protein, 0.2 g fat, 10 mg calcium, 0.4 mg iron, 0.6 mg vitamin A, 25 mg vitamin C per 100 g serving.
INDUSTRIAL PROCESSING: Bottling or canning, making into juice, purée and ketchup.

△ Round, red tomato, $2\frac{1}{2}$ in (62 mm) across ▽ Red marmande tomato, $3\frac{1}{2}$ in (90 mm) across

▽ Yellow marmande tomato 'Oranjezon', $3\frac{1}{2}$ in (90 mm) across

△ Tomato 'Tussentype', 4 in (100 mm) across ▽ Tomato 'Romatype', 3 in (75 mm) long

▽ Round, yellow tomato 'Gouden koningin', $2\frac{1}{4}$ in (56 mm) across

Varieties

The varieties are divided into a number of types. For growing under glass mainly hybrid types of round tomatoes are used, evenly greyish-green in the unripe state, and red when ripe. Many varieties are used for Marmande tomatoes, green or greenish while unripe.

Ronde rode tomaat Most widely grown under glass. Very attractive in shape and colour, two to three segments, slightly acid flavour.

Tussentype Large, round, red tomato, with three to five segments, rather fleshy with a good taste.

Marmande tomato Large, ribbed, red fruits with several segments and firm flesh, and rather sweet.

Romatype Oval to pear-shaped, red fruits with a sweet flavour. Used for purée, canning and bottling.

Cherry tomato Small, round, red or yellow fruits, with a very good flavour, mainly sold loose, but sometimes in bundles. If so, not all will be ripe.

Gouden koningin Round, yellow tomato with a thick skin and a sweet taste.

Oranjezon Yellow marmande type, slightly ribbed.

African aubergine
(Solanum macrocarpum)
Juicy, flattish, spherical fruits, greenish-white ripening to shiny orange-yellow or brownish-yellow, mostly with a crackled surface. The fruit has a thick skin and a green core. Usually unripe fruits on sale, with a rather bitter flavour.
ORIGIN: East Africa (Madagascar).
PRODUCTION: Tropical Africa and Asia.
SEASON: Most of the year.
USE: Remove stem and sepals, cut fruit into slices or chunks. Rub with lemon juice to prevent turning brown. Use in casseroles. Cooking time about 25 minutes. Can also be eaten raw.
STORAGE: For a long time.
NUTRITIONAL VALUE: 42 kcal, 4.8 g protein, 525 mg calcium, 6 mg iron, 6.4 mg vitamin A per 100 g serving.

Aubergine or **eggplant**
(Solanum melongena)
Oblong, pear- or egg-shaped, fleshy berry fruits, 4 to 12 inches (10 to 30 cm) long and generally deep purple. The egg-shaped varieties usually have white fruits.
ORIGIN: Tropical Asia, India, China.
PRODUCTION: China, Turkey, Indonesia, Japan, Italy, Netherlands.
SEASON: Throughout the year.
USE: Stuff the halved ripe fruits, preferably unpeeled (the skin is rich in vitamins), or dice and mix with other vegetables. Alternatively, slice and then boil or bake. Ripe fruits are a dull, dark purple, the flesh should be rather springy. Light-coloured, soft fruits are over ripe, and a brown calyx is a sign that the fruit is too old.
STORAGE: Seven to ten days at 46 to 50°F (8 to 10°C) in high humidity. Deteriorates if kept cooler.
NUTRITIONAL VALUE: 14 kcal, 3 g carbohydrate, 0.5 g protein, 10 mg calcium, 0.4 mg iron, 0.6 mg vitamin PP, 10 mg vitamin C per 100 g serving.

△ African eggplant, 2⅜ in (61 mm) long ▽ Purple aubergine, short type, 6⅞ in (175 mm) long

Varieties

Adona Long, pear-shaped fruit, shiny and deep purple with green calyx margins.

Dobrix Similar but shorter and lighter coloured.

Potato
(Solanum tuberosum)
Tubers rich in starch, usually round or oval with 'eyes'. Size varies considerably. Colour of skin from light yellow to purplish red. There are yellow-fleshed and white-fleshed varieties.
ORIGIN: Peru, north-west Argentina, Mexico.
PRODUCTION: Soviet Union, China, Poland, West Germany, France, Britain, Netherlands, Italy.
SEASON: Throughout the year.
USE: Peel and then boil, bake, mash, fry as chips, or scrub and bake unpeeled in their skins.
STORAGE: Very long at 39 to 41°F (4 to 5°C) in high humidity. At lower temperatures tubers can become sweet.
NUTRITIONAL VALUE: 85 kcal, 19 g carbohydrate, 2 g protein, 0.1 g fat, 10 mg calcium, 0.5 mg iron, 15 mg vitamin C per 100 g serving.
INDUSTRIAL PROCESSING: On a large scale as chips, crisps, mashed and dried.

△ Potato 'Eigenheimer', 3¼ in (83 mm) long ▽ Potato 'Eersteling' (left) and 'Doré', 3¼ in (85 mm) and 3 in (75 mm) long respectively

Varieties

Each potato-growing country has its own regional varieties. Here they are divided into three groups: early, mid-early and mid-late/late.

Early varieties

Eersteling
Very early with long, oval tubers, a yellow skin and shallow eyes. Firm when boiled, not floury. Has a good taste and smell.

Doré Very early with round-oval tubers, dark yellow skin and flaky, shallow eyes. When boiled the early potatoes are crumbly, those from the later crop become mushy. Good taste and colour.

Première Early variety with long, oval tubers, yellow skin and shallow eyes. Good for making chips.

Gloria Very early with long oval tubers, yellow skin, shallow eyes. Stays firm when boiled and keeps its colour well.

△ Potato 'Lekkerlander', 2¾ in (72 mm) long

△ Potato 'Bintje', 4½ in (115 mm) long

▽ Potato 'Desirée', 4¾ in (120 mm) long

Barima Very early, round tubers, light yellow flesh, rather deep eyes. Flavour not as good as Eersteling.

Alcmaria Early with large, long oval tubers, shallow eyes and light yellow flesh. When boiled quite firm with a clean taste.

Lekkerlander Early with rather flattened round tubers, dark yellow skin and shallow eyes. When boiled keeps its colour but is rather floury.

Mid-early varieties

Bintje Mid-early with long, oval tubers, light yellow skin and shallow eyes. Not very floury with a good flavour. Good for chips and crisps.

Eigenheimer Mid-early with oval tubers, yellow skin and quite deep eyes. When boiled it is quite floury, keeps its colour and has a good flavour. In some years it boils away easily.

Parel Early to mid-early with round to oval tubers, a yellow skin and deepish eyes. Floury, but keeps its colour and has a good flavour.

Meerlander Mid-early with round to oval tubers, a yellow skin and shallow eyes. Quite light when boiled, tastes excellent.

Provita Mid-early with oval, sometimes flattish tubers, a light yellow skin and shallow eyes. Keeps its colour but is floury.

Rosonant Mid-early with round to oval tubers, yellow skin and shallow eyes. Floury, keeps it colour, very good flavour.

Désirée Moderately large, red-skinned variety with long, oval tubers and light yellow flesh. Remains firm when boiled, with a neutral flavour.

Mid-late and late varieties

Irene Fairly late with round tubers, red skin and deep eyes. When boiled keeps its colour but often disintegrates.

Eba Fairly late to late, with oval to pear-shaped tubers, yellow skin and shallow eyes. Quite firm when boiled, keeping its colour. Good flavour.

Surprise Mid-late with round to oval tubers, yellow skin and shallow eyes. Floury when boiled with a definite colour.

Woudster Quite late with round to oval tubers, yellow skin and shallow eyes. Keeps its colour well when cooked, but is floury and sometimes disintegrates.

Pimpernel Late to very late with round to oval tubers, dark red skin and shallow eyes. Greyish when boiled, but generally tastes and smells good.

Saturna Mid-late with round to oval tubers, yellow skin and quite deep eyes. Suitable for making crisps.

Alpha Late variety with large, round to oval tubers, rather flat eyes and light yellow flesh. Definite colour but rather floury.

△ Potato 'Alpha', $4\frac{3}{4}$ in (120 mm) long

△ Potato 'Alcmaria', $5\frac{1}{4}$ in (135 mm) long

△ Potato 'Irene', 3 in (75 mm) long

△ Potato 'Barima', $3\frac{3}{4}$ in (95 mm) long

Umbelliferae

There are 3,000 members of the carrot family *(Umbelliferae)*, many to be found in the northern hemisphere, including various aromatic plant species rich in volatile oils. Usually these plants are regarded more as spices than as vegetables, because such small quantities are used as flavouring. A number of them are an important ingredient in many vegetable dishes and some are used as vegetables in their own right. Two unmistakable vegetable species from the family are the carrot and the parsnip.

The name of the family is derived from the small flowers that combine to form white or yellow umbels. A good example is the cow parsley *(Anthriscus sylvestris)*, that turns the wayside verges snow-white in late spring. On the ribbed fruits of many species there are many small ducts containing an aromatic oil, which is released if the fruits are rubbed, and the seed smells strongly. This pleasant smelling and tasting seed is often used as a flavouring in food and drinks. Well-known examples are aniseed *(Pimpinella anisum)*, caraway *(Carum carvi)*, and cumin *(Cuminum cyminum)*. Pieces of leaf, stem or root of other *Umbelliferae*, such as parsley, lovage and angelica *(Angelica archangelica)*, are used as seasoning.

Some *Umbelliferae* were earlier thought to have a medicinal effect, like parsley, regarded as an excellent diuretic under the name of *aqua petroselinii* until the sixteenth century. In ancient Greece the death penalty was carried out using a poisonous drink made of the unripe seeds of the hemlock *(Conium sp.)*. Socrates was said to have been killed in this way.

Internationally the most important species of vegetable from the *Umbelliferae* family is the carrot, the fleshy thickened root of a herbaceous species from the Mediterranean region and south-west Asia. In Roman writings 'white root' is mentioned, but this was probably the parsnip. The first reports of yellow and purple roots date from around the tenth century, from Afghanistan and Turkey. They were probably brought to Europe in the twelfth century by the Arabs, who occupied part of Spain at that time. Around 1300 the carrot was also reported in Italy and during the fourteenth century it appeared in France, Germany and the Netherlands. In 1554 Dodonaeus described three types: a wild carrot, a yellow carrot and a red carrot. The red or purple carrot afterwards disappeared from western Europe, but still occurs in Asia.

The familiar orange-coloured carrot was probably developed from the yellow type, and so was the white type that still exists today.

The total area devoted to carrot cultivation is now about 1.3 million acres (526,000 hectares), including 300,000 acres (125,000 hectares) in Europe.

Before the discovery of America and the arrival of the potato in Europe, the parsnip was a very important food plant. It grows wild in northern Europe, on roadside verges and grassy banks. As a cultivated species the parsnip is biennial, forming the long, white, fleshy roots in its first year. At present it is cultivated only in Britain.

The cow parsley is a wild umbel plant. At the beginning of summer its flowers can transform grass verges into a glorious sea of white

Celery and parsley

Parsley comes originally from quite a small area round the Mediterranean, but celery is a true cosmopolitan. Celery, preferring moist places with brackish water, originally grew in Europe, western Asia, north and south Africa and South America. It has quite a long history as a cultivated species: remains of celery have been found in Egyptian tombs of 1100 BC, and some 200 years later Homer refers to its medicinal effect.

The Roman Pliny (AD 24-79) was the first to distinguish between a wild form and a cultivated form: the wild form was blanched to remove some of the bitter taste. Later celery, celeriac and self-blanching celery developed from the wild celery, presumably in the Mediterranean region. The first mention of any difference between celery and celeriac was in 1543, and by 1600 we find all three described as separate species. Until the eighteenth century celery was mainly used as a medicine (it has a blood-cleaning effect), and it only later became known as a vegetable. The celery flavour is caused by the oil *lactan sedanoline,* only to be found in this plant.

In the case of blanched celery, we must further distinguish between the so-called self-blanching varieties (with golden-yellow leaves and leaf stems) and those that stay green. The green varieties must be blanched artificially by earthing up or covering with some opaque material. Their leaf stems are less fibrous and more aromatic in flavour than those of the self-blanching types. They are mainly grown in Britain, Israel and the United States.

Parsley has become native to many European countries over the years. The wild parsley was originally smooth-leaved and probably the first cultivated plants were too. Only in the second half of the sixteenth century is there any mention of curly parsley. In some parts the turnip-rooted parsley is also grown, a smooth-leaved type with a large, white, fleshy root, eaten as a vegetable.

Fennel and chervil

Fennel and chervil have one thing in common: the aniseed flavour, stronger in fennel than in chervil. Fennel comes from the Mediterranean, and its taste is caused by an aromatic substance called anethole. The most important variety is the Florence fennel. The fleshy bottom ends of the leaf stems form a white bulb eaten as a vegetable. There is also the sweet or spicy fennel *(var. dulce),* with its sweet, aniseedy fruitlets, used to make drinks like Pernod. This is mainly grown in France.

Chervil, a rapid-growing annual plant from south-east Europe, has spread over central and western Europe. It is used mainly for making chervil soup. Bulbous-rooted chervil *(Chaerophyllum bulbosum)* is a biennial plant belonging to a different plant genus, though its small, top-shaped bulbs are eaten. The Roman chervil or sweet cicely *(Myrrhis odorata)* is often found in gardens, a sturdy plant with a mild aniseed taste.

Other cultivars

Dill is a member of the *Umbelliferae* used as a seasoning and also widely eaten as a vegetable in Scandinavia and some east European countries. Amateur gardeners plant dill to keep greenfly away from their bean plants, and the sharp-smelling umbels are sold as cut flowers. The lovage *(Levisticum officinale),* used in soups, salads and stews, is a medicinal herb (especially the root), and is said to stimulate the libido. There is also the skirret *(Sium sisarum),* a root vegetable of unknown origin, mainly grown in Mongolia and Korea.

The vegetables of the *Umbelliferae* family are described below in alphabetical order of their Latin names.

Lovage is a popular kitchen spice and the root has a medicinal effect

△ Dill, 15 in (380 mm) long

Dill

(Anethum graveolens)

A herbaceous plant with needle-shaped, yellowish-green leaves, a fibrous stem and yellow umbels. The young leaf is used as a seasoning and as a vegetable.

ORIGIN: South-east Europe and western Asia.

PRODUCTION: Europe.

SEASON: Young dill herb practically throughout the year, flowering plants in summer and early autumn.

USE: Chop finely and use in cheese dishes, with fish, chicken, mashed potato, soups. Chopped flowering plants and seeds give a spicy taste to pickled gherkins.

STORAGE: Very limited, in the refrigerator.

INDUSTRIAL PROCESSING: Deep freezing and drying.

△ Chervil, 7 in (180 mm) long

Chervil
(Anthriscus cerefolium)
A herbaceous plant with rather small, indented, finned green leaves, with a rather aniseedy flavour when fresh.
ORIGIN: South-east Europe.
PRODUCTION: Belgium, France, and other western European countries.
SEASON: May to October in open ground, later under glass.
USE: Young leaf (as fresh as possible) in soups, salads, egg and cheese dishes, ragouts. When dried the leaf loses nearly all its taste and smell. Can be deep-frozen.
STORAGE: A few days in the refrigerator. Leaf becomes limp and the taste rapidly disappears.
NUTRITIONAL VALUE: 30 kcal, 4 g carbohydrate, 3.5 g protein, 0.1 g fat, 28 mg calcium, 5 mg iron, 80 mg vitamin C per 100 g serving.
INDUSTRIAL PROCESSING: Deep-freezing, making into chervil soup.

Varieties

Ordinary chervil
Smooth-leaved variety with indented finned green leaves.

Fijne krul Rather curly, deeply-indented, finned leaves.

△ Self-blanching celery 'Goudgele zelfblekende', $10\frac{1}{4}$ in (260 mm) long

Self-blanching celery or **winter celery**
(Apium graveolens, var. dulce)
Herbaceous plant with strongly-developed leaf stems. There are two groups of cultivars: the self-blanching, with golden-yellow stems, and the non self-blanching, that may be artificially blanched or eaten green. This is less fibrous and fresher-tasting than the self-blanching variety. The oil content of self-blanching celery is lower than that of ordinary celery.
ORIGIN: Mediterranean region.
PRODUCTION: Self-blanching type: Netherlands, Belgium, France, Spain. Green type: USA, Israel, Britain.
SEASON: Throughout the year.
USE: Remove any green leaves and eat the leaf stems raw or boiled. Leaf can be used as seasoning or in soup.
STORAGE: Three to four weeks at 32 to 34°F (0 to 1°C) in high humidity.
NUTRITIONAL VALUE: 14 kcal, 2 g carbohydrate, 1 g protein, 0.2 g fat, 80 mg calcium, 25 mg vitamin C, 0.8 mg vitamin PP per 100 g serving.
INDUSTRIAL PROCESSING: Canning or bottling. Drying or making into powder or celery salt.

△ Self-blanching celery 'Lathom self-blanching', 20⅛ in (510 mm) long

△ Self-blanching celery 'Utah 52.70', 16¾ in (427 mm) long

Varieties

Goudgele zelfblekende
Compact rosettes with fibrous, sharply-ribbed, yellow-green leaf stems. This type also includes improved LPD and Golden self-blanching.

Lathom self-blanching
Compact rosettes with fleshy, sharply-ribbed leaf stems, remaining light green. The outer leaf stems are particularly fibrous.

Golden spartan Heavy, quite compact rosettes with fairly long, light green leaf stems, fleshy and strongly ribbed.

Utah 52.70 American green celery type with long, fleshy, ribbed non-fibrous leaf stems and an aromatic flavour. The varieties Clairette and Improved belong to this type.

Celeriac
(Apium graveolens, var. rapaceum)
Herbaceous plant with a large, fleshy root tuber and dark-green, strongly aromatic leaves. The tubers are on sale with and without leaves.
ORIGIN: Mediterranean area.
PRODUCTION: Netherlands, West Germany, Denmark, Belgium, France, Italy, East Germany, Poland.
SEASON: July and August small tubers with leaves, September to May large tubers with or without leaves.
USE: Wash and/or peel the tubers, cut into strips or slices and boil, bake or stew. Cut into chunks, use in thick soups (such as pea soup). Grated raw, in salads. Cut and grated celeriac rapidly turns brown, which can be prevented by immersion in water with a little lemon juice.
STORAGE: Fully-grown tubers without leaves five to six months at 32 to 34°F (0 to 1°C) in high humidity.
NUTRITIONAL VALUE: 32 kcal, 5 g carbohydrate, 2 g protein, 0.4 g fat, 80 mg calcium, 1 mg iron, 12 g vitamin C, 0.8 mg vitamin PP, 0.13 vitamin B6 per 100 g serving.
INDUSTRIAL PROCESSING: Drying, deep-freezing, canning and bottling.

△ Celeriac 'Subliem', $7\frac{7}{8}$ in (200 mm) across

Varieties

Celeriac divides into long-leaved and short-leaved varieties. The long-leaved are slow growers, often trapezium shaped, with a heavy root. The tubers of the short-leaved varieties grow faster and are usually smoother and rounder. The degree of sensitivity to discoloration depends on the amount of anthocyanin in the tuber.

Monarch Very leafy, with a trapezium shaped, smooth tuber, pure white with firm flesh. Does not discolour easily.

Roem van Zwijndrecht Very leafy variety with round to trapezium shaped grey tuber. Firm flesh has a good smell but is sensitive to discoloration.

Subliem Short-leaved variety with a smooth, round, white tuber. Firm flesh, does not discolour easily.

Iram Short-leaved with small, round, white tuber. Not sensitive to discoloration.

△ Celery, 13⅜ in (340 mm) long

Celery
(Apium graveolens, var. secalium)
Herbaceous, leafy plant, with green leaves. Young leaves are cut off above ground and sold loose or in bunches.
ORIGIN: Mediterranean area.
PRODUCTION: Western Europe, Israel, Asia.
SEASON: Throughout the year.
USE: Finely-chopped leaf as seasoning in soups and other dishes.
STORAGE: A few days in the refrigerator. About two weeks at 30°F (-1°C) in high humidity.
NUTRITIONAL VALUE: 13 kcal, 2 g carbohydrate, 1 g protein, 0.1 g fat, 80 mg calcium, 40 mg phosphorus, 0.1 mg iron, 60 mg vitamin C, 1.3 mg vitamin A, 1 mg vitamin PP per 100 g serving.
INDUSTRIAL PROCESSING: Drying, deep-freezing, in soup mixtures.

Varieties

Amsterdamse fijne donkergroene A stocky plant with small green aromatic leaves and very small leaf stems.

Gewone snij A sturdy variety with coarse leaves and leaf stems. Leaf colour lighter than the other, and fewer leaf stems per plant.

Carrot
(Daucus carota)
Early summer carrot sold with or without leaves. Long cylindrical, slender root, firm leaves and a vivid orange colouring. Can also be found in different shapes, according to variety.
ORIGIN: Mediterranean area and south-west Asia.
PRODUCTION: Netherlands, Belgium, France, West Germany, Britain.
SEASON: April to December, peaking between May and August.
USE: Wash, scrape or peel the roots and eat raw (grated if you like) in salads. Or boil and eat as a vegetable on its own or mixed with other types of vegetable, such as sugar peas.
STORAGE: With leaves, ten days at 32 to 34°F (0 to 1°C). Without leaves about four weeks.
NUTRITIONAL VALUE: 28 kcal, 6 g carbohydrate, 0.5 g protein, 0.2 g fat, 40 mg calcium, 0.5 mg iron, 6 mg vitamin A, 5 mg vitamin C, 0.6 mg vitamin PP per 100 g serving.
INDUSTRIAL PROCESSING: Canning, bottling, deep-freezing.

△ Carrot 'Amsterdamse bak', root length 5⅞ in (150 mm)

Varieties

Amsterdamse bak Early variety with slender, longish cylindrical or slightly conical root. Like the skin, the small core is orange-red.

Mokum Hybrid variety, similar but longer.

Nantes Fairly early with coarser root than Amsterdamse bak and more flavour. There are two types, the Slender nantes and the Coarse nantes with a shorter, more conical root. In both types the small core is lighter than the skin.

△ Carrot 'Parijse broei', $\frac{1}{2}$ in (14 mm) across

△ Carrot 'Chantenay', 14¼ in (360 mm) long including leaf

Touchon Longish, cylindrical root with a blunt point, often with a green head. An old variety with a distinct orange-yellow core and orange-red skin.

Juwarot Rather early with longish, rather conical root, deep orange-red. High carotene (vitamin A) content.

Parijse broei Very short, almost round carrot with a sunken head and quite a large yellow core. Very sweet taste, mostly goes for processing.

Chantenay Short, conical, summer carrot with a broad head. Quite a large core, the same colour as the skin.

Washed carrot
(Daucus carota)
It can be hard to tell if you have a sample of this type, for it is very similar to the true carrot. The difficulty arises because it comes on to the market without leaves or stems. All other characteristics are similar to those of true carrots, except for the following:

INDUSTRIAL PROCESSING: Washed carrots are preserved in large quantities either in glass or deep frozen. They are graded by diameter: superfine or miniature (less than ½ inch/10 mm), extra fine (½-¾ inch/10-17 mm), fine (¾-⅞ inch/17-21 mm) and normal (⅞-1 inch/21-25 mm). Consumers tend to prefer the slenderest grades, although the thicker ones have more flavour. The carrots are also used in sliced form, and mixed with selected Parijse Broei carrots.

△ From left to right: carrot 'Nantes,' 5¼ in (136 mm) long, carrot 'Juvarot,' 7¼ in (184 mm) long, winter carrot 'Berlikummer' 7½ in (190 mm) long, winter carrot 'Flakkeese' 8¾ in (220 mm) long

Winter carrot
(Daucus carota)
Large, reddish-orange, fleshy roots, with a lighter core. Colour of root depends on the variety and where it is grown. In dry, warm summers it grows better than in cool, wet summers. A good red colour usually means a high carotene content.

ORIGIN: As carrot.

PRODUCTION: Netherlands, France, West Germany, Britain, Spain, Italy, USA, Israel, Asia.

SEASON: End of July to beginning of June.

USE: Wash and peel. Use raw (shredded if you like) in salads, or boil on its own or mixed with other types of vegetable, for instance in broth with onions and potatoes.

STORAGE: Unwashed, four to six months at 32 to 34°F (0 to 1°C), in high humidity. Two to three months at 36 to 41°F (2 to 5°C).

NUTRITIONAL VALUE: As carrot.

INDUSTRIAL PROCESSING: Drying (for vegetable soup mixtures), canning or bottling (diced), in root vegetable salads (cut into thin strips), or making into carrot juice.

Varieties

Berlikumer Long, cylindrical or slightly conical, smooth, blunt root with core and skin the same colour. Does not keep as well as Flakkeese and has a higher carotene content.

Flakkeese Strong, winter carrot, shape varying from long and cylindrical to medium and conical. The first type grows a green head, penetrating deep into the core.

Karotan Late variety with a pointed, conical root and a very attractive colour, outside and inside. Head does not turn green. High carotene content, suitable for root vegetable salad.

△ Fennel 'Florentiner,' $7\frac{1}{2}$ in (190 mm) high

Florence fennel
(Foeniculum vulgare, var. azoricum)
Herbaceous plant with finely-divided green leaflets. The lower ends of the leaf stems thicken to form a tuber. Tuber shape varies from flat to spherical, colour from pure white to greenish-white. The tubers have quite a strong aniseed flavour. There are two types, the Bolognese, with short, tender leaf stems, eaten raw, and the Florentine, with longer leaf stems, that must be cooked.
ORIGIN: Mediterranean area.
PRODUCTION: Italy, France, Spain, Switzerland.
SEASON: Throughout the year.
USE: Shred the tubers raw for use in salads (for instance with beetroot and apple) or boil (with spaghetti and tomato sauce) or bake (with cheese and bacon) or stew.
STORAGE: Two weeks in the refrigerator, best packed in paper or plastic to prevent drying out, when the tubers become tough and fibrous.
NUTRITIONAL VALUE: 12 kcal, 2 g carbohydrate, 1 g protein, 70 mg calcium, 1.4 mg iron, 5 mg vitamin C per 100 g serving.
INDUSTRIAL PROCESSING: Sometimes canned or bottled, also used in the manufacture of liqueurs such as Anisette and Chartreuse.

Varieties

Fino A Swiss variety with flattish-round, white tubers.

Tardo Also Swiss, with flat, greenish-white tubers.

Grosse d'Italia Large tubers, made up of short, broad, fleshy leaf stems.

Florentiner Small, soft tubers, flatter than the others.

△ Parsnip 'Lange witte holkruin', $11\frac{3}{4}$ in (300 mm) long

Parsnip
(Pastinaca sativa)
Fleshy, thickened, creamy-white tap-root with a rather aromatic flavour.
ORIGIN: Temperate Europe.
PRODUCTION: Britain, West Germany, Netherlands.
SEASON: November to May.
USE: Wash and peel (if necessary), dice, slice or cut in strips. Use in soups or stews or bake.
STORAGE: A few months at 32 to 34°F (0 to 1°C). At higher temperatures the roots quickly become woolly.
NUTRITIONAL VALUE: 64 kcal, 15 g carbohydrate, 1.3 g protein, 0.4 g fat, 51 mg calcium, 0.6 mg iron, 18 mg vitamin C per 100 g serving.

Varieties

Lange witte holkruin Long, up to 16 inches (40 cm), tapering, white roots with a broad, indented head. Taste usually sweet, but can be bitter.

Halflange Guernsey Medium-length white root, about 9 inches (22 cm) long, and conical. Taste similar to the last variety.

Avonresister Relatively new English variety, resistant to black spot on the root. Rather small roots.

△ Parsley, 9 in (230 mm) long

Parsley and **curly parsley**
(Petroselinum crispum, ssp. crispum)
Herbaceous plant with smooth or curly leaves. Smooth-leaved parsley has a stronger flavour than curly parsley and is used mainly as a seasoning, while curly parsley is also used for garnishing.
ORIGIN: Mediterranean area.
PRODUCTION: Netherlands, Italy, France, Israel. Also elsewhere in Europe and Asia.
SEASON: Throughout the year.
USE: Chop finely and use as a seasoning in soups, sauces, ragouts. Use curly parsley as a garnish.
STORAGE: About five weeks at 30°F (-1°C) in high humidity.
NUTRITIONAL VALUE: 26 kcal, 4 g protein, 1 g carbohydrate, 0.7 g fat, 40 mg calcium, 10 mg iron, 125 mg vitamin C, 3.2 mg vitamin A, 1.4 mg vitamin PP per 100 g serving.
INDUSTRIAL PROCESSING: Drying, deep-freezing, making into mixed vegetable soups.

Varieties

Gewone snij Fairly robust, with upright, smooth, dark greyish-green, rather dull leaves, and long, thickish leaf stems.

Gekrulde Fairly robust, with semi-upright, very curly, mid to dark greyish-green leaves, with thickish, medium-length leaf stems.

Turnip-rooted parsley
(Petroselinum crispum, ssp. tuberosum)
Herbaceous plant with a smooth leaf and a fleshy white tap root. Both leaf and root can be eaten.
ORIGIN: Mediterranean area.
PRODUCTION: West Germany, eastern European countries.
SEASON: October to May.
USE: Leaf like smooth-leaved parsley. Root shredded in salads, diced in soups and stews, or boiled like a carrot.
STORAGE: A few months at 32 to 34°F (0 to 1°C). At a higher temperature the roots soon become woolly.
NUTRITIONAL VALUE: 22 kcal, 2 g carbohydrate, 2.9 g protein, 0.6 g fat, 40 mg calcium, 0.6 mg iron, 41 mg vitamin C per 100 g serving.
INDUSTRIAL PROCESSING: Drying and grinding into powder.

△ Turnip-rooted parsley 'Lange gladde', root 9½ in (240 mm) long

Varieties

Hamburger Mid-early variety with medium-length, smooth, conical roots. **Berliner** is a similar variety.

Korte dikke Early with short, thick, stumpy roots.

Lange gladde Late, with long, slender, pointed roots, that are liable to branch and are therefore difficult to harvest.

Valerianaceae

The small valerian family *(Valerianaceae)* is made up of about 400 species, most of them to be found in the temperate regions of the northern hemisphere. The best-known is undoubtedly the genus *Valeriana.* This includes the common valerian or all-heal *(V. officinalis),* a strong-smelling, perennial plant with a thickened rootstock. Oils are extracted from the dried roots and used in the manufacture of pharmaceutical preparations such as valerian drops.

The genus *Valeriana* also includes some species eaten as vegetables, like the ordinary corn salad and the Italian corn salad *(V. eriocarpa).* Some botanists regard the corn salads as a separate genus called *Valerianella.*

Corn salad originated in Europe: in the wild there are various species living between 60 degrees North and a southern boundary running through the Canary Islands via North Africa to the Caucasus. Although the annual plant is a wholesome winter vegetable, there is no evidence that our ancestors ate it. There are two methods of cultivation, which produce different vegetables. To grow forced salad, fine seed is used, sown thickly. The young plants are harvested root and all and sold in trays. These plants are grown in winter and early spring, heated under glass. They are very tender, unlike the so-called asses' ears. To grow this other type of corn salad, in a cold frame or in the open, the seeds are sown much more thinly. The plant has then got room to form a vigorous rosette with oblong, spatula-shaped leaves. The rosette is harvested by cutting it from the root with a sharp knife just below the surface of the soil, and it is then sold loose, packed in boxes. The leaf of asses' ears is usually greyish-green.

The leaf of the Italian corn salad mentioned above is yellowish-green. This plant is only grown in southern Europe.

Corn salad or **lamb's lettuce**
(Valeriana locusta, syn. Valerianella locusta)
Herbaceous leaf vegetable, grown and sold mainly during the winter months. See above for a description of the two types.
ORIGIN: Europe.
PRODUCTION: France, Italy, West Germany, Belgium, Britain, Netherlands.
SEASON: November to May.
USE: Raw in salads, or in soups and stews.
STORAGE: Forced salad one to two days in the refrigerator, asses' ears a few days longer.
NUTRITIONAL VALUE: 24 kcal, 3 g carbohydrate, 2 g protein, 0.4 g fat, 25 mg calcium, 4 mg iron, 40 mg vitamin C, 1.5 mg vitamin A per 100 g serving.

△ Corn salad 'Valgros', 4¼ in (110 mm) long

Varieties

Grote noordhollander Flat rosettes with oblong, greyish-green leaves, about 4⅜ inches (11 cm) long and 1 to 1¼ inches (2.5 to 3 cm) wide. The fine seed of this variety is sieved and used for growing forced salad.

Valgros Leaves slightly broader and lighter in colour.

Volhart Rosettes with upright, dark green shiny leaves, shorter and broader than the first two varieties. Leaf also keeps better.

Verte de Cambrai Rosettes with large, green, indented leaves. A winter hardy variety, popular in France.

Verte d'Etampes A bushy growth, not so rosette-shaped, with dark green shiny leaves that keep well.

Italian corn salad or **Regence** A variety with long, narrow, yellowish-green leaves, 5⅛ inches (13 cm) long and ¾ inch (2 cm) wide. Not resistant to frost.

Zingiberaceae

There is room for disagreement as to whether the ginger family *(Zingiberaceae)* belongs among the vegetables or among the herbs and spices. We have decided to include it here, after some hesitation, because the young blooms of some of these species are eaten as vegetables in the tropics, either raw or cooked. In one single case the core of the young stems is also used, although this soon becomes unpleasantly bitter. Neither flowers nor stems are exported to Europe, but the roots of several family members are to be found in the shops, fresh, dried, ground or candied.

The *Zingiberaceae* form a family of about 1,500 species. With one exception, they all belong in the tropical rain forests of south and east Asia. They are herbaceous, perennial plants, often with vigorously developed rootstocks *(rhizomes)* containing different aromatic substances. These substances are often contained in the seeds as well, so the dried or ground roots and seeds are used in cakes, sweetmeats, curries, drinks and perfumes.

The fruit and seed of two *Aframomum* species were the first *Zingiberaceae* representatives to arrive in Europe. These grow in the west African coastal region between Guinea and Angola. In the first century AD these 'grains of paradise' with their strongly aromatic flavour travelled in Sahara caravans to Tripoli, and from there to southern Europe. This was soon a flourishing trade, especially when the Portuguese began to import these peppery spices in large quantities by sea. Eventually higher-quality spices from other lands became more popular, and it is now used only in its country of origin, and in a few other countries where slaves took their 'grains of paradise'.

In India and many other countries in Asia, root ginger is an essential ingredient in national dishes

Just as old is the spice known as cardamom, made from the dried seed of *Elettaria cardamomum*, originally from east Asia, but now grown in Central America. The seeds contain an aromatic oil that gives a distinctive flavour to some liqueurs as well as to cakes and biscuits. The Bedouin put a few cardamom seeds in the long spouts of their coffee pots to give their coffee its characteristic taste.

The genus *Curcuma*, also from south-east Asia, is much better known. This genus includes the turmeric, whose branching, yellowish rootstocks are ground into turmeric powder. The rootstock of a related species, the zedoary root *(C. zedoria)*, has a camphor-like smell, and the young shoots are eaten as a vegetable, especially on Madagascar and Sri Lanka. The bitter-tasting, orange-coloured rootstock of *C. xanthorhiza* is used as a remedy for liver and gall complaints.

Ginger and the greater galangal are the two *Zingiberaceae* whose fresh rootstocks are regularly on sale, as well as their dried and powdered forms. The greater galangal belongs to a genus originating in south-east Asia, and cultivated in tropical Asia on quite a large scale for its edible rootstock. The yellowish-white or light-red roots have young side-shoots, mainly eaten as a vegetable with rice. When raw the roots are too hot and strongly flavoured, so they are always cooked. A related species, *Alpinia officinarum*, has a brownish-red rootstock and is known as soft ginger.

No wild form is known of the true ginger: the plant has been cultivated since time immemorial in India and the south of China. The Arabs introduced ginger into east Africa in the thirteenth century, and the Portuguese brought the roots in the sixteenth century from east to west Africa, and then to Europe. This African ginger was later superseded by better-quality Chinese ginger. The fairly thick, hard rootstocks are yellowish when young and later greyish-brown. Apart from fresh ginger, we are also familiar with white ginger (scraped or peeled roots, blanched in the sun and dried), black ginger (the same, but unpeeled), and candied ginger (pieces of root boiled in sugar). Ginger is also available in powdered form.

△ Galangal root, 9¾ in (250 mm) long

Greater galangal

(Alpinia galanga)

Yellowish-white or light red rootstocks with reddish side-shoots and a very hot, strong flavour when raw.

ORIGIN: South-east Asia.

PRODUCTION: All tropical Asia.

SEASON: Throughout the year.

USE: Boil the root and use in rice dishes.

INDUSTRIAL PROCESSING: Drying and grinding into powder.

Turmeric

(Curcuma longa)

Branched rootstocks, round in cross-section, deep orange in colour.

ORIGIN: South-east Asia.

PRODUCTION: China, India, Malacca, Malaysia.

SEASON: Throughout the year.

USE: In powder form, for colouring and as a curry ingredient.

NUTRITIONAL VALUE: 345 kcal, 4 g protein, 5 g fat, 71 g carbohydrate, 150 mg calcium, 18 mg iron, 0.05 mg vitamin A per 100 g serving.

INDUSTRIAL PROCESSING: In powder form as a curry ingredient, and as a colouring in piccalilly and some kinds of mustard.

△ Root ginger, $6\frac{7}{8}$ in (175 mm) long

Ginger

(Zingiber officinale)

Vigorously developed, irregularly shaped, yellowish or brown rootstocks with an aromatic flavour.

ORIGIN: Not known.

PRODUCTION: India, China.

SEASON: Throughout the year.

USE: Peel, grate, and use in curries, sauces, chutneys. Shredded or sliced, preserved in sherry or spirits.

INDUSTRIAL PROCESSING: Drying and grinding into ginger powder, candying, using in sweet dishes, making into drinks.

Recipes

The main aim of the following recipe section is to suggest new ways to cook some of the less familiar vegetables ignored by most cookbooks. The recipes use fresh vegetables and are all for four people. Whether you prefer the light or the substantial, the simple or the elaborate, *bon appétit.*

Sweet potato soup

5 to 6 large sweet potatoes
9 cups/3½ pints/2 litres fish stock
1 tablespoon tomato purée
a generous sprinkling of white pepper
salt
1 cup/8 oz/250 g boiled cod
½ cup/4 oz/100 g peeled shrimps
1 leek
chopped parsley

Peel and wash the sweet potatoes and cut into pieces. Boil until cooked with the tomato purée in the fish stock. Season to taste with salt and freshly ground pepper. Flake the cod and stir it into the soup with the shrimps. Garnish with thin rings of leek and chopped parsley.

Jerusalem artichoke with rice

2 lb/1 kg Jerusalem artichokes
4 shallots (chopped)
¾ cup/scant ½ pint/300 ml olive oil
1 cup/8 oz/250 g tomatoes (peeled with pips removed)
salt
pepper
1¾ cups/14 oz/400 g rice
juice and grated peel of 1 lemon
2 tablespoons chopped dill

Wash, peel and slice the artichokes. Heat the oil and fry the shallots for a couple of minutes and then add the tomatoes. Let the mixture simmer for about 5 minutes. Lay the artichoke slices on the tomato mixture, pour over 4 tablespoons of water and simmer with the lid on, stirring occasionally. Add salt and pepper, cover with water, and leave to simmer for about 7 minutes. Boil the rice and sprinkle it over the vegetables. Add the lemon juice and grated peel, stir gently and leave to simmer uncovered for a further 5 to 10 minutes. Pour into a bowl, leave to cool, and then refrigerate. Serve cold, garnished with dill.

Adzuki salad

½ cup/4 oz/125 g adzuki beans
1 cup/8 oz/200 g rice
salt
2 stems of self-blanching celery (chopped finely)
1 shallot (sliced thinly)
1 small courgette (diced)
¼ cup/2 oz/40 g seedless raisins
5 walnuts (chopped)
¼ cup/2 oz/50 g sweetcorn (cooked)
¼ cup/2 oz/50 g haricot beans (chopped)
Chinese chives (chopped)

For the dressing:
6 tablespoons lemon juice
salt
freshly ground black pepper
3 tablespoons nut oil

Soak the adzuki beans overnight and boil in the same water for about 1 hour until cooked. Leave to drain. Mix the beans with the boiled rice. Make the dressing from the ingredients given and stir into the mixture. Add the celery, shallot, courgette, walnuts, raisins, sweetcorn and haricot beans and mix together carefully. Leave to cool in the refrigerator. Before serving, stir once more and garnish with finely chopped Chinese chives.

Stewed amaranth

2 lb/1 kg amaranth
2 cloves garlic (chopped finely)
2 tablespoons corn oil
salt

Clean the leaves and the tops of the amaranth and leave to drain. Heat the oil in a pan, fry the garlic, and then add the drained amaranth and allow it to boil down, stirring from time to time. Add a little salt and stew for about 15 minutes until done. Amaranth may be chopped up like spinach.

Fried mustard greens

3 cups/1½ lb/750 g mustard greens
3 tablespoons oil
2 onions (chopped)
1 clove garlic
2 teaspoons curry powder
¼ cup/2 oz/50g lean beef mince
salt
freshly ground black pepper

Remove the leaf ribs from the mustard greens. Wash the greens and drain well, then cut into small strips. Fry the onion until glazed in the hot oil, add the curry powder and fry for a minute or two, then add the mince and garlic and fry for about 10 minutes, stirring gently. Add the mustard greens and fry for a further 10 minutes. The mustard greens should still be crisp. Season to taste with salt and pepper.

Marinaded artichoke hearts

1¾ cups/14 oz/400 g cooked artichoke hearts
3 tablespoons wine vinegar or dry sherry
4 sprigs of tarragon
2 cloves garlic (crushed)
a piece of lemon rind
salt
freshly ground pepper
8 tablespoons olive oil

Make a marinade of the ingredients. Blend thoroughly. Add the cooked, drained artichoke hearts and marinade for at least 12 hours. Serve as a starter or as a light lunch (hot or cold) with fresh crusty French bread.

Asperges à la Colin

2 cups/1 lb/500 g asparagus
streaky smoked bacon, (thinly sliced)
½ cup/4 oz/100 g butter
2 hard-boiled eggs (sliced)
3 tablespoons cream

Peel, wash and boil the asparagus. When cooked, leave to drain well. Grease an ovenproof dish with butter. Roll the asparagus in bundles of four inside the slices of bacon and lay them on the greased dish. Garnish with the sliced hard- boiled eggs. Melt the butter and mix with the cream. Pour the mixture over the asparagus and bake in a moderately hot oven for 15 minutes. Serve immediately.

Asparagus pea salad

1 lb/500 g asparagus peas
salt
1 hard-boiled egg (sliced)
a few leaves of red-leaved chicory

For the dressing:

1 tablespoon wine vinegar
2 tablespoons of cold chicken stock (with the fat removed)
1 clove garlic (crushed)
freshly ground black pepper
3 tablespoons olive oil

Clean the asparagus peas and blanch for 7 minutes in boiling water with a little salt. Rinse in cold water and leave to drain. Arrange the chicory leaves in a salad bowl and fill with the drained asparagus peas. Make the dressing from the ingredients shown and pour it over the peas. Garnish with a few slices of hard-boiled egg.

Aubergine and lamb

2 aubergines
olive oil
2 cups/1 lb/500 g minced lamb
freshly ground black pepper
salt
2 cloves garlic (chopped)
2 shallots (chopped)
1 tablespoon chopped parsley
a few rosemary leaves
½ tablespoon chopped marjoram
2 tablespoons tomato purée
¼ cup/2 oz/50 g flour
1 cup/½ pint/300 ml milk
1 egg

Wash the aubergines and cut into ¼-inch/5 mm slices. Fry in a little olive oil until brown on both sides and leave to drain on kitchen roll. Fry the shallots and garlic in a little olive oil. Add the crumbled mince and cook until separated. When it begins to brown, add the salt, pepper, parsley, rosemary, marjoram and tomato purée and leave to simmer for 10 minutes, stirring frequently. Place a layer of aubergines in a greased oven dish, pour over the meat mixture and then cover with the rest of the aubergines. Make a smooth sauce from the flour, milk and egg and pour over the top. Bake for ½ hour in a preheated oven at 350°F/180°C/gas mark 4.

Mixed salad with bamboo shoots

2 cups/1 lb/500 g bamboo shoots
$\frac{1}{2}$ lb/250 g iceberg lettuce
1 cup/$\frac{1}{2}$ lb/250 g bean shoots
1 cup/$\frac{1}{2}$ lb/250 g Chinese kale
1 bunch Chinese chives

For the sauce:
2 tablespoons vinegar
2 tablespoons dry sherry
salt
$\frac{1}{2}$ teaspoon grated ginger root
1 clove garlic
1 tablespoon ketchup
5 tablespoons sesame oil

Wash the bamboo shoots and boil until tender in plenty of water. Drain and cool, then cut into matchstick-sized strips. Wash the other vegetables, cut the lettuce into small strips and break the kale into small pieces and chop the chives. Mix all the vegetables together. Blend the dressing ingredients in the order given. Mix the smooth, spicy dressing into the salad and serve immediately.

Winter cress soup

1 cup/8 oz/250 g winter cress
$4\frac{1}{2}$ cups/2 pints/1 litre chicken stock
$\frac{1}{4}$ cup/2 oz/50 g butter
$\frac{1}{4}$ cup/2 oz/50 g flour
3 tablespoons cream
freshly ground white pepper
salt

Wash cress, drain, and then simmer for 10 minutes in the pre-heated chicken stock. Meanwhile make a roux with the butter and flour and leave to cool. Sieve the stock and rub the cress through the sieve back into the stock. Bring to the boil, stirring continuously, then add to the roux a little at a time, stirring until smooth. Leave to simmer for a for a few minutes. Season to taste with salt and pepper and add a blob of cream. Garnish with a little left-over cress.

Basella casserole

$1\frac{1}{2}$ cups/12 oz/350 g basella stems
4 potatoes (peeled and diced)
$\frac{1}{2}$ cup/4 oz/100 g pork
$\frac{1}{2}$ cup/4 oz/100 g smoked streaky bacon
$\frac{1}{4}$ cup/2 oz/50 g butter
1 tablespoon olive oil
4 tablespoons stock
2 teaspoons tomato purée
salt
freshly ground black pepper
1 red onion (chopped)

Clean the basella stems, remove the leaves and cut the stems into pieces about $1\frac{1}{2}$ inches/4 cm long. Save the leaves for another recipe. Do not use the thickest ends of the stems. Dice the meat and the bacon and fry in a mixture of butter and olive oil. Add the chopped onion and stir-fry. Then add the potatoes and the basella and continue to stir-fry. Add the stock and simmer till tender, for about 25 minutes. Season to taste with tomato purée, salt and black pepper.

Borage cucumbers

1 large cucumber
$\frac{3}{4}$ cup/6 oz/150 g streaky bacon (diced)
2 tablespoons butter
1 small onion (chopped)
salt
1 teaspoon strong mustard
a pinch of sugar
a generous amount of finely chopped borage
a few borage flowers
freshly ground black pepper

Peel the cucumber, remove the seeds and cut into pieces. Melt the butter in a pan and fry the diced bacon in it until it begins to change colour. Then add the onion and cucumber pieces and fry for about 5 minutes, stirring frequently. Season to taste with salt, pepper, mustard and sugar. Mix in borage and garnish with a few flowers.

Borage sauce

2 tablespoons butter
2 tablespoons flour
$2\frac{1}{2}$ cups/1 pint/600 ml chicken stock
salt
freshly ground white pepper
1 egg yolk
a pinch of sugar
grated nutmeg
plenty of finely chopped borage
a little lemon juice

Make a roux of butter and flour, leave to cool. Then stir it gradually into the hot chicken stock so that it makes a smooth sauce. Leave to cook for a few minutes on a low heat. Season to taste with salt, white pepper, sugar and a little grated nutmeg. Stir in the egg yolk. Then add a generous quantity of borage and finish the sauce with a few drops of lemon juice. Goes well with poultry, and is also suitable for fish dishes if made with fish stock.

Broccoli soup

2 lb/1 kg sprouting broccoli
9 cups/$3\frac{1}{2}$ pints/2 litres veal stock with fat removed
$\frac{1}{4}$ cup/2 oz/60 g butter
$\frac{1}{4}$ cup/2 oz/60 g flour
salt
pepper
grated nutmeg
2 tablespoons cream
2 egg yolks
young broccoli leaves

Clean the broccoli, reserve a few attractive small rosettes and chop the rest finely. Blanch the small rosettes for a few minutes in the hot veal stock and put on one side. Add the rest of the broccoli to the stock and cook until tender. Sieve the stock and rub the broccoli through the sieve back into the stock. Make a roux from the flour and butter and leave to cool. Then add the hot stock gradually, stirring until smooth. Season to taste with salt, pepper and nutmeg. Add the blanched rosettes and at the last moment stir in the mixture of cream and egg yolk. Garnish with a finely chopped broccoli leaf.

Chinese kale salad

1 lb/500 g Chinese kale
1 tablespoon chervil (chopped)

For the dressing:
2 tablespoons white vinegar
salt
pepper
1 small clove garlic
6 tablespoons corn oil
2 hard-boiled eggs (chopped)
1 tablespoon chopped chives

Wash the kale and cut into pieces, leaving the flower bunches intact as far as possible. Cut the stems and add to the leaves. Boil for about 10 minutes in lightly salted water until tender. Rinse in cold water and drain. Make a dressing from the ingredients shown, in the order given, and stir this into the kale. Garnish with chopped chervil.

Fried cassavas

2 good-sized cassava roots
2 cloves garlic (crushed)
salt
pepper
4 tablespoons corn oil

Peel the cassavas, wash, dry and cut into $1\frac{1}{2}$-inch/4 cm cubes. Mix the crushed garlic with the cassava, cover and leave to stand for $\frac{1}{2}$ hour. Heat the oil in a good-sized pan and fry the cassava cubes until cooked through. Take the cassava out of the pan, leave to drain and sprinkle with salt and pepper.

Choisum with melted butter

$2\frac{1}{2}$ cups/$1\frac{1}{2}$ lb/600 g choisum
salt
1 cup/7 oz/200 g butter
4 hard-boiled eggs (chopped)
grated nutmeg
chopped chervil

Remove the coarse leaves from the choisum and wash it. Cut into pieces of about 4 inches/10 cm but leave the buds intact. Cook in a little salted water for about 4 minutes until tender and then leave to drain. Place in a heated dish, melt the butter and pour a spoonful over the choisum. Spread the chopped eggs over the top. Garnish with chervil and serve the rest of the butter separately.

Stuffed courgettes (zucchini) with sardines

4 courgettes (not too big)
1 tin of sardines in tomato sauce
breadcrumbs
1 shallot (sliced wafer thin)
2 tomatoes (peeled with pips removed)
1 tablespoon olive oil
salt
freshly ground black pepper

Wash the courgettes and boil in salted water for about 7 minutes until tender. Cut in half lengthwise, remove the flesh and chop it up. Mix it with the sardines (filleted and chopped) and the tomato sauce. Bind with breadcrumbs if necessary. Put the mixture into the hollowed-out courgettes. Place the courgettes in a greased oven dish. Fry the shallot and the sliced tomato in the oil, season to taste with salt and pepper, and pour it over the courgettes. Place in the oven pre-heated to 350°F/180°C/gas mark 4 and bake for about 10 minutes.

Fried Japanese artichokes (crosnes)

1 lb/500 g Japanese artichokes
$2\frac{1}{2}$ cups/1 pint/600 ml chicken stock
salt
1 small onion
butter
chopped parsley or chives

Wash the Japanese artichokes well and boil for 3 minutes in the chicken stock with a little salt and the onion. Drain carefully. Then fry them in butter until golden brown and serve sprinkled with chopped parsley or chives.

Mixed salad with Japanese artichokes

1 cup/8 oz/250 g Japanese artichokes
1 cup/8 oz/250 g lightly boiled potatoes (diced)
1 cup/$\frac{1}{2}$ pint/300 ml stock
2 stems self-blanching celery
1 cup/8 oz/250 g cooked mussels
black olives
dry white wine

For the dressing:
2 tablespoons tarragon vinegar
salt pepper
1 tablespoon Dijon mustard
6 tablespoons olive oil

Clean the Japanese artichokes well and boil them for about 3 minutes in the lightly salted stock until tender. Leave to drain and cool. Mix with the diced potato and marinade for a few hours in plenty of dry white wine. Leave to drain again. Mix with the finely chopped celery and the mussels. Make a dressing from the ingredients shown above and toss the salad in it.

Garnish with black olives.

Pigeon peas with broccoli

2 cups/1 lb/500 g pigeon peas
parsley stems
a sprig of rosemary
a pinch of thyme
1 red pepper (diced)
1 broccoli (cut in strips)
1 onion (finely chopped)
salt
freshly ground black pepper
oil
1½ cups/12 oz/350 g spiced meat balls

Soak the pigeon peas overnight. Put in a linen bag and close tightly. Boil the peas together with the parsley stems, rosemary and thyme in plenty of water for about 1 hour until tender. Heat the oil in a good-sized pan and fry the pepper and the onion in it. When they start to change colour add the broccoli and continue frying. Everything should be tender but not over-cooked. Add the drained pigeon peas and stir well. Season with salt and pepper. Bake the meat balls separately until brown all over and mix them into the pigeon pea dish.

Red oakleaf lettuce salad

½ to 1 red oakleaf lettuce head

For the dressing:
1 tablespoon lemon juice
salt
freshly ground white pepper
a pinch of sugar
1 tablespoon chopped chervil
3 tablespoons corn oil

Strip the leaves from the head, wash and dry carefully. Make a dressing from the ingredients shown, and add just before serving. This salad is so attractive that it needs no other garnish.

Patience dock with bacon

2 lb/1 kg patience dock
½ cup/4 oz/100 g bacon (chopped)
½ cup/4 oz/100 g onions (chopped)

Clean the patience dock and blanch it several times in salted boiling water. Immerse at once in cold water and leave to drain. Fry the onions in the butter until they begin to change colour. Add the bacon and the roughly chopped dock and stew until tender. Season to taste with salt, pepper and nutmeg.

Garland chrysanthemum salad

30 just-opened flowers of garland chrysanthemum
1 lb/500 g potatoes
a few garland chrysanthemum leaves

For the dressing:
2 tablespoons vinegar
salt
freshly ground white pepper
1 tablespoon chopped chives
1 teaspoon Dijon mustard
1 tablespoon very finely chopped gherkin
5 tablespoons sunflower oil

First make the dressing from the ingredients shown, in the order given. Peel, wash and boil potatoes until done (but not floury). Dice and mix into the dressing while still hot. Pull the petals from the flowers and mix them into the salad. Leave the salad covered in the refrigerator to cool. Turn into a serving dish and garnish with garland chrysanthemum leaves and a few flowers.

Sugar loaf au gratin

2 lb/1 kg sugar loaf
½ cup/4 oz/100 g bacon
2 tablespoons butter
salt
juice of half a lemon
2 tablespoons grated cheese

Wash the sugar loaf and cut into small pieces. Blanch for 5 minutes in boiling water with a little salt and lemon juice. Leave to drain well in a colander. Cut the bacon into thin strips and fry in the butter. Then add the sugar loaf and cook for about 10 minutes on a low heat. Turn out into a greased gratin dish and sprinkle grated cheese on top. Place in a pre-heated hot oven or under the grill until the cheese is golden-brown.

Mixed buckshorn plantain salad

1 cup/8 oz/250 g buckshorn plantain
1 head of cabbage lettuce
½ cup/4 oz/100 g sugar peas
1 red onion (sliced in rings)
½ red pepper cut in strips

For the sauce:
3 tablespoons tomato ketchup
2 teaspoons Dijon mustard
6 tablespoons cream
salt
freshly ground white pepper
1 clove garlic (crushed)

Clean the plantain thoroughly and divide it into 2-inch/5 cm pieces. Do the same with the lettuce. String and wash the sugar peas and cut them into diagonal ¾-inch/2 cm pieces. Mix vegetables together. Make a sauce from the ingredients shown, stir a few spoonfuls into the salad and leave to stand before serving. Serve the rest of the sauce separately.

Hop shoots à la crème

2 lb/1 kg hop shoots
salt
freshly ground white pepper
1 cup/scant ½ pint/300 ml cream
lemon juice

Clean the hop shoots and boil in a little salted water for about 10 minutes until tender. Leave to drain and chop roughly. Mix with the cream and heat well. Season with a little lemon juice, salt and pepper.

Hop shoots with poached eggs

2 lb/1 kg hop shoots
2 tablespoons butter
4 poached eggs
salt
chopped parsley

Prepare the hop shoots as in the previous recipe. Boil them with the butter and season to taste with a little salt. Lay the poached eggs on the hop shoots.

Indonesian water spinach

$1\frac{1}{2}$ lb/700 g water spinach leaf
$\frac{1}{4}$ cup/2 oz/50 g butter or margarine
1 onion (chopped)
1 tomato (peeled with pips removed)
1 clove garlic (crushed)
salt

Clean the water spinach, remove the thick stem, wash and leave to drain. Melt the butter and fry the onion, garlic and tomato. Then add the drained water spinach and cook for about 15 minutes until tender. This vegetable should remain crisp.

Cardoon à la crème

2 lb/1 kg cardoon
1 tablespoon flour
salt
pepper
2 lemons
$\frac{1}{4}$ cup/2 oz/50 g butter
1 cup/scant $\frac{1}{2}$ pint/20 cl cream

First make a white sauce by mixing the flour with 3 to 4 tablespoons of water. Bring a large saucepanful of water to the boil, add salt and the juice of one lemon, beat in the white sauce and bring to the boil, stirring continuously. Clean the cardoon. Peel the stems to remove all strings. Halve the second lemon and rub over the stems. Then cut into pieces of about 2 inches/5 cm. Put them into the boiling sauce and boil for about 1 hour until tender. Then leave to drain well. Heat the butter in a pan, add the cardoon and fry, stirring occasionally, for 5 minutes on a low heat. Then pour over the fresh cream and allow it to warm, without boiling. Season with salt and pepper to taste.

Chick-peas and bacon

$1\frac{3}{4}$ cups/1 lb/500 g chick-peas
$1\frac{1}{2}$ cups/12 oz/350 g lean unsmoked bacon
1 tablespoon butter
2 shallots (diced)
1 cup/8 oz/250 g carrots (diced)
$\frac{3}{4}$ cup/6 oz/150 g mushrooms
1 clove garlic (crushed)
1 tablespoon tomato purée
1 cup/scant $\frac{1}{2}$ pint/300 ml stock
salt
freshly ground black pepper
chopped parsley

Soak the chick-peas for 24 hours and boil them in the water they were soaked in for $1\frac{1}{2}$ to 2 hours. Cut the bacon into strips and fry slowly. As it begins to change colour add the carrots, shallots and garlic. Fry evenly and then add the quartered mushrooms. Then add the tomato purée and pour on the stock. Finally add the cooked, drained chick-peas and leave to cook through. Garnish with plenty of chopped parsley.

Burdock with egg

2 lb/1 kg young burdock
milk
salt
2 tablespoons butter
lemon juice
1 hard-boiled egg
chopped parsley

Clean the burdock and cut into 2-inch/5 cm pieces. Boil for about 20 minutes until tender in lightly salted water with a dash of milk added. Leave to drain. Melt the butter in a pan, lay the burdock in it and fry over a low heat until it is golden yellow. Sprinkle a little lemon juice on top and a mixture of finely chopped egg and parsley.

Burdock salad

2 cups/1 lb/500 g burdock
milk
salt
½ cup/4 oz/100 g ham (diced)
1 small red pepper (diced)
chopped parsley

For the dressing:
2 tablespoons lemon juice
salt
freshly ground white pepper
½ teaspoon mustard
a pinch of sugar
5 tablespoons sunflower oil

Clean the burdock, cut into 1½-inch/3 cm pieces and boil until tender as in the previous recipe. Leave to drain and cool. Mix the burdock with the ham and the red pepper. Make a smooth dressing from the ingredients shown and stir into the salad. Garnish with finely chopped parsley.

Fried garden turnips

6 whole turnips
4½ cups/2 pints/1 litre stock
celery salt
fat or oil for frying

Peel the turnips and cut into chip-sized pieces. Blanch for 5 minutes in the boiling stock, drain, and then deep fry for a few minutes until golden brown. Sprinkle with celery salt.

Lamb with Florence fennel

4 tablespoons olive oil
1¾ lb/800 g lamb (cut up)
1 onion (chopped)
salt
freshly ground black pepper
1¾ cups/14 oz/400 g tomatoes (peeled with pips removed)
1½ lb/650 g fennel tubers (quartered)

Heat the oil in a pan and brown the meat in it. Add the onion and cook for a couple of minutes. Then add the tomatoes (cut up) with a little salt and pepper and simmer with the lid on for about 50 minutes on a low heat. Boil the fennel for 10 minutes in a little salted water. Add the fennel and 1 cup/scant ½ pint/300 ml of its water to the lamb and simmer for a further 10 to 15 minutes until the meat is tender.

Mustard spinach salad

2 cups/1 lb/500 g mustard spinach
2 firm bananas (sliced)
2 hard-boiled eggs
2 tomatoes
1 small leek

For the sauce:
3 tablespoons mayonnaise
aromat flavouring
4 teaspoons Dijon mustard

Clean the mustard spinach and cut into 1-inch/2 cm pieces. Blanch for 5 minutes in lightly salted boiling water. Then leave to drain and cool. Make a sauce from the ingredients shown. Mix the bananas with the mustard spinach in the sauce. Garnish the salad with the eggs, tomatoes and leek, all in thin slices.

Baked balsam pear with shrimps

2 balsam pears
1 cup/8 oz/250 g fresh peeled shrimps
1 large onion (chopped)
2 cloves garlic
1 tomato (peeled and cut up with the pips removed)
3 tablespoons corn oil
3 teaspoons curry powder
salt

Wash the balsam pears, cut them in half lengthwise and remove the pips. Then cut the halves into ½-inch/1 cm pieces. Heat the oil in a deep pan or wok, fry the onion and garlic, then add the tomato pieces and leave to fry for a little longer. Mix in the curry powder and the balsam pears, and leave to cook slowly. If necessary add a little water. Finally stir in the shrimps, season to taste with a little salt and warm through.

One-pan meal with kohlrabi

2 lb/1 kg kohlrabi
1 lb/500 g potatoes
4 sausages
salt
pepper
4 tablespoons whipped cream
1 tablespoon flour
young kohlrabi leaves

Peel the kohlrabi and potatoes, wash them and cut into 1-inch/2 cm thick strips. Put in a pan together with the sausages, salt, pepper and water, and cook gently for 20 minutes. Thicken the remaining liquid with a mixture of flour and cream and add to the kohlrabi mixture again.

Chinese cabbage with pork

2 lb/1 kg Chinese cabbage
1¾ cups/14 oz/400g pork (cut into strips)
salt
1 teaspoon powdered ginger
3 tablespoons soya sauce
2 tablespoons potato flour
3 tablespoons oil
2 onions (sliced in rings)
2 carrots (sliced)
1 clove garlic (crushed)
1 cup/scant ½ pint/300 ml chicken stock
2 tablespoons tomato ketchup

Marinade the pork for at least 1 hour in a mixture of soya sauce, salt and powdered ginger. Cut the Chinese cabbage into strips, wash and leave to drain. Take the meat from the marinade, drain well and coat in 1 tablespoonful of the potato flour. Fry the meat until tender in the hot oil, take it out and keep it warm. Fry the onion rings in the oil, then add the Chinese cabbage, garlic and carrots and fry for 5 minutes. Then add the chicken stock, the marinade and the tomato ketchup and bring it all to the boil. Thicken the mixture with potato flour and add the meat. Warm through and season to taste with salt and a little more powdered ginger if necessary.

Baked cowpeas (yard-long beans)

1 lb/ 500 g cowpeas
2 tablespoons sunflower oil
1 small clove garlic (sliced)
salt or stock cubes
powdered ginger

Clean the cowpeas and cut them into 2½-inch/6 cm pieces. Heat the oil, fry the garlic and then add the cowpea pieces. Fry for about 3 minutes on a high heat stirring continuously. Season the cowpeas to taste with salt and a pinch of powdered ginger.

Curly lettuce salad

1 head of curly lettuce
1 hard-boiled egg (sliced)
1 tomato (sliced)
a few cucumber slices
chopped parsley

For the dressing:
1 tablespoon wine vinegar
salt
freshly ground pepper
1 shallot
1 small clove garlic
3 tablespoons vegetable oil

Clean the lettuce thoroughly, dry carefully and break into pieces. Make a dressing from the ingredients shown and mix into the salad immediately before serving. Garnish with slices of tomato, cucumber, egg and finely chopped parsley.

'Lamb's ears' (sea aster)

1 lb/500 g sea aster
1 shallot (chopped)
2 tablespoons butter
freshly ground white pepper
salt

Fry the shallot lightly in the butter. Add the washed and drained sea aster and fry, stirring continuously. Add pepper and salt to taste.

Bean stew with lima beans

1¾ cups/14 oz/400 g lima beans
1¾ cups/1 lb/500 g beef (cut into cubes)
1 tablespoon flour
salt
freshly ground pepper
1 large onion (chopped)
4 large potatoes
1 winter carrot
4 May tubers

Soak the lima beans overnight. Boil for 1 hour in fresh water. Drain and save the water. Coat the meat in seasoned flour. Heat the butter, and brown the meat and the onion in it. Put the lima beans in a casserole with a little of their water, sprinkle a little salt and pepper over them and place the meat and onions on top. Cook covered for 1 hour in an oven pre-heated to 350°F/180°C/gas mark 4. Meanwhile clean the potatoes, the carrot and the May tubers. Dice all the vegetables and mix together. Add this mixture to the meat and beans, sprinkle a little salt on top, add a little more of the bean water and stew for about 1 hour until tender.

Brown lentils with lamb's liver

1½ cups/12 oz/350 g brown lentils
2 cups/1 lb/500 g lamb's liver (sliced thinly)
⅜ cup/4 oz/100 g streaky smoked bacon (diced)
1 large onion (chopped)
3 tablespoons oil
1 clove garlic (crushed)
1 red pepper (diced)
1 green pepper (diced)
½ tablespoon flour
freshly ground black pepper
salt
chopped parsley

Soak the lentils for 1 hour and boil in the same water for about 30 minutes. Leave to drain and save the water. Sprinkle salt and pepper over the slices of liver and dust them with a little flour. Heat the oil in a large pan and fry the bacon gently until golden brown. Add the onion, garlic and pepper and fry thoroughly. Then add the liver and fry for a few minutes longer, stirring continuously, until light brown and tender. Then stir in the lentils and heat through. If necessary add a few spoonfuls of the bean water, but do not boil any longer. Season to taste with salt and pepper and garnish with plenty of chopped parsley.

Indian red lentils

1¾ cups/14 oz/400 g red lentils
2 large onions (chopped)
2 cloves garlic (crushed)
2 tablespoons finely chopped raw spinach
3 tablespoons oil
salt
⅔ cup/¼ pint/150 ml sour cream
herb mixture of:
½ teaspoon of cumin,
½ teaspoon coriander,
1 pinch cayenne pepper,
½ teaspoon coarsely ground black pepper
1 pinch of cinnamon
4 hard-boiled eggs (quartered)
2 tablespoons curry powder

Soak the lentils if necessary, then boil for ¾ hour. Heat the oil and fry one of the chopped onions with the garlic until golden yellow and then add the spinach, the herb mixture and a little salt. Leave to simmer and add the mixture to the lentils. Mix well and keep warm. Fry the other chopped onion with the curry powder in a little oil until golden yellow, add the eggs and stir carefully until the eggs turn yellow. Place the curried eggs on the lentil mixture. Add the sour cream separately.

Mixed sweetcorn salad

1 large cob or 2 small cobs sweetcorn
2 red onions
3 tomatoes (peeled with pips removed)
1 red pepper
1 green pepper
6 oz/150 g iceberg lettuce

For the dressing:
2 tablespoons vinegar
salt
pepper
2 cloves garlic (crushed)
6 tablespoons oil

Remove the leaves and silk from the corn and boil for about 20 minutes until tender in unsalted water. Leave to cool and then remove the grains from the cob. Clean the onions and the peppers and slice them into thin rings. Slice the tomatoes and cut the lettuce into strips. Mix all the vegetables together. Make a dressing from the ingredients shown and toss the salad in it. Cover the salad and leave for about 1 hour in the refrigerator, stirring once just before serving.

Stewed garden turnips

1¾ lb/750 g garden turnips
salt
a pinch of sugar
2 tablespoons butter
2 tablespoons (altogether) of chopped parsley, chervil, chives and celery

Peel the washed turnips and cut into ¼-inch (5 mm) strips. Boil for about 15 minutes until tender in water with a little salt and sugar. Leave to drain and then fry in the butter. Before serving sprinkle with the mixed herbs.

Horseradish sauce

4 tablespoons grated horseradish
1 teaspoon lemon juice
1 teaspoon sugar
2½ cups/1 pint/300 ml fresh cream

Mix the grated horseradish with the lemon juice, cover and leave to stand for 10 minutes. Then stir in the sugar and leave to stand again. Finally mix in the cream.

Dandelion salad

1 lb/500 g dandelion leaves
2 stems of self-blanching celery (cut in strips)
1 cooked red beetroot (grated)
2 tablespoons vinegar
5 tablespoons oil
salt

Wash the dandelion leaves and leave to stand in water for a few hours. Then drain well and mix with the small strips of celery and the grated beetroot. Make a dressing of the oil, vinegar and salt and stir into the salad.

New Zealand spinach with macaroni

1 lb/500 g New Zealand spinach
4 cups/1 lb/500 g macaroni
2 tablespoons olive oil
2 cups/1 lb/500 g coarse-mince
4 shallots (chopped)
4 eggs
grated nutmeg
salt
freshly ground white pepper
¾ cup/6 oz/150 g grated Gouda cheese
2½ cups/1 pint/300 ml spicy tomato sauce

Use only the leaves and tops of the New Zealand spinach. Clean thoroughly and cook in a little water for about 2 minutes. Leave to drain in a colander. Boil the macaroni in plenty of water with a little oil for about 8 minutes. Leave to drain. Heat the olive oil in a pan, stir in the mince and add the shallots. Fry until the shallots are golden yellow, stirring continuously. Then add the macaroni, eggs, nutmeg, pepper and a little salt and mix well. Place the mixture around the edge of a greased oven dish. Pour the drained spinach into the middle and sprinkle with grated cheese. Bake for 10 minutes in a pre-heated oven at about 400°F/200°C/gas mark 6. Serve with a spicy tomato sauce.

Okra curry

1 lb/500 g okra
1 large onion (chopped)
1 clove garlic (crushed)
1 large red pepper (seeded and chopped)
3 tablespoons corn oil
3 teaspoons curry powder
salt
1 teaspoon grated lemon peel
6 tablespoons fresh cream

Wash the okra, cut away the stalks and dry thoroughly. Heat the oil and fry the okra, onion and garlic for a few minutes, stirring gently. Cook for 5 minutes over a low heat with the lid on. Add the curry powder, salt, lemon peel and red pepper. Mix carefully and heat through. Lastly add the fresh cream and serve immediately.

Okra salad

12 oz/350 g okra
4½ cups/2 pints/1 litre water
1 tablespoon vinegar
1 cup/8 oz/250 g tomatoes (peeled with pips removed)
3 stems of self-blanching celery (cut in strips)
1 tablespoon chopped parsley
3 tablespoons chopped garden cress

For the dressing:
3 tablespoons lemon juice
salt
freshly ground white pepper
a pinch of sugar
1 clove of garlic
4 tablespoons olive oil

Wash the okra and blanch for 15 minutes in boiling water with vinegar. Leave to drain and cool. Remove and discard the stalks. Mix the okra with the sliced tomato, celery, cress and parsley. Make a dressing from the ingredients shown and pour this over the salad. Then cover and leave to cool for a few hours. Stir carefully just before serving.

Pak-choi hotpot

4 bunches of pak-choi
2 lb/1 kg mashed potato
4 tablespoons suet
1 onion (chopped)
salt
freshly ground pepper
grilled sausages

Wash the pak-choi, cut into small pieces and blanch for a few minutes in lightly salted boiling water. Leave to drain. Save a little of the water and add it to the mashed potato. Stir the pak-choi into the mashed potato. Allow the suet to melt slowly in a frying pan and then add to the hotpot. Fry the onion in the suet until it changes colour, add it to the hotpot and stir well. Serve with the grilled sausages.

Bacon stew with parsnips

1¾ lb/750 g parsnips (diced)
1¾ lb/750 g winter carrots (diced)
2 cups/1 lb/500 g onions (chopped)
2 cups/1 lb/500 g white beans (soaked)
2 cups/1 lb/500 g unsmoked bacon (diced)
salt
pepper

Boil the beans in their soaking water for at least 20 minutes, together with the bacon. Then add the parsnips, carrots and onions and leave to cook for a further 45 minutes. Stir well and season to taste with salt and pepper.

Pumpkin purée

1½ lb/700 g pumpkin (Table King)
1¼ cups/½ pint/300 ml good beef stock
4 tablespoons milk
a piece of lovage
¾ cup/6 oz/150 g boiled potatoes
1 egg yolk
pepper
salt
grated nutmeg

Peel the pumpkin, remove the seeds and cut into cubes. Boil for 5 minutes in the beef stock (already stewed with the lovage for 15 minutes). Sieve the stock and reduce to about 4 tablespoons. Mash the pumpkin and the potatoes, and beat together with the stock, hot milk and egg yolk. Season to taste with salt, pepper and grated nutmeg. Pour into a dish and brown under the grill.

Custard marrow with salad

4 young custard marrows, (not too large)
stock (from a cube)
salt

For the filling:
2 boiled potatoes (diced)
4 tablespoons mixed cooked vegetables
1 tablespoon boiled ham (chopped finely)
3 tablespoons mayonnaise
salt
pepper

For the garnish:
1 hard-boiled egg
chopped parsley

Wash the custard marrows, cut away the stalks and scoop out the flesh. Chop finely, raw or blanched: the flesh can be used in the salad. Heat up the stock, add a little salt and blanch the hollowed-out custard marrows for about 5 minutes. Then place them immediately in cold water and leave to drain and cool. Shave a slice off the undersides, if necessary, so each marrow has a firm base to stand on and will not fall over. Make a filling from the ingredients shown, and fill the custard marrows with it. Top with a few slices of egg and sprinkle with chopped parsley.

Vegetable pumpkin

2 lb/1 kg pumpkin (Golden Nugget)
2 tablespoons butter
$\frac{2}{3}$ cup/$\frac{1}{4}$ pint/150 ml stock
3 to 4 tablespoons vinegar
dill (finely chopped)
parsley (chopped)
salt
pepper
a pinch of sugar
2 tablespoons sour cream

Peel the pumpkin and remove the seeds. Cut into long strips and fry evenly in the butter. Add the stock and leave to cook for about 8 minutes. Season the vegetables to taste with vinegar, salt, pepper and sugar. Pour the sour cream over it and sprinkle on the dill and parsley.

Stir-fry runner beans

$1\frac{1}{2}$ cups/12 oz/350 g dried runner beans
a sprig of lovage
1 cup/8 oz/250 g streaky unsmoked bacon (diced)
$\frac{1}{2}$ cup/4 oz/100 g pig's liver (cut in strips)
$\frac{1}{4}$ cup/2 oz/50 g boemboe nasi herbs
1 leek (chopped)
1 green pepper (cut in strips)
2 cloves garlic (crushed)
4 tablespoons olive oil
salt or soup flavouring

Soak the beans in plenty of water and boil for about 1 hour in the same water with the sprig of lovage. Leave to drain. Heat the oil in a frying pan or wok and fry the liver and bacon. When they begin to change colour add the leek, the green pepper, the garlic and the soaked nasi herbs and stir-fry. Add the drained beans and heat through. Season to taste with salt or soup flavouring.

Black radish salad

$1\frac{1}{2}$ cups/12 oz/350 g black radish
3 large stems of chives
6 tablespoons sour cream
a little lemon juice
salt
freshly ground white pepper
chopped parsley

Peel and wash the radish and cut into narrow strips like matchsticks. Cut the chives into rings. Stir the radish, chives and parsley into the sour cream and season to taste with salt, pepper and lemon juice.

Redleaved chicory (radicchio) salad

4 heads of red-leaved chicory
a bunch of garden cress
half a Florence fennel (cut in strips)

For the dressing:
2 tablespoons wine vinegar
salt
pepper
1 clove garlic (crushed)
1 teaspoon mustard
15 tarragon leaves
6 tablespoons olive oil

Clean the chicory heads, break the leaves into pieces and slice a little of the bitter core wafer-thin. Mix everything with the Florence fennel and the cress. Make a smooth dressing from the ingredients shown and mix it into the salad.

Grilled red-leaved chicory (radicchio)

2 firm heads of red-leaved chicory
2 tablespoons corn oil
freshly ground black pepper
salt

Clean the chicory heads, dry and cut lengthwise into four. Mix the corn oil with plenty of black pepper and draw the chicory through it. Leave to drain and then place under a hot grill, turning occasionally. When the heads are crisp, sprinkle them with a little salt.

Salad rocket à la Margarethe

1 lb/500 g salad rocket
1 kohlrabi (cooked and diced)
1 cup/8 oz/250 g young snap beans (cut up and cooked)

For the dressing:
2 tablespoons vinegar
salt
pepper
1 shallot (finely chopped)
2 tablespoons (altogether) of chopped parsley, chervil, tarragon and chives
5 tablespoons oil

Clean the salad rocket, leave to drain and then cut up roughly. Mix with the other vegetables. Make a dressing from the ingredients shown and toss the salad in it.

Fried scorzonera à la George

2 lb/1 kg scorzonera
3 tablespoons vinegar
4 tablespoons milk
1 onion (in half rings)
$\frac{1}{4}$ cup/2 oz/50 g bacon (cut in strips)
chopped parsley
2 tablespoons butter
salt

Clean the scorzonera, cut into 2 inch/5 cm pieces and immediately place in water with vinegar. Wash well and rinse. Boil the pieces for about 15 minutes until tender in water with milk. Heat the butter and fry the bacon and the onion in it until golden brown. Then add the scorzonera and stir-fry. When it begins to change colour mix in the chopped parsley and season to taste with a little salt.

Piquant Swiss chard

$1\frac{3}{4}$ lb/750 g Swiss chard
6 tablespoons fresh cream
2 shallots (finely chopped)
2 teaspoons freshly grated horseradish
1 teaspoon chopped tarragon leaves
salt
pepper
2 tablespoons butter
chopped parsley or celery

Wash the Swiss chard and cut into pieces about $1\frac{1}{2}$ inches/4 cm long. Boil in a little salted water for about 10 minutes until tender. Fry the shallots in the butter until golden brown. Leave the Swiss chard to drain and then mix with the cream, fried shallots, tarragon leaves and grated horseradish. Heat through but do not boil. Season to taste with salt and pepper and garnish with chopped parsley or celery.

Grandmother's red Swiss chard

$1\frac{3}{4}$ lb/750 g red Swiss chard
a drop of vinegar
1 onion (chopped)
freshly ground black pepper
a pinch of ground cloves
1 teaspoon cinnamon
$\frac{1}{2}$ tablespoon sugar
2 tablespoons butter
1 tablespoon potato flour
chopped parsley

Wash the chard and cut into pieces about $1\frac{1}{2}$ inches/5 cm long. Boil in a little water with a drop of vinegar, and the onion, pepper, cloves and cinnamon for about 30 minutes. Then add the sugar and butter and cook for a few more minutes. If necessary thicken with a little potato flour paste and garnish with chopped parsley.

Maltese stem lettuce (celtuce)

$4\frac{1}{2}$ lb/2 kg stem lettuce
salt
a pinch of sugar
2 blood oranges
$\frac{1}{2}$ cup/4 oz/100 g butter
6 tablespoons whipped cream
juice of 2 blood oranges
grated peel of 1 blood orange

Remove the leaf from the stem lettuce and use for a salad. Peel the stems, especially the lower ends, and cut into pieces about 6 inches/15 cm long. Thick stems should also be cut lengthwise. Barely cover the stems in water and boil for about 10 minutes until tender. Meanwhile peel 2 oranges, removing the pith, and cut into slices. Take the stem lettuce out of the pan, drain carefully and place on a hot serving dish. Drench the stem lettuce with the orange juice and the melted butter. Sprinkle the grated peel over it and garnish with orange slices. Serve the whipped cream separately.

Welsh onion soup

$3\frac{1}{2}$ lb/$1\frac{1}{2}$ kg Welsh onions
1 medium winter carrot
3 tablespoons butter
3 tablespoons flour
1 teaspoon curry powder
a pinch of oregano
1 cup/8 oz/250 g cooked chicken (chopped)
9 cups/$3\frac{1}{2}$ pints/2 litres good chicken stock
salt
freshly ground white pepper
celery
croutons
grated cheese

Wash the onions and cut them diagonally into rings including the green part. Peel and slice the carrot thinly. Melt the butter in a pan, stir in the carrot and fry evenly. Then add the curry powder and the oregano and continue to stir-fry. Sprinkle the flour over the top and leave to cook gently on a low heat. Leave to cool. Heat the chicken stock and gradually add to the vegetables, stirring continuously until you have a smooth soup. Leave to simmer for 15 minutes. Add the onions for the last 5 minutes. Then add the chicken and the celery, and season the soup to taste with the pepper and salt. Pour the soup into bowls, sprinkle some croutons on top, and sprinkle the grated cheese over the croutons. Brown under the grill.

Soya beans Indienne

$1\frac{1}{2}$ cups/12 oz/350 g soya beans
8 shallots (chopped)
6 tablespoons oil
2 cm fresh ginger (chopped)
1 teaspoon ground curcuma
6 cloves garlic (chopped)
4 green chillies (chopped)
2 tablespoons grated coconut

Soak the soya beans for 24 hours in plenty of water and then boil for $1\frac{1}{2}$ to 2 hours. Fry the shallots and garlic in the oil until golden brown. Add the chillies, the ginger and the ground curcuma to the shallots and garlic and fry together. Then add the drained beans and the coconut and allow to cook for a few more minutes on a low heat. Serve with rice.

Vegetable spaghetti with tomato sauce

$\frac{1}{2}$ vegetable spaghetti

For the sauce:
2 tablespoons butter
1 tablespoon oil
$\frac{1}{2}$ cup/4 oz/100 g minced beef
2 cups/$\frac{3}{4}$ pint/450 ml stock or water
1 tablespoon tomato purée
$\frac{1}{3}$ cup/3 oz/80 g shallots (chopped)
$\frac{1}{4}$ cup/2 oz/50 g leek (chopped)
$\frac{1}{4}$ cup/2 oz/50 g mushrooms (quartered)
$\frac{1}{2}$ tablespoon ketchup
$\frac{1}{4}$ teaspoon of five-spice powder
salt
cornflour

Boil the vegetable spaghetti in plenty of water for about 20 to 25 minutes, depending on size. Leave to cool and then cut in half lengthwise. Remove the seeds and strings and scrape out the flesh with a fork. Heat the butter and the oil in a pan and fry the meat in it. When it begins to change colour, stir in the shallots and the mushrooms. Add the tomato purée with the five-spice powder and, at the last moment, the leek. Stir everything well and pour in the stock. Leave to cook gently. Season to taste with ketchup and a little salt. If necessary thicken with cornflour. Heat the vegetable spaghetti in the sauce.

Sugar peas with lemon butter

1 lb/500 g sugar pea pods
1 lemon
2 tablespoons butter
a pinch of sugar
grated nutmeg
freshly ground white pepper
salt
chopped parsley

Cream the butter in a bowl. Add a teaspoonful of chopped lemon peel with a little sugar, salt and freshly ground white pepper. Top and tail the pods, wash and boil in a little water for about 5 minutes. Drain, add the lemon butter and stir this well into the pods. Season to taste with a pinch of grated nutmeg and garnish with chopped parsley.

Braised tannia leaf

2 lb/1 kg tannia leaf
$1\frac{1}{4}$ cups/$\frac{1}{2}$ pint/300 ml water
$\frac{1}{4}$ cup/2 oz/50 g butter
salt
grated nutmeg
1 hard-boiled egg (chopped)
1 tomato (sliced)

Remove the leaves from the stems and wash them. Cut the larger leaves into small pieces. Bring the water to the boil with a little salt and put in the tannia leaf. Simmer on a low heat for about 15 minutes, then rinse in cold water and drain thoroughly. Chop finely if preferred. Braise the tannia leaf with a little butter and season to taste with salt and grated nutmeg. Garnish with eggs and tomato.

Braised orache

2 lb/1 kg orache
a handful of sorrel leaves
salt
2 tablespoons butter
a pinch of freshly ground white pepper
1 hard-boiled egg (chopped)

Clean the orache and the sorrel leaves and cook for 5 minutes with a little water and salt on a high heat, stirring continuously. Take the vegetables from the pan, chop finely and braise with the butter. Season to taste with a little salt and pepper, and garnish with egg.

Springtime salad with orache

equal quantities of orache, dandelion leaves, sorrel and garden cress
2 spring onions
1 hard-boiled egg (sliced)
chopped parsley

For the dressing:
1 tablespoon lemon juice
pepper
salt
a pinch of sugar
3 tablespoons sunflower oil

Clean the vegetables and tear off the leaves in small pieces. Cut the spring onions into rings. Mix the vegetables together. Make a dressing from the ingredients shown and stir this into the salad. Garnish with egg slices and chopped parsley.

Broad beans with mint

7 lb/3 kg broad beans
1 tablespoon lard
$\frac{3}{4}$ cup/6 oz/150 g salted fat bacon (diced)
5 shallots (chopped)
1 clove garlic (chopped)
1 small bay leaf
2 glasses of dry white wine
1 cup/scant $\frac{1}{2}$ pint/250 ml salt water
1 generous tablespoon of finely chopped mint
freshly ground black pepper

Wash the beans and leave to drain. Heat the lard in a pan with a thick bottom and fry the bacon in it. Leave to drain on kitchen paper. Fry the shallots and the garlic until they change colour, and then add the bay leaf and the white wine, the water and the beans. Cook the beans in the pan with the lid off, so that when the beans are ready the liquid will have boiled away. Remove the bay leaf, add the bacon and the mint and mix well. Season to taste with a little pepper.

Broad beans with red pepper

7 lb/3 kg broad beans
milk
salt
2 red peppers (cut in strips)
1 onion (chopped)
2 tablespoons butter
freshly ground white pepper

Wash the beans and boil for about 15 minutes in water with milk and salt. Fry the onion and the red pepper in the butter, pour this mixture over the beans and stir gently. Season to taste with pepper.

Corn salad with omelette

1 lb/500 g corn salad
2 eggs
1 tablespoon fresh cream
salt
grated nutmeg
croutons

For the dressing:
2 tablespoons red wine vinegar
salt
pepper
a pinch of sugar
3 tablespoons olive oil

Clean the corn salad and drain thoroughly. Stir the eggs into the fresh cream, salt and nutmeg and make an omelette of them. Leave to cool and cut into squares. Make a dressing from the ingredients shown and pour it over the corn salad, stir in the omelette pieces and garnish with croutons immediately before serving.

Corn salad

14 oz/400 g corn salad
1 soft onion (cut in rings)
1 hard-boiled egg (sliced)
2 tablespoons vinegar
1 tablespoon salad oil

Clean the corn salad and dry it carefully. Mix in the onion rings, add oil and vinegar and garnish with egg slices.

Wax gourd stew

1 cup/8 oz/250 g lamb (in $\frac{3}{4}$ in/2 cm cubes)
1 lemon or lime
2 tablespoons corn oil
2 tablespoons butter
1 onion (chopped)
2 tomatoes (peeled with pips removed)
2 cloves garlic (chopped)
salt or stock cube
freshly ground black pepper
4 medium-sized potatoes
2$\frac{1}{4}$ lbs/1 kg wax gourd
1 teaspoon tomato purée
1 teaspoon sugar

Mix the cubes of lamb with the lemon juice. Leave for $\frac{1}{2}$ hour and then drain. Heat the oil and the butter and brown the meat. Cut the tomatoes into pieces, add them to the meat with the onion and garlic and continue frying. Add salt, pepper and water and simmer for 1 hour on a low heat. Peel the wax gourd and remove the seeds. Peel the potatoes and then dice the wax gourd and the potatoes. Add to the stew and leave to cook for 20 minutes. Then add the tomato purée and season to taste with sugar, pepper and salt. You can use fish (hake for instance) instead of lamb.

Chicken soup with watercress

1 boiling fowl
1 onion (chopped roughly)
parsley stems
a few leaves of lovage
10 peppercorns (crushed)
1 leaf of mace
$\frac{1}{2}$ cup/$\frac{1}{4}$ lb/100 g watercress

Bring the chicken to the boil in water, skim and add the onion, parsley stems, lovage, peppercorns and mace. When the chicken is cooked, sieve the stock and remove the fat. Bone the chicken and cut up the breast for the soup. Clean the watercress carefully and cut it up finely. Heat the stock with the chicken breast and stir in the watercress just before serving.

Winter purslane soup

1$\frac{1}{2}$ cups/12 oz /350 g winter purslane
4$\frac{1}{2}$ cups/2 pints/1 litre good chicken stock
3 tablespoons boiled rice
salt
3 egg yolks
6 tablespoons cream

Wash the purslane and leave to drain. Bring the chicken stock to the boil, add the purslane and the boiled rice and leave to simmer for 5 minutes. Sieve the stock. Blend the purslane and rice in the blender and sieve the purée into the chicken stock. Bring the soup to the boil and season to taste with a little salt. Just before serving stir in the mixture of egg yolks and cream.

Parijse broei carrots with caraway

1 lb/500 g Parijse broei carrots
salt
2$\frac{1}{2}$ tablespoons butter
1 tablespoon flour
1 pinch caraway seed
1 tablespoon chopped parsley

Scrape and wash the carrots and boil in lightly salted water for about 10 minutes. Drain and reserve the water. Make a light brown roux with the butter and flour and add to the water, stirring continuously, to make a smooth sauce. Season to taste with the caraway seed and a little more salt. Stir in the carrots, heat through and garnish with parsley.

Winter carrots with swede

$\frac{1}{2}$ lb/250 g winter carrots
$\frac{1}{2}$ lb/250 g swede
2 tablespoons butter
1 tablespoon brown sugar

Clean the carrots and the swede and cut them into strips 2 inches (5 cm) long and $\frac{1}{4}$ in (5 mm) thick. Boil together in plenty of water until cooked and then drain. Caramelize the sugar in the butter and mix into the vegetables.

Summer carrots with pumpkin

1 lb/500 g small carrots
1 lb/500 g pumpkin
salt
1$\frac{1}{2}$ teaspoons dill seed
$\frac{1}{4}$ cup/2 oz/50 g butter
1 tablespoon sugar
dill leaves

Scrape and wash the carrots, peel the pumpkin and cut into cubes. Put the carrots and pumpkin in a pan with the butter, sugar and dill seed, and braise for about 10 minutes. If necessary add a spoonful of water. Garnish with finely chopped dill.

Turnip-rooted parsley au gratin

1$\frac{1}{2}$ lb turnip-rooted parsley
juice of half a lemon
2 tablespoons butter
a blob of cream
freshly ground white pepper
salt
grated hard cheese

Peel and wash the parsley. Place in water with lemon juice and boil for about 10 minutes. Leave to drain. Then braise in butter, add a blob of cream and a little pepper. Put in a fireproof dish, sprinkle the cheese on top and brown under a pre-heated hot grill.

Baked yams

8 medium-sized yams
4 tablespoons oil or clarified butter
salt
pepper

Wash the yams, dry them and make a cross on one side with a sharp knife. Coat them liberally with oil or clarified butter and put in an ovenproof dish. Bake for about 35 minutes in an oven pre-heated to 400°F/200°C/gas mark 6. Then scoop out the insides with a spoon and sprinkle on salt and pepper to taste.

Boiled yams

$1\frac{3}{4}$ lb/800 g yams
water
salt

Peel and wash the yams and cover with salted water. Boil until tender, drain and cook on a low heat so that they steam through. Serve with a spicy sauce.

Iceplant salad

1 lb/500 g iceplant
1 hard-boiled egg
1 tomato (sliced)

For the dressing:
2 tablespoons tarragon vinegar
freshly ground white pepper
1 teaspoon mustard
a pinch of sugar
6 tablespoons sunflower oil

Remove and discard the coarse stems from the iceplant. Wash the leaves and dry carefully. Make a dressing from the ingredients shown and toss the iceplant in it. Garnish with crumbled hard-boiled egg and a few slices of tomato.

Braised iceplant

2 lb/1 kg iceplant
2 tablespoons butter
grated nutmeg
1 beaten egg

Wash the iceplant, discarding the coarsest stems. Boil in a little water for 3 minutes. Drain and cut into diamond shapes. Then braise in butter and bind with beaten egg. No salt is needed, because the iceplant itself is so salty.

Seakale with hollandaise sauce

2 lb/1 kg seakale
salt
chopped parsley
$2\frac{1}{2}$ cups/1 pint/300 ml hollandaise sauce

Use only the young, 6-inch/15 cm long, blanched stems of the seakale. Wash and boil for about 15 minutes in lightly salted water. Drain, place on a warmed serving dish and pour over a few spoonfuls of hollandaise sauce. Garnish with chopped parsley. Serve the rest of the sauce separately.

Glasswort

1 lb/500 g young glasswort
2 tablespoons butter
cornflour (cornstarch)
grated nutmeg

Wash the glasswort thoroughly and boil for about 20 minutes in a little water. If necessary, thicken with a little cornflour. Mix in the butter and season to taste with a pinch of grated nutmeg.

Acknowledgements

All photographs in this book are the work of Kees Jansen, except for:
the cover and pages 1, 2, 161 to 180 inclusive: Chris Steffens Fotografie, Amsterdam
page 6 (right): Fotobureau Koninklijk Institut voor de Tropen, Amsterdam
page 7 (left): Atlas van Stolk, Rotterdam
page 7 (middle): Ron Putto, Zuid-Scharwoude
pages 7 (right), 9 (left), 96 and 129: Rinus Wilms, Amstelveen
page 8 (top): Archief 'Vakblad', The Hague
page 8 (bottom): Nico van der Stam, Amsterdam
page 9 (right): GroDam, Roermond
pages 14, 40, 124 and 141: Dick J.C. Klees, Duiven
page 39: Toon Fey, Heukelum
page 63: Bejo Zaden BV, Noord-Scharwoude
page 127: Willemse Holland
page 130: Machiel de Vos, Leusden
illustrations on page 11 (map) and 106: Gieb van Enckevort, Eindhoven

This book is the result of the enthusiastic cooperation of many people, companies and institutions. For supplying information, vegetable samples, recipes and additional photographs, the publishers would like to thank Fa. Van Bakel, Heesch; Bejo Zaden, Noord-Scharwoude; W. E. H. Braun, Alkmaar; J. Broeksteeg, Oss; Gebr. Dollevoet, Oss; H. Duggen, Kiel; G. J. H. Grubben, PAGV, Lelystad; Hecor BV Int., Rotterdam; H. A. M. Heerkens, Nistelrode; I.S.P.C., Breda; Fa. Jonkergouw, Schaijk; J. van Lieverloo, Heesch; Fa. Limex, Haarlem; J. Linssen, Veghel; N.A.K.G., Roelofarendsveen; J. V. A. Ploegmakers, Heesch; Produktschap voor Groenten en Fruit, Den Haag; Royal Sluis, Enkhuizen; Fa. P. A. F. Ruhe, Lelystad; S. Schalken, Oss; Sprenger Instituut, Wageningen; Stichting Flevohof, Biddinghuizen; Stichting Proeftuin Noord-Limburg, Horst; Fa. Strik, Herpen; Tuinbouwschool 'Warmonderhof,' Tiel; A. Vissers, Oss; Windig BV, Amsterdam.

Index

Bold page numbers refer to recipes